Holman *QuickSource*™

GUIDE TO

UNDERSTANDING JESUS

Holman *QuickSource*™

GUIDE TO

UNDERSTANDING JESUS

Jeremy Royal Howard

HOLMAN
REFERENCE

NASHVILLE, TENNESSEE

Holman QuickSource Guide to Understanding Jesus
© 2009 by Jeremy Royal Howard

ISBN: 978-0-8054-9521-8   -

A Holman Reference Book
published by
B&H Publishing Group
127 Ninth Avenue, North
Nashville, Tennessee 37234
http://www.broadmanholman.com

Dewey Decimal Classification: 232
Subject Heading: JESUS CHRIST—BIBLICAL TEACHING\BIBLE. N.T.
GOSPELS AND ACTS

Cover Design by Greg Pope
Interior Design by Doug Powell

Printed in Italy

1 2 3 4 5 6 • 12 11 10 09 08

LEGO

Dedicated to

. . .

My wife, Simone Howard

Eu amo minha querida Simone e
faço votos de ama-la para sempre.

Table of Contents

Part I:
Jesus' Inheritance

Part II:
Jesus' Life

Part III:
Jesus' Cross

Part IV:
Jesus' Teachings

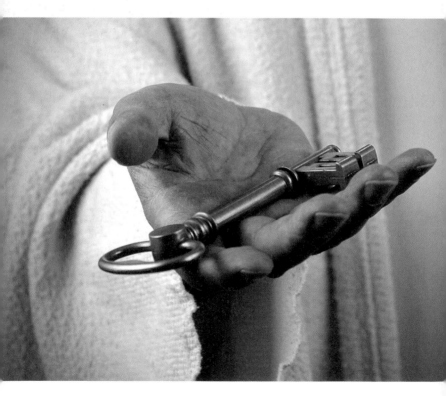

Part V:
Jesus' Followers

Introduction

Imagine that a man moves in next door to you and starts proclaiming that he is God. You are stunned at first, but this feeling soon gives way to alarm. Is the man dangerous? What might he be planning to do? Will he attempt to call down fire if your dog crosses into his yard? Will he picket your street like one of the apocalyptic crazies you've seen in the movies? And just how far will your property value plunge once he's in full swing?

You waste no time rallying the neighbors. Everyone joins in "The Watch." Round-the-clock observation soon reveals what you expected from the start: except for the God complex, this man seems perfectly ordinary. He walks, dresses, sleeps, and eats like a normal man. He pays taxes. He even mows his lawn with the same brand of mower you use. What kind of God would do these things?

But you begrudgingly notice other things about him as well, things not common to mere men. He has a way of speaking about God that sends your soul soaring. He can also pierce your conscience like no one else. So far as you can judge, his every act is truly selfless. He resolves conflicts that arise among neighbors and shows no discrimination or favoritism. Rumors have it that he has done some pretty remarkable things for the sick; plus there was the amazing thing he did (or *appeared* to have done, you insist) on your neighbor's pool. And then there's the difference he's made in people's lives. Some folks seem like entirely new people since they started hanging out with the new guy. You begin to drop your guard a bit, but every time you start to form a decent opinion of the man he starts in again about the God thing.

This cannot be permitted to go on forever. Being a person committed to truth, one day you get a few of the neighbors together and go down to the courthouse. You dig up the old yellowed documents, the ones with the state seals and big, looping signatures. You seize the birth certificate and shout out the news: "This man didn't come from heaven! Right here in plain print is his mother's name. His dad is on the certificate as well. And of all things, he was born in that ramshackle town down the road. Nothing good ever came from there!"

As you bask in the glow of these discoveries, the clerk comes over to join the conversation. She has overheard your comments.

"I grew up in that 'ramshackle' town," she reports with a slight edge in her voice.

You start to apologize, but she waves you off.

"I was a kid when this guy was born," she continues. She pauses to scan the room for eavesdroppers. "I remember it like it was yesterday. Folks back home like to keep it all hush-hush because it's embarrassing."

"What's embarrassing?" you ask. "The guy's God complex?"

"No," she quickly says but then reconsiders. "Well, yes.

That *is* sort of embarrassing." She shifts her weight and considers her next words carefully. "What I meant was the things that happened surrounding his birth. It wasn't natural." She stops and looks around again. A slight sweat has broken out over her lip. What is this woman going to say?

And then she unloads it. "His momma was a virgin. Sure as anything. She had never been with a man when she had that baby."

You and your friends hang there for what seems like an eternity of silence. You don't even dare to breathe as you turn her crazed words over in your mind, trying to find a different meaning, a *rational* meaning. And then none of you can fight it anymore. You and your pals break out in raucous laughter. A virgin birth!

Before turning to leave, the red-faced clerk says, "See what I mean? People laugh like we're nuts. But I'm telling you how it happened. And it's nothing to laugh at."

You beg to differ. It *is* something to laugh at. But as soon as you say it, you find you can't go on laughing. Something about the lady stops you short. She's sincere, not a trace of sarcasm or deception. And then there's the man himself, the enigmatic neighbor who says he's God. He's the same as every man and yet so very different as well.

No one says a word on the way back to the car. As you all pile in, you ask aloud the questions everyone wants answered: "What are we going to do with this guy? Is he God or what?"

No one offers an answer. You're not even sure where to begin.

The Two-Thousand-Year Dilemma

Whether you realize it or not, you face a dilemma that is similar to the one illustrated in the above scenario. Two thousand years ago, at a crossroads in time and culture, a Jewish boy was born in Roman Palestine to a woman who was reportedly a virgin. As amazing a start as that was, the boy's story only increased in wonderment as he grew older. He wowed his elders at a tender age, turned water to wine as a young man, and shortly thereafter there were reports of healings, exorcisms,

Two thousand years ago, at a crossroads in time and culture, a Jewish boy was born in Roman Palestine to a woman who was reportedly a virgin.

and mastery over nature. People flocked to him out of love, hatred, and simple curiosity because his teachings were both inspiring and controversial. Before long the whole nation of Israel was ignited in a firestorm over his claims to divinity.

This man, of course, is Jesus of Nazareth. Like the man in our opening illustration, Jesus polarized all who met him. The outstanding questions he left in his wake as he strode from town to town were: "What are we going to do with this guy? Is he God or what?" But unlike the fictitious man in our illustration, Jesus was real, and he was *killed* over his radical claims and deeds. His shocking execution set the stage for an even bigger drama, his purported resurrection. Jews and Gentiles, family and friends, folks from every walk of life were deeply divided over reports that Jesus had risen from the dead. Believing this message of hope, some people gave up everything to spread the good news Jesus had brought. Others

Is Jesus dead or alive today? Your entire view of life and its ultimate purpose hangs on how you answer this question.

spent their lives fighting off the religious fervor that steadily built around him. Which side was right? Is Jesus dead or alive today? Your entire view of life and its ultimate purpose hangs on how you answer this question.

But the questions about Jesus do not begin and end with the resurrection. There are numerous other issues of vital importance, and for two thousand years people have grappled with, divided over, and contended for these matters as well. Did Jesus really claim to be God? What of his miracles? Real,

fake, or misunderstood? Did he fulfill Old Testament prophecies for the sought-after Messiah? Did the Gospel writers pen faithful stories about Jesus' life, or did they blend fiction with fact? For that matter, did the Gospel writers even know Jesus personally, or did they just hand down what they heard from others? Were the authentic stories of Jesus' life suppressed and thereby lost to history? These and dozens of other important questions naturally arise when you explore the life and claims of Jesus Christ.

This Book's Purpose and Approach

The purpose of this book is to help you find solid answers about the life, teachings, and identity of Jesus Christ. We will examine the biblical testimony plus summarize important points about historical context, theological meaning, various evidences, and the origin of Scripture. If in the end you are helped in the quest to see and proclaim Jesus for who he is, this book has served its purpose.

The purpose of this book is to help you find solid answers about the life, teachings, and identity of Jesus Christ.

Part I
Jesus' Inheritance

Chapter 1
Originations

If you wish to understand Jesus, you must start by looking into his inheritance. I don't mean the monies, heirlooms, and odd pieces of furniture that may have been lined up for his enjoyment after the passing of his earthly parents, had he outlived both of them. What I have in mind is the religious, cultural, and political heritage that came down to him at birth. These are factors whose roots reached far back into history, help-

If you wish to understand Jesus, you must start by looking into his inheritance.

ing to shape his beliefs about God, his ethnic and national identity, and even his views on such things as taxes and politics.

We all have such inheritances; they are ours whether we like them or not. At the outset it's not a matter of choice, for we are all set in place at birth; and, assuming you came into the world in the standard way, no one consulted your preferences prior to your debut on the world stage. Your beginning and your inheritance were handed to you no-questions-asked on day one. Though returns are not possible, you can choose whether you will live in accordance with your inheritance. Many of us live within its walls, never realizing how they hem us in. Others relish the rebel image; they drive against the flow of cultural traffic and wave dismissively at all the lemmings that go diving off high places *en masse*. But even rebels are shaped by their inheritance, for it has helped define their choices by serving as the foil against which they strive to forge a unique identity.

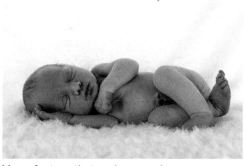

Many factors that make you who you are were handed to you no-questions-asked on the day of your birth.

For the above reasons all biography starts out as an exercise in history. If I wish to learn about you, I will need to roll up my sleeves and dive into details about things that came and went long before you arrived to jam a foot in life's door. Naturally the same is true if we wish to reach an accurate understanding of Jesus. We cannot just look at his time trekking around Israel. When Jesus dropped onto the scene at the turn of history (the *hairpin curve* of history, actually), he picked up a backstory or inheritance that we must comprehend before we

When Jesus dropped onto the scene at the turn of history, he picked up a backstory or inheritance that we must comprehend before we begin to examine the memoirs of his life.

begin to examine the memoirs of his life, which are collected in the volume known as the New Testament. This means we must go back in time to the era before Jesus was born. Fortunately, we are not forced to scramble around the hills and vales of the Middle East in search of whatever dusty traces may remain of Jesus' ancestral world. Instead, we enjoy the opportunity of cracking open an ancient set of books we call the Old Testament. But there is something unique in this maneuver. In researching Jesus' inheritance documented in the Old Testament, we are looking into a book that millions of people have taken to be *from God*. We will further examine this belief—its source, rationality, and feasibility—as we go along in the following chapters. For now the important point to note is that by the Old Testament's own testimony we are reading the words of God given through his chosen prophets, priests, and kings.

The Old Testament records the words God gave through his chosen prophets, priests, and kings. Photo: Merlin (CC Lisence 2.5).

God's Autobiography

The Old Testament is the beginning of what is essentially God's autobiography; for in this collection of books, God repeatedly reveals himself by words of disclosure and works of power. He tells us who he is, who *we* are, how we came to be, and what this buzzing, careening world is all about. In other words, God tells us about ultimate meaning and purpose, and it all centers on *him*. Certainly the Jews of Jesus' day believed these things of the Old Testament (known then simply as the Scriptures), and Jesus held fast to this belief. So here is our first insight to Jesus' inheritance: he believed that the Old Testament

The Old Testament is the beginning of what is essentially God's autobiography.

Here is our first insight to Jesus' inheritance: he believed that the Old Testament was written by men who had a commission from God to reveal truths about God and the world he made.

was written by men who had a commission from God to reveal truths about God and the world he made. Comprehending the message of these Scriptures is therefore our first chore in the quest to understand the cultural, religious, and historical foundations that grounded Jesus' identity.

Moses Speaks and Writes from God

According to long-standing tradition the first five books of the Bible were written by Moses as he and his fellow Hebrews (descendants of a renowned man named Abraham) sojourned in the wilderness between Egypt and modern Israel from roughly 1440 to 1400 BC. Having spent several hundred years in Egypt, first as guests and then eventually as slaves, the majority of the Hebrews had forgotten many important truths that had been handed down to them from ancestors who had had life-changing encounters with God. This heritage of relations with God marked the Hebrew family line as unique among the peoples of Earth. Naturally stories of the old encounters with God were treasured and passed down with care generation after generation.

Moses by José de Ribera.

But Egypt had beaten these treasures back into the deepest recesses of the Hebrew consciousness, and so Moses was led by God to cast light in these dark corners by teaching about beginnings—their beginning as a distinct people but also the beginning of the universe and human history.

How could Moses write accurately about things that preceded his lifetime by many centuries? Some people suggest that God miraculously gave Moses details about far-gone people, places, and conversations. God is capable of working such miracles, but the Bible nowhere hints that the histories were written in this manner. Instead, the Genesis narratives read like straight-forward accounts that have been handed down in the usual way: through oral and written records that originated soon after the events occurred. Thus it is best to concentrate on two sources for Moses' writings. First, Moses drew significantly from a collection of oral and written histories that had come down to him through his ancestors. Accomplished scholars such as Duane Garrett and K. A. Kitchen have reasonably suggested that thoughtful persons well in advance of Moses learned early forms of writing and thus took steps to preserve seminal stories that previously had been transmitted only as oral history.[1] These stories would have covered topics such as early human history and God's dealings with humankind, especially concerning Abraham and his descendants since God kept up regular dealings with them. In both their oral and early written versions, the stories would have been carefully guarded against error due to the important nature of the topics they conveyed. After all, it's not every day that God Almighty shows up and has a talk with humans or directs them to undertake heroic ventures. The guardians of these stories, being the descendants of Abraham and in many cases sharing similarly fantastic experiences with God themselves, would not dare handle the reports loosely. They were passed down faithfully with reverence and gratitude to the God who had involved himself in the human story.

> *How could Moses write accurately about things that preceded his lifetime by many centuries?*

> *Long before Moses, stories about God's dealings with humanity were passed down faithfully with reverence and gratitude to the God who had involved himself in the human story.*

An Egyptian scribe's tablet from around the time of Moses. Photo: David Liam Moran (CC License 3.0).

Later in Hebrew history a descendant of Abraham named Joseph moved to Egypt and rose to a position of great power. He married an Egyptian woman of high standing, and his family naturally had access to education in the advanced Egyptian writing arts. When the rest of the Hebrews migrated to Egypt to shelter under Joseph's wings, they came to venerate him as head of their tribe. In such a situation he would become chief guardian of the sacred Hebrew histories; and as a man of education and privilege, he almost certainly would have ensured that everything was written down in permanent fashion and placed in a repository for safeguarding. Four hundred years later, God's hand piloted a water-borne baby named Moses into Pharaoh's care. This Moses grew up in Pharaoh's beneficent shadow as an

Finding of Moses by Lawrence Alma-Tadema.

adopted family member. This allowed him to receive the best Egyptian education on offer. Known to be the son of a Hebrew woman, Moses was in a fine position to access the written Hebrew histories. Hence it is reasonable to suppose that he would have made off with these documents when he left Egypt permanently after his confrontations with Pharaoh. These documents would then be on hand when Moses set out to write the ancient histories. Lest you think it seems far-fetched to suppose that Moses would have used older, nonsacred documents as source material for writing Genesis, please note that the Old Testament frankly admits the use of nonbiblical sources. For instance, Numbers 21:14, authored by Moses, openly quotes from the "Book of the Lord's Wars," a nonbiblical book which has been lost to history. The principle seems obvious: if the source (be it written or oral) is telling truth about the histories it records, it is fit for contributing information to the Holy Bible.

But is this all Genesis is—a patchwork of documents and oral histories brought together by Moses? Certainly not. The second and most significant factor in Moses' authorship of Genesis is the fact that he wrote with the guidance of God. Several years before Moses set out to write Genesis, God selected him to be spokesperson to Pharaoh and the Hebrew slave-force that suffered under Egyptian suppression. Trouble is Moses was not an eloquent man. Words were not his craft, and so he worried that God had made a poor selection. In response to these misgivings, God promised to help Moses speak and teach him what words he should say (Exod 4:12). God kept this promise. The inspired books Moses wrote are the chief lasting result.

> *God promised to help Moses speak and teach him what words he should say (Exod 4:12). God kept this promise. The inspired books Moses wrote are the chief lasting result.*

Creation and Creator(s) According to the Ancients

The ancients were smart. No less so than we are today. After all, they built far-reaching empires, erected impressive monuments that could hardly be duplicated today, and established

cultures whose creativity and perception move us deeply. Some of them even charted the stars, figured out the basics of our solar system, and calculated with startling accuracy the circumference of Earth.

The pyramids of Giza, one of the seven wonders of the ancient world.

Yes, the ancients

were gifted with the same smarts as us, but we don't have to do much digging to find their shortcomings. With inadequate access to God's revelation in nature (since science and scientific instruments were only rudimentary at the time) and no access to God's personal revelation (through prophets, personal appearances, or Scripture), the non-Hebrew ancients were left to sheer speculation when it came to forming beliefs about the ultimate origins of the universe and supernatural beings. For instance, a popular Egyptian myth held that in the beginning a temple rose up in the midst of a timeless ocean called Nu. This stone temple produced a god called Atum (don't bother asking how because no one knew), and he in turn generated a host of other gods. No explanation is given for the origin of the ocean or the temple which sat sentinel-like above it. They're just *givens*. Of course today we know full well that material things such as water and stone temples cannot just *be*. They do not have eternal natures; in fact they are made of things that inevitably pass away as they bleed off energy and dissipate, bit by bit, to powder and dust. Further, neither stone nor water has the power of generation. Rocks do not beget gods, and a vast tub of lifeless water left standing full for all of eternity will forever be just that, a vast tub of lifeless water. So though the Egyptians accomplished much that commands our respect, their dabblings in cosmology (the study of origins) reveal their incapacities to discover ultimate truth.

> *The non-Hebrew ancients were left to sheer speculation when it came to forming beliefs about the ultimate origins of the universe.*

> *Though the Egyptians accomplished much that commands our respect, their dabblings in cosmology (the study of origins) reveal their incapacities to discover ultimate truth.*

Not to be outdone by the Egyptian efforts, the equally accomplished Babylonians put forward their own take on how it all began. It also involved eternal waters. In this case there were two bodies of water: a salty ocean named Apsu and a

Marduk killed Tiamat and fashioned the world from her corpse.

body of fresh water called Tiamat. When Apsu and Tiamat commingled, out sprang a host of ham-fisted new gods who reckoned the whole world was theirs to rule. Apsu and Tiamat were put off by these ungrateful latecomers, and so they decided to put them to death. But Apsu was slain by his upstart son, Ea, before the plan came off. When Tiamat saw this, she created a fearful army and prepared to launch it against her children. Recognizing their need for a champion, the gods rallied around Ea's son, Marduk. Marduk agreed to go do battle with his mother on the condition that his fellows agreed to name him chief among the gods. They did so eagerly, and so off he went. Marduk proved to be a fine selection. He defeated Tiamat and tore her corpse into two portions. With one part he created the sky, and with the other he formed land. From her unseeing eyes he caused the Tigris and Euphrates Rivers to flow. Finally he chased down the remnant of Tiamat's allies and from their corpses formed everything from the human race to the stars of the heavens.

These are just two examples of the sorts of stories the ancients put forth to explain the universe. Needless to say such tales are fascinating but deeply problematic. There is nothing in them that can hold our attention today as believable explanations for ultimate origins. They are stories told fireside, long ago, by imaginative people who could only guess at such things. Not so among the Hebrews. As we will see in greater detail in the coming pages, God chose to reveal to Abraham and his descendants grand

God chose to reveal to Abraham and his descendants grand truths that no human could attain if left to his or her own efforts.

truths that no human could attain if left to his or her own efforts.

Genesis and True Beginnings

The outstanding feature of nonbiblical creation stories among the ancients is that there are many, many gods. Some are great (in power); others are quite ordinary as gods go. Some are devoted to feasting and protracted bouts of drinking and are only rarely distracted by human affairs. Others lord over hunt or harvest and demand supplication if humans wish to keep themselves well fed.

The account given in the book of Genesis could hardly be more different. Here there is but one true God. We have strong hints from the outset that there is a plurality within the godhead (see "Us" in Gen 1:26), meaning God is one and yet somehow plural as well. As biblical revelation progressed beyond Genesis and into the New Testament, it was shown that God is Father, Son, and Holy Spirit. In this light theologians refer to God as Trinity, which means he is one in divine essence and three in person. In any case the emphasis in Genesis and the entire Old Testament is that there is only one true God. "I am God, and there is no other," says the Lord (Isa 45:22). It is hard to exaggerate how avant-garde this belief was in that day. At a time when *all* cultures believed in a plurality of gods, Genesis revealed that there is in fact only one.

At a time when all cultures believed in a plurality of gods, Genesis revealed that there is in fact only one.

We saw above that the Egyptians and Babylonians believed the gods were material beings. They came from stone temples or brooding waters, and in Tiamat and Apsu's cases they became the stuff of the physical world on the occasion of their violent deaths. In contrast to this, the God of the Old Testament is Spirit, not material. Neither did he have a beginning. He is invisible, immaterial, and self-sufficient, meaning he has no need of anything. When he created the world, he did so for a purpose (there was no accidental creation via mixing of waters), and he created it from nothing. By creating the world from nothing and for a purpose, God established his uncondi-

God chose to create humans in his own image and bestow upon them a degree of dignity and freedom that is unparalleled among other creatures.

tional rights over everything. The world is at his disposal; nothing can counter him. But this claim is nuanced by the fact that God chose to create humans in his own image and bestow upon them a degree of dignity and freedom that is unparalleled among other creatures. In the Babylonian conception Marduk killed one of Tiamat's allies and created humans from his blood. This ignoble start was reflected in the purpose Marduk bestowed on humans: they were to be slaves in service to the gods. This differs remarkably from Genesis, where humans are made in the image of God and are given assignments that bless them and honor God. As Old Testament scholar Eugene Merrill has said, "God elected to reign through a subordinate, a surrogate king responsible only to him."[2]

We are all kings and queens of creation. The diadem on your head is given by God, but for what purpose has he bestowed this privilege? Taking stock of the whole Old Testament witness, Merrill makes the following summary statement of God's purposes in creating us:

> [God] created all things in order to display his glory and majesty over a kingdom of time and space. Concomitant with that work was his desire for fellowship with sentient beings with whom he could share the responsibilities of universal dominion.[3]

How well have we borne these responsibilities? In many ways that is a central concern of the Old Testament.

Border Wars

By God's appointment we are the regents of creation, but we've thrown out our wise Counselor and sacked the kingdom. The trouble all began in the garden of Eden where God set down some rules. Actually, just one rule: Adam and Eve

By God's appointment we are the regents of creation, but we've thrown out our wise Counselor and sacked the kingdom. were not to take from the tree of the knowledge of good and evil. We know next to nothing about this tree. Though popularly depicted as an apple tree, it may have been any variety of fruit. Most likely there was nothing extraordinary about the fruit itself. The power was in the act of obedience (or disobedience), not in the skin, pulp, or seed of the forbidden food.

Why did God place the restricted tree in the garden? The Bible never answers this question, but it seems reasonable to suggest something along the following lines: God had given Adam and Eve many good things. The garden included more than enough to satisfy their needs and desires. The only sensible response was contentment and gratitude to God for his goodness. The restricted tree provided them with the opportunity to *demonstrate* these attitudes by obeying God's lone prohibition. Proof is found in actions rather than just

The Temptation of Adam and Eve by Lucas Cranach.

words. Here, hanging from the boughs of a forbidden tree, was Adam and Eve's chance to prove their esteem for God.

All might have gone well had Adam and Eve been genuinely alone in the garden, but in the shadows lurked a malevolent spirit-being who aimed to graft them into his plan to

Satan turned from devotion to the ultimate good (God) to infatuation with a lesser good (himself). overthrow God. This was Satan. As with all of God's creations, Satan was originally good. Piecing together several multilayered biblical passages, we learn that Satan was an angelic being whose mismanagement of his God-given beauty and privilege led to his rebellion (Ezek 28:11–19; Isa 14:14). He turned from devotion to the ultimate good (God) to infatuation with a lesser good (himself). Ruin was the inevitable result. God cursed him and threw him down from the heavenly realm to writhe and roam over a world that he hoped to corrupt in bitter payback to God (Isa 14:12–17). As an angelic being Satan does not have a material body. Nevertheless he is able to take on or indwell material substance for the purpose of interacting with the stuff of this world. Adam and Eve were citizens of a garden teeming with animals.

The Fall of Satan by Gustave Doré.

They were comfortable in the presence of many creatures, including the serpent. Satan took advantage of this by using a serpent as host for his appearance to Eve.[4] Eve did not seem surprised that the serpent could speak. Might she have taken it as just another discovery in a world brimming with newness?

Adam stole away into shadow as his wife faced the enemy of her soul.

In any event Satan struck up a conversation with Eve and coaxed her into doubting God's goodness. Adam was supposed to exercise noble masculinity at times like this (after all, it was to *him* that God had given the prohibition, which he in turn was to convey to Eve), but instead he stole away into shadow as his wife faced the enemy of her soul. But Eve was no guiltless victim. She willingly pushed past clear boundaries to take the fruit. Thus the original sin was a joint venture, though Adam rightly received the lion's share of blame.

The result of their infraction was spiritual death immediately, physical death eventually. God had told Adam, "On the day you eat from [the tree], you will certainly die" (Gen 2:17). Adam lived on for many years after this, and Eve bore children. Thus the more direct result of their sin was severance from God and banishment from the posh garden. But there was no escape from their error. The boughs of the forbidden tree grew over all the earth, overshadowing their every step. Whereas Adam and Eve had originally loved one another selflessly, the new reality was that relationship became difficult.

Expulsion of Adam and Eve by Masaccio.

God himself said it would be this way in the curse. Adam would labor hard to harvest his foods, and Eve would cry out in increased pain during birthing, but worst of all God said to Eve, "Your desire will be for your husband, yet he will dominate you" (Gen 3:16). The "desire" God said Eve would feel for her husband is a tainted desire. It's a quest for control and a wresting for power, as the word's usage elsewhere demonstrates (see "desire" in Gen 4:7). Adam's response to this was to lead by force (physically or by a domineering will) instead of by love. Control and suspicion, plot and maneuver—relationship realities we all experience because our first parents set their hearts on selfish gain rather than God's will.

The Bible explains human sinfulness and relational border wars (with God and one another) as a product of misused choice. In contrast to this, ancient non-Hebrew creation stories explained sin as the product of divine intention. For instance, a Babylonian text says the gods "gave perverse speech to the human race; with lies, and not truth, they endowed them forever."[5] This view means we're stuck with the mess we've made because this is what the gods desired. We're *designed* to be bad. Further, in the Babylonian worldview we cannot look to the gods for

Ancient non-Hebrew creation stories explained sin as the product of divine intention.

a hand up because they are a rowdy bunch of miscreants for whom fighting is a way of life. A lifeline from them would only tow us into darker waters.

Blood and Water

Children are the jewels in a family's crown. Adam and Eve had a couple of them after Eden: Cain and Abel. Would they strike a better chord than their parents? Not hardly. When Abel offered a sacrifice that pleased God, Cain became furious

and downcast because his own sacrifice had been deemed unworthy (Gen 4:5). God warned him about these feelings, but stony Cain would not listen. He rose up and killed his brother, spilling Abel's lifeblood into unwilling soil. This was history's first murder, but it was made possible by the events back in Eden. In the years after Abel's murder, wonton brutality and boastfulness became prominent among men. One of Cain's descendants, a bawdy man named Lamech,

Cain and Abel by Titian. Cain rose up and killed his brother, spilling Abel's lifeblood into unwilling soil.

bragged that he had killed a boy who had merely struck him and that his standard for vengeance was seventy-seven times greater than the offense (Gen 4:24). Here is a man who plays god and runs to tell it to his devoted fans. How long will a holy God abide such behavior? Not much longer, it turns out. In Genesis 6:6 we are told that God became fed up with humanity and even "regretted that He had made man on the earth." This does not literally mean God thought, *I made a mistake by making humanity.* After all, he knows the end from the beginning and nothing about the human fall into sin surprised him (Isa 46:10). Talk of God's

Genesis 6:5 says God became fed up with humanity and even "regretted that He had made man on the earth."

"regret" in Genesis 6:5 conveys the reality that he detests human sin and finds the whole situation intolerable. Thus God decided to wipe humanity from the face of earth in a devastating flood. But in the midst of moral darkness, God did find one point of light—Noah, a man of righteousness. Noah was not perfect, mind you, but he came off pretty well in comparison to the rest of the natives. God had regard for this and so elected to spare Noah and his family from destruction.

Interesting confirmation of the flood's assured place in history comes from several ancient flood stories that were recorded even before Moses penned the Genesis account in the fifteenth century BC. The existence of these earlier accounts demonstrates that various peoples remembered something of the flood and its aftermath. But it also raises a common and

Confirmation of the flood's assured place in history comes from several ancient flood stories that were recorded even before Moses penned the Genesis account in the fifteenth century BC.

important challenge: Does the fact that other cultures have similar flood stories suggest that the Genesis account is just one among equal peers or that the Hebrews may actually have gotten the core elements of Noah's story from other cultures? The answer on both counts is no. First, recall that by writing down the flood account and other histories, Moses was fixing on parchment the true stories that had been handed down to his people from folks like Abraham. Thus, other cultures may

have beaten the Hebrews to the punch in disseminating the ancient stories (on clay tablets), but that in no way implies that the other cultures

Noah's flood as envisioned by Michelangelo.

"had the stories" before the Hebrews did. Second, the extreme fancifulness and moral poverty of the non-Hebrew flood stories illustrate that the Hebrews kept the story pure whereas the non-Hebrews went off on fantastic flights of imagination when retelling the old histories. The best known nonbiblical flood story, the Atrahasis Epic, is a case in point. "In the Atrahasis Epic, the gods are annoyed by the noise which the increasing population of mankind makes. The gods decide to create a great flood to destroy man for only doing what he was made to do."[6] In this flood story there is no high divine morality; neither is there a base human sinfulness that deserves punishing. It is just a story about short-tempered gods and their ill-fortuned human subjects.

Tongue and Tower

After the flood humanity gradually rebuilt based on the eight persons in Noah's family, but if the flood was meant to be instructive, the lesson didn't take. Though Noah was regarded as a righteous man and though his family presumably drafted much the same lifestyle based on his example, his descendants nevertheless carried on living by the curse. Dogged by spiritual corruption inherited from Adam, Noah's descendants were sinners, and their progeny could be no different. Centuries after the flood, the sin problem once again came to a head when humanity banded together to erect a monu-

The Tower of Babel by Bruegel.

ment symbolizing their defiance of God's purposes. In the beginning God told humans to "fill the earth" (Gen 1:28), and no doubt this ordinance was passed down to each generation as, starting with Adam and Eve, parents told their children of God's purposes. But true to form humanity set its heart on other plans. The folks gathered at Babel said, "Come, let us build ourselves a city and a tower with its top in the sky. Let us make a name for ourselves; otherwise, we will be scattered over the face of the whole earth" (Gen 11:4). This was a direct countermeasure to God's command to fill the whole earth (to "be scattered"). So the test of wills continued even after the flood, and God again answered by a stunning show of sovereign power. To thwart their unity God confused the languages of the peoples. This inclined them to clump together according to common tongues and eventually to shunt off to different parts of earth. Thereafter the early histories of humanity (the oral accounts that were passed down generation after generation) began to diverge, such that the old stories were corrupted as each culture mixed truth with fiction, memory with fantasy.

The tower of Babel was a direct countermeasure to God's command to fill the whole earth.

As part of this process, many family lines (and thus many cultures) eventually forgot everything they had known about God. For them the line of transference was clipped. Vital truths that were once passed down father to son, mother to daughter, were lost. As a result the world dipped ever deeper into theological and moral error. False gods and contrived religions proliferated, as did immoralities and despair; before long the earth reached a point where even rudimentary knowledge of God was rare. But the light would not go out altogether. God himself saw to that.

Notes

1. Duane Garrett, *Rethinking Genesis: The Sources and Authorship of the First Book of the Pentateuch* (Fearn, Ross-shire, UK: Christian Focus Publications, 2000), chapters 3, 10–11. See also, K. A. Kitchen, *On the Reliability of the Old Testament* (Grand Rapids: Eerdmans, 2003).

2. Eugene Merrill, *Everlasting Dominion: A Theology of the Old Testament* (Nashville: B&H Publishing, 2006), 136.

3. Ibid., 161.

4. The Old Testament elsewhere confirms that "serpent" serves as imagery for the spiritual being who stands in hateful opposition to God (e.g., Job 26:13 and Isa 27:1). The New Testament makes this connection clear (e.g., Rev 12:9; 15; 20:2).

5. Cited by Paul House and Eric Mitchell, *Old Testament Survey*, 2nd ed. (Nashville: B&H Publishing, 2007), 25.

6. Ibid., 25.

Chapter 2
By the Light of Stars

By the twenty-second century BC humanity had spread across the globe and founded cultures that had lost all substantial contact with their ultimate beginnings and Beginner. Darkness reigned even at midday as whole nations bowed to stone idols, worshipped flesh-and-bone kings, and prayed to the sun above. It was into such a scene as this that Abram of Ur was born. Though everyone alive was a descendant of the far-gone Noah, Abram's family had apparently kept hold of this heritage to an unusual degree, for they retained memory of Noah and could name Shem (one of Noah's sons) as their ancient patriarch (Gen 11:27). Most likely this family's persistent

> *Darkness reigned even at midday as whole nations bowed to stone idols, worshipped flesh-and-bone kings, and prayed to the sun above.*

efforts kept memories of Noah and key events preceding him from going extinct. The data link to beginnings in Eden was strained and thin yet unbroken.

Ur was a prominent city in Sumer, the first known society to have achieved a status we now call civilization. Writing was so prominent in Ur that over 20,000 clay tablets dating to

Abram's day have been recovered. The biblical evidence indicates that Abram was from a wealthy family of herders. Picture a family of mobile sheiks, not transient shepherds, when you think of his lifestyle in Ur. While grown-up Abram was still under his father's rule, the family moved from Ur (in modern Iraq) to Haran, situated to the north of modern Israel. If Abram dreamed of a life of permanence and ease in this adopted homeland, his hopes went unfulfilled. Not since Noah's day had God put in personal appearances with mankind, but with Abram he broke this string of silence. We are not told that Abram was a particularly good man. Nothing about him commends him to God. God has simply made a

Writing was so prominent in Ur that over 20,000 clay tablets dating to Abram's day have been recovered.

choice: Abram will be his instrument for initiating a plan of hope. The event is recorded in Genesis 12:1–3.

> Go out from your land, your relatives, and your father's house to the land that I will show you. I will make you into a great nation, I will bless you, I will make your name great, and you will be a blessing. I will bless those who bless you, I will curse those who treat you with contempt, and all the peoples on earth will be blessed through you.

Abram and his wife Sarai were aged and childless at this time, but God's promise was that their descendants would bless all the earth. We can only imagine what Abram thought of his encounter with God. Then as now, encounters with God were simply unheard of. Whatever he thought, the important thing is that he followed through in obedience. He left Haran with Sarai and other members of his entourage and set out for the bushlands of Canaan where God was set to carve out a niche for this couple and their promised descendants. God was deadly earnest about this business, as he demonstrated in one of the most shocking scenes in the Bible.

Terror and Torch

After promising Abram that his descendants would be as numerous as the stars (Gen 15:5), God instructed Abram to bring sacrificial animals and cut them in halves to be placed opposite one another down a line, forming a gauntlet of destruction. As the sun set on this scene, God put Abram to sleep, "and suddenly a terror and great darkness descended on him" (Gen 15:12). It is a fearful thing to be in the presence of holy God. Awakened and awed, Abram listened as God foretold the four-hundred-year Egyptian enslavement his descendants would undergo. God then threatened violence against *himself* should he fail to keep his promises to Abram and the generations which would issue from him. "When the sun had set and it was dark, a smoking fire pot and a flaming torch appeared and passed between the divided animals" (Gen 15:17). This imagery is foreign to us today, but Abram certainly got the message. In that era such an action meant, "May I be ripped apart like these carcasses if I go back on my word to you." In other words, God vowed to bless the world by the light of Abram's stars (children), and he put his own life in the balance of that commitment. Of course this meant God would carry the matter through, for it is impossible that he should die. By faith, therefore, Abram had confidence in the blessings God promised him.

God vowed to bless the world by the light of Abram's stars (children), and he put his own life in the balance of that commitment.

God soon changed Abram and Sarai's names to Abraham and Sarah in recognition of their roles in his plan. Sarah's womb was barren and lifeless in her old age, but God overturned nature to gift the couple with Isaac, the son of the promise. This conception was a miracle, of course, an intervention by God, which proved that he had not walked away from sinful humanity. Any hope that existed would be given through the life of this boy.

Egyptian Sands

The family line progressed from Abraham to Isaac to Jacob, whom God chose over his brother Esau as recipient of Abraham's blessing. Jacob strove with God on a night of contention and was renamed Israel by the Almighty (Gen 32:24–32). This Israel fathered 12 sons, one of whom was sold to nomadic slavers by his jealous brothers. This son was named Joseph. He had a rough go of it in Egypt after he was sold to a governmental executive whose wife subsequently had him jailed on trumped-up charges. Ironically, however, it was his stay in the jailhouse depths

Joseph Sold into Slavery by Flavitsky.

that set him on high. Throughout the Bible God is keen to work in hopeless situations to bring about redemption. In this way there is no mistaking who gets the credit. *He* does. Thus it was from the depths of incarceration in a foreign dungeon that Joseph won renown for his God-given ability to interpret dreams. Soon he became vice-regent over all Egypt, charged with managing the nation's food supplies during a famine. Surrounding peoples came to Joseph for relief, including his own backstabbing brothers. They had no idea they were standing before Joseph, whom they presumed was dead. Here was Joseph's chance for revenge. A few words of command and all but one of Abraham's stars would have been eclipsed. But Joseph chose mercy instead. He revealed his identity, and soon his entire extended family moved to Egypt. Because of Joseph's high standing, they enjoyed Pharaoh's favor and were given land (Gen 47:1).

Shifting Egyptian sands eventually covered over Joseph and his legacy of aid to Egypt. The Hebrews became slaves rather than favored guests, and as they multiplied, they came to be seen as a threat to Pharaoh's rule. A rat cannot rule over mice when mice overrun the kingdom, and so the screws of oppression tightened. After several centuries God raised up a deliverer—Moses, a Hebrew who was raised in Pharaoh's own household. He fled Egypt as a relatively young adult because he bashed to death an Egyptian who had been roughing

Moses was a murderer and a fugitive from justice when God called him to holy service.

up a Hebrew slave (Exod 2:11–15). For all intents and purposes Moses was a blue-blooded Egyptian, but he knew of his Hebrew heritage, and he could not stand idly by and watch a man of his own ethnicity receive abuse. Thus Moses was a murderer and a fugitive from justice when God called him to holy service. Furthermore, he struck cowardly colors when God commissioned him to be heaven's spokesperson to the Hebrews and to Pharaoh, but these facts could not pry him loose from God's plan (Exod 3:11–4:17). Thus after 40 years of wasteland exile, Moses slinked back to the scene of his crime in the Nile Valley, sent by God to announce deliverance for the beleaguered Hebrews.

Death of the Pharaoh's Firstborn Son by Alma-Tadema.

Pharaoh only scoffed at this message. He was unwilling to lose his labor force and unwilling to humble himself before God. Thus by several rounds of plague and wonder, God laid Pharaoh low for his stubbornness—stubbornness God himself had ordained so he could demonstrate his power by overcoming the Egyptian monarch (Gen 4:21). Here, in the setting up and knocking down of Pharaoh, is one of many biblical indications that God's highest good is his glory and honor. Humans are important since they are made in God's image, but by no means are we the center of his universe or his thought. This is a difficult lesson for many of us today. We have grown accustomed to thinking that God's highest priority is that humans should be happy and endowed with peace, even at the expense of his holy nature, his demands for justice, and his fame as a God of unmatched power. We must renounce this humanistic habit of mind. With trembling we note that it greatly resembles the sort of bent Satan's thoughts took before he was cast down in shame and curse by the God who shares glory and place with no one. God made all things for himself. The story of creation will unfold in a way that maximizes his renown as the highest imaginable good. Among humans some will glorify God by humbly receiving his offer of mercy. Others (such as Pharaoh) will choose obstinacy and ongoing sin. These too will glorify God insomuch as they invite a demonstration of power and judgment in which God highlights his excellencies (Rom 9:14–24).

God made all things for himself. The story of creation will unfold in a way that maximizes his renown as the highest imaginable good.

Ramses II, possible Pharaoh of Exodus.

Back to Pharaoh. By fire and ice, death and darkness, God pushed him to the precipice of submission. When he could no longer withstand the judgments against his nation and household, Pharaoh granted the Hebrews the right to leave Egypt. It was a stunning blow to Egyptian esteem. As citizens of the world's greatest superpower, they believed their greatness was made possible by their gods. Even so no Egyptian imagined that their gods controlled anything outside the national borders. This is because in their worldview gods were strictly territorial. Drag a deity outside his homeland and he is powerless. In defiance of this expectation, the Hebrew God demonstrated that he is at home anywhere. After all, it was far away from the place of Hebrew origins that he thwarted foreign priest, regent, and god.

The Hebrews skipped town in the middle of the night as Egypt cried for her slain sons. All firstborn males, from those in Pharaoh's household on down to those born to the lowest Egyptian laborer, fell to God's final and definitive judgment (Exod 12). The Hebrews were spared this penalty because at God's command they sprinkled the blood of lambs

over their doorposts. This act of faith honored God and placed them under his mercy. As they spilled out into the reaches beyond Egypt proper, the Hebrews tasted freedom for the first time in 400 years. We may wonder why they became enslaved in the first place. After all, God had promised that Abraham's children would occupy the land of Canaan. Why foreordain that they should first be oppressed by a pagan power? The answer is that in God's

The Egyptians Urging Moses to Depart by Gustave Doré.

wisdom he often plots the path to blessing through a land of trouble. Ironically, it is the journey through trouble that makes later success possible. Consider Joseph again, the venerated forefather of the Hebrews. It was his time in prison that primed him for the leadership and administrative roles he acquired after his release. In much the same way the Egyptian furnace served as a womb for Abraham's descendants. Mighty Egypt fed them and protected them from marauding bandits and petty nations that would otherwise assail them. Thus

In God's wisdom he often plots the path to blessing through a land of trouble.

nourished and protected, the Hebrew population increased exponentially. Egypt also unintentionally fostered solidarity and national identity among the Hebrews by warding them away from choice lands and favored occupations. Theirs was a grotto experience. As a result of these factors, several hundred years into their Egyptian experience the Hebrews had formed a great mass of people capable of mustering armies for the conquest of Canaan, a land filled with seasoned warriors. This population expansion would not have been feasible had they carried on the nomadic lifestyle set down by Abraham and his sons, for the nomadic way is hard and meager. So, what at the outset seemed like a broken promise (the sons of Israel were enslaved and living outside the promised land) ended up being the means of fulfilling the promise.

Rules of Engagement

After making a miraculous escape through the Red Sea, the Hebrews met with God at Mount Sinai for an orientation meeting in which he spelled out what it means to know him and be a people set apart for holy living. God told Moses that he would come person-ally to speak to the people. On the appointed day, "there was thunder and lightning, a thick cloud on the mountain, and a loud trumpet sound, so that all the people in the camp shuddered. . . . Mount Sinai was completely enveloped in smoke because the LORD came down on it in fire. Its smoke went up like the smoke of a fur-nace, and the whole mountain shook violently. As the sound of the trumpet grew louder and louder, Moses spoke and God answered him in the thunder" (Exod 19:16–19). The people had been warned to keep their distance lest they tempt God to "break out in anger against them" (Exod 19:22). God is not a man that one can sim-ply stroll up to him at ease.

Moses with the Ten Command-ments by Rembrandt. The Hebrews met with God at Mount Sinai for an orientation meeting in which he spelled out what it means to know him and be a people set apart for holy living.

Now that they faced him the people understood this clearly enough. It is a fearful thing to be near the Creator. Soon the tension became too much, and the people begged Moses to ascend the mountain and meet God by himself. You be our intercessor, they said. In response Moses explained that God's show of force was a test "so that you will fear Him and will not sin" (Exod 20:20). Believing that they had learned this lesson, Moses left to meet the Lord.

Though the Hebrews saw an entire mountain tremble and crack at its roots under the burden of God's presence, they defied that lesson once Moses went missing up the mountain

After Aaron made the idol, the people said, "Israel, this is your God, who brought you up from the land of Egypt!" (Exod 32:4). *The Golden Calf* by Poussin.

slope. Having given him up for dead after forty days, they figured they were on their own with the fearful deity. Recalling the sphinx-like idols and crafts of Egyptian religion, the people commissioned Moses' brother Aaron to shape a calf from the gold that had been hauled out from under Pharaoh's nose. "Israel, this is your God, who brought you up from the land of Egypt!" they announced (Exod 32:4). In keeping with this degradation, the people then sacrificed to the idol and drank themselves into an orgy, sealing this as a day of infamy for all time.

In the aftermath of the rebellion at Sinai, the Hebrews were forced to wander in the wilderness for 40 years as punishment. None of the adults who participated in the atrocities were permitted to enter the land promised to Abraham's descendants. Sadly, Moses himself came under this restriction because at some point after Sinai he lost his temper and treated the Lord's instructions disdainfully (Num 20:7–12). It is hard not to be troubled at

In the aftermath of the rebellion at Sinai, the Hebrews were forced to wander in the wilderness for 40 years as punishment.

Moses' fate. He put up with a lot of griping and rebellion from the people, saved their lives on several occasions by averting God's wrath, and on the whole was faithful to the hard path God called him to walk. Is it not unfair that he was debarred from the promised land for a minor infraction? The problem with this question is that it is out of focus. Rather than eyeing Moses' mistake, we must eye his *task*. In his role as mediator between sinful humanity and holy God, Moses had to satisfy two parties: God and the Hebrews. Both parties expected Moses to meet the highest standards. God wanted complete holiness, and the Hebrews wanted bold leadership that met all their needs and inspired immovable trust. Moses failed to meet these expectations; indeed, he could hardly have done otherwise since he was a sinner leading sinners. His failures therefore highlight the desperation of the human condition. We cannot put forward a merely human representative whom God will find complete, nor can we select a representative in whom we can trust enough to lead us safely to the foot of God's throne, a place where utter holiness is the only accepted standard. If you are a man and nothing more, I have grave misgivings about your judgment in matters pertaining to God. What if you are wrong about God's rules, his mercies, or his offer of forgiveness? What if God has not chosen you as a messenger to humanity? The failures of a merely human

> *Moses failed as a mediator because he was neither good enough for God nor good enough for sinners.*

Moses lost his temper and treated the Lord's instructions disdainfully (Num 20:1–12). *Moses Striking the Rock* by Nicolas Poussin.

mediator could lead to final doom for everyone. Ultimately, therefore, Moses failed as a mediator because he was neither good enough for God nor good enough for sinners. This is an important point, and we shall return to it again in the discussions that follow. For now we must break away and follow Israel down the warpath to the promised land. How did they get there, and what does their method of entry say about God?

Holy War

The Hebrew occupation of the promised land is often

referred to as a holy war because it was by God's plan, God's command, and God's power that the Canaanites were eliminated, town by town, as the children of Abraham tore across the land in a great red swath. The Canaanites had lived in this land for at least a thousand years; they had even been mostly peaceable with Abraham when he sojourned among them many years earlier. So the question arises: Why was it necessary to eliminate them? In the first place the Hebrews needed a homeland. Since two large and dissimilar people groups cannot occupy the exact same territory, something had to give. God had chosen to set his covenant love upon the Hebrews, so it was fitting that he should give them the land of his own choosing. Second, the Canaanites had roused God's anger by worshipping false gods such as Baal and Asherah. Imagine a human father whose children run off after another man, a *lesser* man, and embrace him with cries of "Our father and benefactor!" Such a jilted father would rightly be angry. How much more should God be angered when his image bearers fold hands and bend knees before false gods? It is the ultimate offence.

But the Canaanites were guilty of more than just mistaken beliefs about God. Beliefs drive actions; wrong beliefs drive wrong actions. For the Canaanites the wrong actions included human sacrifice and ritualistic prostitution, both of which aimed to entice Baal into bestowing fertility upon the wombs and fields of the region. One

The Canaanites were mistreating God and one another, and they did it all in the name of religion.

can only imagine the horror of human sacrifice, and ritualistic prostitution would deeply scar the female victims, especially since a great many of them were unwilling participants. Hence the Canaanites were mistreating God *and* one another, and they did it all in the name of religion. God is not obligated to put up with such things. As the holy one who created the universe

As the holy one who created the universe for his glory, God is right to punish sins in whatever manner he chooses.

for his glory, God is right to punish sins in whatever manner he chooses. In this case he chose to conduct a sustained war against a whole region. We must emphasize that this is a very *rare* thing in history. Subsequent to Bible times it is absolutely illegitimate to say, "God is calling for holy war." In contrast to regular wars, the campaign we are examining was deeply marked by symbols of holy ritual and divine sanction. For instance, Joshua 3:1–4 reports that the priests marched before the Hebrew host, carrying the ark

Subsequent to Bible times it is absolutely illegitimate to say, "God is calling for holy war."

of the covenant as they entered the doomed lands. It was God who went to war here, and he did it for the sake of his holiness and for his chosen people. Of all the nations on earth, it was the Hebrews alone with whom God had established his covenant. He had created them from scratch by taking an old couple (Abraham and Sarah) and gifting them with a child out of season. Now that his people were huddled on the borders of their inheritance, God elected to clear the land of false beliefs and wicked practices that would cause them to stumble if the natives were allowed to remain. In the debacle at Sinai, the Hebrews had already proven how susceptible they were to peer influence. God's instruction to eliminate all Canaanite presence in the new Hebrew homeland was therefore aimed at giving them a distraction-free environment in which their devotion to God could be fostered and unchallenged. But as Bible history tells us, the Hebrews failed to make a clean sweep of the land. Too often they let the Canaanites live. In so doing they let Canaan's false gods live on in rituals and beliefs that would eventually grab them around the heart.

Summary

God announced a plan to bless the world by the light of Abraham's stars. That this plan provided for actions such as the war against Canaan indicates the gravity of sin, the primacy of God's redemptive plan, and the lengths to which he is prepared to go to fulfill that plan. Nothing can thwart God's plan of redemption, but as we will see in the next chapter, this assurance rests on God's faithfulness, not the faithfulness of his covenant people.

Chapter 3
National Treasure

While spiritual poverty gripped the peoples of the world, the Hebrews were given a treasure of incalculable worth: true knowledge of God. It came to them not because they sought it or stumbled upon a key that opened divine secrets. It was theirs because God picked Abram, struck a deal with him, and kept at it with his bumbling descendants down through the years. The treasure was a free and unmerited gift in the truest sense possible. But it was not meant to be horded. Once the Hebrews settled in the promised land, one of God's chief purposes for them was that by keeping true to his revelations they would be a beacon of light to the world. This means, for instance, that their adherence to God's moral laws would promote a more peaceful and equitable society than was seen in the surrounding nations. The He-

One of God's chief purposes for the Hebrews was that they would be a beacon of light to the world.

brews would thus be seen as distinct because of lifestyles that were driven by their unique theological beliefs. This means the Hebrew God would stand out as different from the so-called gods of nearby nations. The principle is this: Live well and the world will notice your God. Jesus hinged much of his teaching on this exact point, as we shall see later in this book.

God could have chosen another method for spreading knowledge of himself among the nations, but it was his delight to invent a people from Abraham and Sarah's aged loins, multiply them under the bonds of slavery, chasten them in the wilderness sojourn, and then deposit them in a land freshly cleared of demoralizing false religion. The question is, What did the Hebrews do with their national treasure? Were they faithful stewards of the blessing God gave them? Some yes and some no? In this chapter we examine the history of the Hebrew nation and their stewardship of God's revelations.

> *Live well and the world will notice your God.*

Lifeblood for the Gods

Most of us would not have the stomach to practice the ancient religions. Without exception they involved sacrifice, sometimes of humans—infant, child, or adult—but most often it was animals and birds that lost their lives for the sake of religion. In these rituals the key element was blood. While the ancients did not have

Early Bronze Age altar at Arad in southern Israel c. 2800 BC.
Photo: HolyLandPhotos.org.

advanced medical knowledge, they could plainly see that the life of a creature is in its blood. For this reason blood was seen as a sort of liquid gold. Spilling it onto an altar was paramount to giving the gods a most precious sacrifice: life itself. But why did people think this was necessary? First, they realized that their lives depended on factors that were out of their direct control. These included the need for rain, fertile soils, and wombs, good health, sanctuary from storms, protection from beasts and pestilences, and so forth. Keeping the gods happy by giving them valuable sacrifices seemed like a sensible way of buying good fortune. Second, all humans sensed their guilt and need for forgiveness. This awareness of sin is a basic result of bearing the image of God. Hardwired into our mental and spiritual makeup is a fundamental understanding of right and wrong. We call it our conscience. We say our conscience accuses us if we do something wrong, but more fundamentally it is *God* who does the accusing as we act against his moral nature, which he has imprinted in us. Sensing their errors however dimly, the ancients sought to appease the gods by sacrificing something of value.

While there are obvious parallels between the sacrificial practices of the Hebrews and all other ancient cultures, there are also fundamental differences. For instance, the gods of the nations were universally regarded as fick-

The gods of the nations were universally regarded as fickle, peevish, and unpredictable.

le, peevish, and unpredictable. The fact that storms blew up from nowhere, that disasters befell innocents for no apparent reason, and that droughts, plagues, and infestations struck even those most devoted to their idols led the nations to suppose that the gods were unpredictable and mean-spirited. One

result of this belief is that the worshippers lived in a perpetual state of fear. Not crippling fear, of course, but a consistent unease and uncertainty about their standing before the lidless eye of divinity. That the gods numbered into the hundreds or even thousands in popular lore meant that the task of achieving right standing was impossi-

Three of ancient Egypt's gods. Photo: Rama (CC License 2.0). That the gods numbered into the hundreds or even thousands in popular lore meant that the task of achieving right standing was impossible.

ble, for by pleasing one god you have likely displeased another whose expectations differ from those of the god you pleased. Confused? So were the ancients. They could never be sure which divinities were for them and which were against them. Thus the pagan sacrifices were varied, hurried, and harried.

A Sure Atonement

While the pagans fumbled with sacrificial innards, hoping to find a sign from the gods in a misshapen liver or a knotted bowel, the Hebrews practiced a much more affirming variety of sacrifice. God himself had shown them the way by revealing concretely his moral standards in the Ten Commandments and various laws. There was no need to guess at right and wrong, nor was there any concern about competing interests among the gods since the Hebrews knew only one God exists. God also gave the Hebrews clear instructions on how to conduct the sacrifices.

The Hebrews did not worry about competing interests among the gods since they knew only one God exists.

The book of Leviticus offers vivid notes on the principles and practices God laid out for the sacred rituals. The priests were

required to approach God in the manner prescribed. It is an undeserved honor to come into the presence of holy God. No man can do it on his own terms, and so the priests were given regulations, clear and strict. The consequences of disobeying these are vividly displayed by an episode involv-

Reconstruction of an ancient Hebrew altar from around the time of King Hezekiah. Photo: Gugganij (CC License 2.5).

ing the sons of Aaron, Israel's first high priest. One day Aaron's sons were conducting ceremonies before the Lord. They knew the regulations but decided to take an alternate approach to their duties. They "presented unauthorized fire before the LORD, which He had not commanded them to do" (Lev 10:1). In other words, they decided that God could be approached on *their* terms. The result is not hard to guess. "Then flames leaped from the LORD's presence and burned them to death before the LORD"(v. 2).

This episode shocks us and seems to call God's goodness into question, but upon further reflection we find a measure of comfort and encouragement in the death of Aaron's sons. Here is what I mean: The swift and drastic punishment of their arrogance proves the reality of God's presence during the atonement ceremonies. God really *is* present, taking note of what goes on. If he takes the whole thing seriously enough to strike out at those who offer "unauthorized fire," then surely he's just as serious when he says that by means of the sacrifices

No merely human mediator is capable of meeting the requirements of God's holiness or the requirements of perfectly representing humanity before God.

people of faith will be forgiven of their sins. Additionally, the high standards of the priestly office and the inability of even Aaron's sons to carry it out to satisfaction demonstrate the theme we mentioned earlier: no merely human mediator is capable of meeting the requirements of God's holiness or the requirements of perfectly representing humanity before God. A better mediator must be found, one whom only God can provide. This he would do in the fullness of time.

Meanwhile the most important sacrifices were offered on the annual Day of Atonement when the high priest made atoning sacrifices on behalf of the nation. The first step in this daylong drama was for Aaron to make sacrifices for himself and his family (Lev 16:6). By this means he was made worthy to conduct the ceremonies on behalf of the people who had gathered solemnly outside the tabernacle. Next the priest gathered two goats and brought them into the presence of God. By the sacred casting of lots, the priests identified which of the goats God had chosen to be slain for the people. This is important, for it reveals that the acceptable sacrifice was *God's* to choose. No one can come into God's presence and dictate what

The high priest sprinkled blood on the mercy seat, the symbol of God's presence. Photo: Ben Schumin (CC License 2.5).

sacrifices are acceptable. As for the sinless animal that was chosen, it was slain as a representation that God's wrath had fallen on it rather than the sinful people to whom wrath was genuinely due. The priest then took some of the goat's blood and sprinkled it against the mercy seat, which was a golden slab that ran like a tabletop across the length of the ark of the covenant. This was kept inside the holy of holies, the highly restrictive inner sanctum of the tabernacle. The altar and other priestly implements were cleansed in the same way. All of these acts served to make the tabernacle and its items acceptable for the day's holy purposes.

The final act of the Day of Atonement was the most dramatic of all. The goat which was *not* chosen to be sacrificed was brought forward in full view of the assembly. The high priest then laid his hands on the head of the goat and confessed the sins of the people. In so doing the guilt and blame for a year's worth of rebellion was transferred to the goat. Then as the people stood in silent awe and gratitude, the goat was driven far into "a desolate land" from which it would never return (Lev 16:22). God's purpose in sending out this "scapegoat" was to demonstrate to the Hebrews that their sins had been transferred and banished from all view. Thus they were in good standing before God by virtue of their

faith participation in the atonement event. By watching the high priest's actions and believing in their hearts that this was God's appointed means of forgiving sins, the people were made holy in the sight of God.

Kings of the Earth

When God told Abraham what his descendants would experience as the covenant relationship unfolded, he said that kings and nations would arise from his bloodlines and that the Hebrew kingdom would be everlasting (Gen 17:6–8). He reiterated the kingship promise to Abraham's descendant Jacob in Genesis 35:11. Therefore the Hebrews were destined to have kings, but God did not intend for them

Solomon by Gustave Doré. The Hebrews were destined to have kings, but God did not intend for them to mimic the nations.

to mimic the nations by naming as king men of iron force who aimed to bolster Israel's status in the panoply of world powers. Instead, they were to wait for God's timing and God's man. Their ambitions were to be toward heaven, not earth. The Hebrews lost sight of this and pined for a king when they saw the deeds of heroic Gideon. They asked him to establish a throne over Israel, but he refused, saying, "I will not rule over you, and my son will not rule over you; the LORD will rule over you" (Judg 8:23). Gideon understood that God must lead in this matter, else the kingship is in vain. But the people would not be dissuaded for long. Intent on jumping the gun and making a name for themselves on the earth, they demanded that Samuel (who served the Hebrews as prophet and priest) "appoint a king to judge us the same as all the other nations have" (1 Sam 8:5). Much like Gideon, Samuel recognized the rashness of this demand. Israel had become like a spoiled son who wanted fulfillment *now*, on his own terms. God chose to meet the demand, though to chastise rather than bless his child. To Samuel he said, "Listen to the people and everything they say to you. They have not rejected you; they have rejected Me as their king" (v. 7). Thus at God's prompting Samuel foretold the people that once their king had abused his privileges, "you will cry out because of the king you've chosen for yourselves, but the LORD won't answer you on that day" (v. 18).

God chose a giant among men to be the premature king over Israel. His name was Saul. He appeared to be the genuine article when judged by flesh and bone, but he was a tragic figure from the start. At his public installation as king, he hid among sacks and crates in a bid to escape the responsibilities that would soon rest on his broad shoulders. The reader is not kept wondering about the cause of this cowardly behavior for long, for Saul revealed weak character early in his kingship. In an episode that reminds us of Aaron's sons and the unauthorized fire, Saul conducted burnt offerings one day because he was too impatient to wait for the arrival of Samuel, the authorized priest. God did not take Saul's life for this infraction, but he did arrange for him to be caught red-handed. When Samuel arrived Saul hastily explained, "When I saw that . . . you didn't come within the appointed days . . . I *forced* myself to offer the burnt offering" (1 Sam 13:11–12). In modern parlance this

runs something like, "I'm sorry, officer, but since you never showed up, I forced myself to go ahead and break the law." Here, O Israel, is the enforcer of your laws and the keeper of the light that was entrusted to Abraham!

David Playing the Harp for Saul by Rembrandt.

Sadly, Saul never corrected this early trajectory. He was nose-down and ill-fated in all his strivings. When he later defied God's commands regarding the destruction of an enemy,

Saul was essentially finished as king. God disclosed the end to Samuel even as Saul was off erecting a monument to his kingship, thus proving in stone effigy what sort of king he was at heart (1 Sam 15:10–12). Soon an "evil spirit" was appointed by God to harry and trouble this maker of monuments (1 Sam 18:10; see also 16:15, 16, 23). While scholars have debated the exact identity of this spirit from God, the results are beyond question: for the rest of his days Saul was pressed and

God chooses emotional engagement instead of detached supervision. By virtue of this, he makes himself vulnerable in ways we cannot capture.

punished by the hand of God for his inexcusable sins. It did not please God to do this. He even expressed "regret" that he had made Saul king over Israel (1 Sam 15:11). The regret God feels here is not like the regret you and I feel when we've made a bad decision due to lack of sound judgment or foresight. God infallibly knows all things past, present, and future (Isa 46:10). The success of his plan to redeem a people for himself is not left to chance or the wiles of fallen human nature. But what God *has* done, and this should catch us breathless, is enter into our experience and lay his own heart on the line. He chooses emotional engagement instead of detached supervision. By virtue of this, he makes himself vulnerable in ways we cannot capture. He foreknows every rise and fall in the affections of his people; and certainly he was never caught gaping in surprise as Saul's kingship disintegrated; but when his holiness and love were denigrated by the people whom he had separated from the nations, his heart was moved to sorrow, regret, anger, and a gamut of strong emotions that are proper to holy God.

Shepherd King and Shattered Kingdom

While broad-chested Saul strode around the kingdom, restless in his consumption, a ruddy lad of humble size and spirit tended sheep on the hillsides of Judah. He was altogether ordinary to look at, and he was kid brother to a set of Saul's warriors. In short, this boy David was invisible to the world —not at all the sort of figure to catch your eye, let alone hold your attention. But God looks at the heart, the true fount of character; and in young David he saw a mighty king. God determined from the outset that David's kingship would be nobler than Saul's: "He will build a house for My name, and I will establish the throne of his kingdom forever. I will be a father to him, and he will be a son to Me. When he does wrong, I will discipline him with a human rod and with blows from others. But My faithful love will never leave him as I removed it from Saul" (2 Sam 7:13–15).

> *God looks at the heart, the true fount of character, and in young David he saw a mighty king.*

Saul never had a head for theology, but David displayed a firm grasp of God's identity and Israel's role in history. "There is no one like You," he said of God, "and there is no God besides You . . . And who is like Your people Israel? God came to one nation on earth in order to redeem a people for Himself,

David by Castagno. In young David the world saw only a shepherd boy, but God saw a king.

and to perform for them great and awesome acts, driving out nations and their gods before Your people You redeemed for Yourself from Egypt" (2 Sam 7:22–23).

Blending together several of God's pronouncements, the Father's assessment of King David can be stated in this way: "I have found David the son of Jesse, a man after My heart, who will carry out all My will" (Acts 13:22).[1] Indeed, David is depicted throughout Scripture as the exemplar for human kingship in Israel. He is God's Son, a willing servant to the divine will, a faultless follower of God. This saintly image was important because it maintained Israel's hope in a future restoration of humankind's place with God, a restoration that would be possible only if God could find a man in whom he was fully pleased and who could bridge the infinite gap between humanity and holiness. David was the prefiguration of that perfect man, but he himself was *not* perfect despite the many biblical passages that highlight his devotions to God. Balancing the "David as saint" passages are several narratives that unflinchingly expose his errors. Not many of us are murderers, though our darkest thoughts bring us to the edge of such poison pools. David has been there and jumped in headlong. He once saw a woman bathe and did not turn away (2 Sam 11). His lingering glance produced a child, a murder, and the early death of a firstborn son. David confessed and repented when God sent a prophet to expose him, but all the same this episode was a window to the inner rooms of a good king's heart. Eden's ancient darkness was found even there. David's sons and daughters fared no better. Plots, ploys, and murders played out among them. When it was Solomon's turn to wield his father's scepter over Israel, he took a thousand wives and concubines, many from other cultures, and sanctioned their pagan religions. The light of Abraham's stars was dimmed as smoke rose from a land dotted with unauthorized fires and rituals. And still the faithful in Israel waited for a perfect mediator.

> *David's saintly image was important because it maintained Israel's hope in a future restoration of humankind's place with God.*

Note

1. Paul's quote blends divine words recorded in 1 Samuel 13:14; Psalm 89:20; and Isaiah 44:28.

Jeremiah Lamenting the Destruction of Jerusalem by Rembrandt.

Chapter 4
Prophets of Doom

King Solomon died amidst a great horde of gold and exotic women, but none of these could hold his dimming eye. In fact, he surely despised his wealth and reputed wisdom as he lay dying, for God had told him that his kingdom was forfeit (1 Kgs 11:11–13). Wise Solomon had played the fool, forsaking God and leaving behind a household in shambles. When the time of succession came, his son Rehoboam leaped onto the throne and called down brash orders that caused revolt and division. The nation split into two factions—Israel to the north, composed of ten tribes, and Judah to the south, based in Jerusalem and centered on what remained of the tattered Davidic lineage. From this point onward the Hebrews were mostly faithless unto God. Stragglers in both kingdoms remained true, but most turned away forever.

Solomon and Sheba by Denim. Neither wealth nor women brought Solomon happiness.

Elijah faced off against King Ahab and 450 priests of Baal on Mount Carmel. Illustration by Gustave Doré.

It was in this era that God sent the prophets—storied men such as Elijah and Elisha, Isaiah and Jeremiah—to announce judgment and restoration, doom and hope over Abraham's stray stars. From these men we learn deep truths about God's nature and his plans to forge a holy people called by his name and for his glory. We also see them struggle to cope with the sins of God's chosen people. Elijah famously believed he was the last of the faithful, and it's little wonder he felt this way as he faced off against King Ahab and 450 pagan priests of Baal at Mount Carmel. Right there in the open, on a hilltop in the promised land, the Hebrews perfected rebellion as they bowed the knee to a mute and false god who could make no fire on the altar even though his servants slashed their veins and cried out for vindication. Elijah suggested that their unresponsive god had gone off on a restroom break or a stroll (1 Kgs 18:27). He then watered down his own altar before asking God to send forth fire. The flames came down and consumed *everything*—wood, stone, offering, and all. Nothing was left because the presence of Israel's *true* God had come in a display of power that all the priests of Baal could not duplicate even with an eternity of chanting.

Hearts feinted toward God as the fire fell, but this kindling of love died away as soon as the flames winked out. Genuine, lasting repentance evaded the Hebrews, and thus they marched on toward disso-

The faith of Israel became so derelict that God told the prophet Isaiah at the outset of his ministry that the people would not heed his voice.

lution. The faith of Israel became so derelict that God told the prophet Isaiah at the outset of his ministry that the people would not heed his voice (Isa 6:9–10). Throughout Israel's spiritual drought we catch glimpses of the sovereignty and power of a God whose people have walked away from him. He is not ruined by their mass defection. In fact, it provided him the chance to demonstrate his status as the unquestioned ruler over all human affairs, both within and without Israel. Having decided to chasten his erring children, God raised up the pagan Assyrians and directed them to sack Judah. The king of Assyria had his own reasons for undertaking this campaign, of course, but God was the higher cause of the aggressions, and he went on to punish the Assyrian ruler for not recognizing that he was just a pawn in the divine hand (Isa 10). Here we see that God will get his way on the earth even if he must use people who neither call on his name nor confess his existence. Deep and awe-inspiring is the mystery of divine sovereignty.

God will get his way on the earth even if he must use people who neither call on his name nor confess his existence.

Banishing Acts

In 722 BC the Assyrian war machine rolled through Israel (the Northern Kingdom) and hauled most of the survivors back to Assyria. Israel was then forcibly repopulated with non-Hebrews. These immigrants mixed with the few native Hebrews who had evaded exile. In this way religion and blood commingled to create a hybrid, syncretistic population known as the Samaritans. As for those who were led away in Assyrian slave caravans, they composed the ten lost tribes who would never return home as tribal entities. The few persons who did eventually return had to assimilate into the tiny Southern Kingdom (Judah), which huddled around

The Taylor Prism, found at Nineveh, dates from the time of the Assyrian captivity. It mentions the siege of Jerusalem and King Hezekiah.

the city of Jerusalem. This sliver of land was all that remained of David's once mighty kingdom, and even it was no safe haven. Jerusalem was overthrown by Babylon in 586 BC. Again the invaders left select natives behind, but most of the Hebrews were hauled away to serve in foreign lands.

Punishment can be redemptive insomuch as it humbles the proud heart, and indeed this was one of God's purposes in the exile of his people. Approximately 70 years after their banishment, God prepared to gather a remnant of his people back to Jerusalem. Speaking through the prophet Ezekiel, he said, "When I bring you from the peoples and gather you from the countries where you have been scattered, I will accept you as a pleasing aroma. And I will demonstrate My holiness through you in the sight of the nations" (Ezek 20:41). God's holiness was displayed by the humbled Hebrews who confessed that their improbable restoration was made possible by God's gracious choice, not their power or merit.

Punishment can be redemptive insomuch as it humbles the proud heart, and indeed this was one of God's purposes in the exile of his people.

The ruins of a wall built by Hezekiah to protect against the siege of Sennacherib. This would have been similar to what the ancient Hebrews found on their return to Jerusalem. Photo: Lior Golgher (CC License 2.5).

It was a moment of resounding triumph when a remnant of Hebrews reentered Jerusalem from abroad, but it did not translate into the rebirth of the Davidic kingdom. Israel was finished as a regional power. The return of a few avid Jews could not change that. This is not to say that all hope was lost, however. For the few who remained faithful to God's covenant, hope was upheld by the firm foundations God had revealed through the patriarchs and the prophets.

Foundations for Hope

Three key foundations kept hope alive among the faithful in Israel: God's love which was secured by his covenants, God's sovereign power, and God's promised Messiah.

God's love for his people is fundamentally elective love, a matter of divine choice. He loves the unlovable because that is what he chooses to do.

Israel's hope for redemption lay first of all in the love of God. Faithful Hebrews understood that God is holy, that human sin is repulsive to him, and that the resulting breach between God and humanity cannot be repaired by our efforts. Hence, God's love for his people is fundamentally *elective* love, a matter of divine choice. He loves the unlovable because that is what he chooses to do. This was the model from the very start, as when God chose Abram from among all the peoples of earth and established a permanent covenant with him. Since God's fidelity to his covenant was on the line (recall God's threat against himself should he ever break the covenant, Gen 15:17), he never let his love die; and he also ensured that a faithful nucleus remained among his chosen people. Thus God promised Israel through the prophet Ezekiel: "I will give you a new heart and put a new spirit within you; I will remove your heart of stone and give you a heart of flesh. I will place My Spirit within you and cause you to follow My statutes and carefully observe My ordinances. Then you will live in the land that I gave your fathers; you will be My people, and I will be your God" (Ezek 36:26-28).

Ezekiel by Michelangelo.

Those who trusted this promise understood that in the final analysis God's love would secure their faithfulness. He would work in their hearts to ensure that the covenant promises came true. Who can find a surer foundation for hope than this? God will love and redeem his people because he holds himself a willing captive to the covenant choices he has made.

Related to trust in God's love is trust in his power. God is able to carry out all of his purposes. Confessions of God's absolute dominion and power dot the entire landscape of Old Testament revelation. He directs the channels of the king's heart (Prov 21:1), conducts the affairs of earth in whatever manner he chooses (Pss 115:3; 103:19; 1 Chr 29:12), holds sway over inanimate natural processes such as weather and the growth of vegetation (Job 37:6–13; Ps 104:14), exercises providence over the entire lifecycle of animals (Pss 104:27–29; 29:9), hems in and bends Satan's hateful actions to achieve holy purposes (Job 1:6–12), and mysteriously reigns over and works through even the sinful choices of humans (Gen 45:5–8; 50:19–20; Isa 10:5–27). Can such a God be thwarted in his plan to redeem a people for himself? Absolutely not.

Confessions of God's absolute dominion and power dot the entire landscape of Old Testament revelation.

Finally, flowing from God's elective love and his unchecked power to accomplish his plans was the people's hope for Messiah, a servant who would fully and finally deliver Israel into good standing with God. Stray allusions to Messiah are sprinkled throughout the Old Testament, typically in the midst of disclosures that have immediate relevance in some nonmessianic application but which also stretch beyond the moment and point to something grander that lies in the future. A chief example of this is when Jacob blessed his sons before he died. Speaking to Judah, he said, "The scepter will not depart from Judah,

Stray allusions to Messiah are sprinkled throughout the Old Testament, typically in the midst of disclosures that have immediate relevance in some non-messianic application.

or the staff from between his feet until He whose right it is comes and the obedience of the peoples belongs to Him" (Gen 49:10). On the surface this fit with the immediate context of Jacob's describing Judah's preeminence among his brothers. But the last part of the verse stretches beyond this and speaks of a man whose coming is in the distant future and who has rights over the people and their kingdom. Because of these prophetic words, an expectation of a future superleader grew among Jacob's descendants.

Isaiah by Grunewald.

As God continued to unfold glimpses of his master plan, there were hints that the superleader would be more than merely human. The prophet Isaiah, writing in a dark and hopeless epoch, prophesied about the coming of a child who is God: "For a child will be born for us, a son will be given to us, and the government will be on His shoulders. He will be named Wonderful Counselor, Mighty God, Eternal Father, Prince of Peace. The dominion will be vast, and its prosperity will never end. He will reign on the throne of David and over his kingdom, to establish and sustain it with justice and righteousness from now on and forever" (Isa 9:6–7). Micah sounded a similar note when he said, "Bethlehem Ephrathah, you are small among the clans of Judah; One will come from you to be ruler over Israel for Me. His origin

Few if any Jewish interpreters understood that Messiah would be God until they looked at the Old Testament afresh after the resurrection of Christ.

is from antiquity, from eternity" (Mic 5:2). The last part of this verse means this child's birth is not the beginning of his existence. Rather, he is eternal. He is *God*. But as we will see in the next chapter, few if any Jewish interpreters understood that Messiah would be God until they looked at the Old Testament afresh after the resurrection of Christ.

Daniel by Michelangelo.

In a final passage alluding to the supernatural identity of the coming Messiah, the prophet Daniel recounted a vision in which he saw "One like a son of man coming with the clouds of heaven. He approached the Ancient of Days and was escorted before Him. He was given authority to rule, and glory, and a kingdom; so that those of every people, nation, and language should serve Him. His dominion is an everlasting dominion that will not pass away, and His kingdom is one that will not be destroyed" (Dan 7:13–14).

Daniel's words gave great hope to the Jews who heard and believed. God would act decisively through the promised Messiah, setting right the world's many wrongs. The question was, When would this happen?

Chapter 5
Time Between Times

The fate of nations turns on the decisions made by kings. Their moods, perceptions, and habits of mind can determine life or death, freedom or bondage. As we saw previously, God is provident over the hearts of kings. This does not ensure that God's perfect moral law is reflected in the decisions of kings. However, it does mean that in ways that escape our recognition, God directs kings and kingdoms to the ends he has appointed for them.

When Nebuchadnezzar and his Babylonian army flew down from the north and wrecked Jerusalem in 586 BC, it was according to God's design. He had announced it through Jeremiah years previously. Thus for a season Nebuchadnezzar and his army were appointed by God to be world beaters, but those days were numbered even before they began. After all, Jeremiah had said that the Jews would be exiled in Babylon for only 70 years, a rounded number indicating an entire generation (Jer 25:11–12). As that term drew to a close, God raised up a new regional power: the Medo-Persians led by King Cyrus. Cyrus

In ways that escape our recognition, God directs kings and kingdoms to the ends he has appointed for them.

The Cyrus Cylinder may record the release of the Jews to return to Jerusalem from Babylon.

was no worshipper of God, but his heart was nevertheless within God's power. After he defeated the Babylonians, he had to assess the situation of the Jewish exiles whom Nebuchadnezzar had kept in Babylon. Ezra tells us that God "put it into the mind of King Cyrus to issue a proclamation" that permitted the Jews to return to Jerusalem (Ezra 1:1). In ways Cyrus never detected, God moved him to this decision.

As road-worn clumps of Jews climbed up into Jerusalem following their Babylonian release, they were on the cusp of an epoch in parentheses—a time between times. Since the far-gone day when God had singled out Abram, he had kept up regular dealings with the Hebrews. He would do so again with the coming of the Christ child 500 years after the exiles returned to Jerusalem, but what the Jews could not have known as they reentered their broken, silent city was that God himself would soon fall quiet. Yes, he continued to send prophets for the next generation or two, but by 433 BC the prophetic voice died out in Israel. Nonbiblical Jewish writings of the era (called the apocryphal books) acknowledged this. The prophets simply disappeared as the voice of God withdrew. Jewish historian Josephus named the reign of Artazxerxes (c. 424 BC) as the time when Scripture ceased to be written.[1] This silence was not a matter of human choice; if it had been up to humans, the faithful remnant would have kicked up a revival and kept the writing and prophecies going. But humans were never the origin of God's Word. The voices of true prophets rose and fell at God's command. When God chooses silence, silent they fall. And so the prophets stopped coming, the visitations ceased, and the people waited in the time between times.

Humans were never the origin of God's Word. The voices of true prophets rose and fell at God's command.

Exile in the Homeland

The Jews who returned to their homeland from exile found that they remained in *virtual* exile for the rest of their history as they were passed from one overlord to another. Some of their masters were harsher than others. Under Persian rule, for instance, they were not allowed to name even a puppet king. The Jews were made to feel like tenants of a dirty little hovel. Their every move was scrutinized, and their religion was despised. By this time there was already a growing hope that God would send the promised messianic king to save them and restore their nation; the Persian restriction against any form of kingship only heightened this desire. Give us Messiah, O God! Simultaneous to this there developed a heightened awareness among the Jews that their infidelity to God had been the cause of the exiles and the destruction of Solomon's majestic temple. Pious Jews began to study the Ten Commandments and the laws of Moses with new intensity. Synagogues had first developed during the exile as Jews gathered regularly to pore over the Scriptures in a quest to understand the troubles that had come to pass. Now, back in Jerusalem and again hemmed in by foreigners, the synagogue movement grew even stronger. The Jews were "people of the holy book" as never before.

First-century BC mural found at Pompeii showing Alexander the Great.

The emphasis on Scripture was a noteworthy attempt to get back to their roots, to understand the covenants and the God who had given them, but with each passing day the task of remaining distinctly Jewish grew more difficult. The region's language changed as Aramaic and Greek gained prominence and pressed in on the flagging Hebrew tongue. Culture changed too, especially after Alexander the Great and his wave of culture agents washed through the land. When he conquered the region in 330 BC, he brought along a veritable train of Hellenists, learned men whose purpose was to reshape backwards native culture into the superior Greek image. Alexander took this to be his mission to humanity, an act of mercy which aimed to haul the world up from barbarism. He was kind enough to allow the Jews their religious freedoms, but many Israelites found the foreign ways appealing, and thus they blended Greek life with Hebrew.

Alexander died at age 32, apparently the result of a nagging illness combined with a series of his infamous drinking bouts. Thus was his campaign to conquer the world halted by a bug and a bottle

Alexander's bid to conquer the world was halted by a bug and a bottle of beer.

of beer. In the aftermath his generals vied for power, with the result that competing power bases were established in Syria (to the north of Israel) and Egypt (to the south). A tug-of-war played out over the next few centuries with the Hebrews trapped in the middle. First from Egypt and then from Syria came occupiers who wished to exact benefit from Abraham's children. Taxes were levied, heightened, and then heightened still more. Benevolent governorship gave way to hostile suppression as later rulers treated the Jews with contempt. Most contemptible of all were the actions of Antiochus IV, a Syrian ruler who came to power in 175 BC. Antiochus styled himself as a god after the Greek tradition. Naturally the Jews despised him; and when rumors reached Jerusalem that he had been killed, they broke out into celebration. Trouble is he was *not* killed. In retaliation for the ill-founded jubilation, Antiochus robbed the holy temple of its sacred implements and massacred thousands of Jews. On his next swing through town, he renamed the Jewish temple after Zeus and even dared to sacrifice a pig on its altar. Here was a man who stood in opposition to everything the Jews held sacred, and yet still Messiah did not come.

Antiochus IV. Photo: CNG (CC License 2.5).

A Priest and His Sword

Tensions eventually boiled over in the Maccabean revolt (167 BC). Already incensed at the atrocities performed by Antiochus, pious Jews erupted when an aged priest named Mattathias was commanded to perform a sacrilegious offering. Mattathias refused, but one of his groveling countrymen stepped forward to obey the command on his behalf. The old man would have none of that. Before any of the stunned bystanders could react, grizzled Mattathias drew his sword and killed the commanding officer plus the compromising Jew. Soon the

Maccabean Revolt by Delacroix.

nation rallied around Mattathias and his sons; *war was on.* So fierce was Jewish anger that they succeeded in driving the powerful Syrians out of Israel, and for roughly 100 years the Jews enjoyed a season of relative peace. But even then Israel was divided over its vision for the future. Some wanted to get back to the old ways; others wanted something new and cosmopolitan, patterned after the things they had seen in the Grecians, Babylonians, Persians, and Egyptians.

Israel was divided over its vision for the future.

These conflicting visions for the future led to civil unrest. Feeling helpless as he faced this, an ill-chosen Jewish leader invited Rome to come help Israel sort out her troubles. The burgeoning empire to the west was only too glad to assist. In almost the next moment Pompey was standing inside the highly restricted holy of holies in the Jewish temple, gazing about like a vulgar tourist as every pious Jew in Israel relived the horrors of Antiochus. The year was 63 BC, and Israel belonged to Rome from this point until she was officially dissolved nearly 130 years later.

One of the most significant Roman rulers was actually a

nominally Jewish Galilean named Herod. Historians call him Herod the Great, although the appellation fits him poorly. The Romans appointed him governor over Galilee, and he ruled from 37 BC to 4 BC, which fell a few years after Christ's birth.[2] Though he shared in the Jewish bloodline, Herod ruled as a Roman and did much to heighten Jewish dislike for foreign rule. We will take a closer look at Herod in chapter 6. For now the important thing to note is that his violence and megalomania, plus the fact that he bequeathed his reign to inept sons at his death, helped to focus Jewish hopes on the promised Messiah. Now more than ever the people longed for deliverance.

> *Though he shared in the Jewish bloodline, Herod ruled as a Roman and did much to heighten Jewish dislike for foreign rule.*

Religion

We do not have exhaustive information about Jewish religious developments during the time between times, but what sources we do have paint a picture of flux and tension. As the Hebrews were passed from one foreign master to another, they repeatedly faced the question of identity: Who would they be and what would they believe? Answers differed. The Pharisees, specialists in the interpretation of the Mosaic laws, were hardline conservatives who opposed foreign influence. "To the Scriptures!" was their cry. In their judgment pagan influences had corrupted Jewish life and invited God's wrath. Taking a much more lax view was a

First-century AD synagogue at Masada near the Dead Sea. Photo: HolyLandPhotos.org.

group known as the Sadducees. By and large they were moderates who embraced new ideas with zeal. "Why stand in the way of progress?" they asked. As for Scripture, the Sadducees accepted only the first five books of the Bible—the ones Moses wrote. None of the other holy books held authority for them. For both parties the center of religious life was the above mentioned synagogue, a place where people gathered to read and discuss the Scriptures and parse the rapidly changing world around them. Of the many topics they likely discussed, three have particular bearing on the religious worldview which predominated when Jesus was born. These are oral law, the afterlife, and the Messiah, all of which we will discuss in the final three sections of this chapter.

Inching closer to Jesus' time there arose a group called the Essenes. They were monastics: men and women who retreated into the desert to escape the moral filth that was stacking up on every cor-

Secular Jews pushed for modernization in just the way Alexander's emissaries had invited them to do.

ner of society. They studied the Scriptures with great intensity and awaited the end of the world, which they supposed was coming soon. And then there was everyone else: average Jewish people whose focus was less on God and more on the demands of the moment. This is the secular mind-set in its essence, and unfortunately a growing number of Jews adopted this framework. To them the covenants, the Scriptures, and the far-gone fathers belonged to another world, one that was quickly disappearing. The world had shifted since Abraham's day, and so secular Jews pushed for modernization in just the way Alexander's emissaries had invited them to do.

Law and Interpretation

"Oral law" is the name given to the traditional interpretations that men built up around the laws and regulations God gave through Moses. Picture a synagogue in which men regularly gathered to discuss the Scriptures. Those who were particularly articulate and studious came to hold considerable influence among the people, for their opinions were backed by knowledge of Scripture. After a time the favored interpretations of such men merged as consensus built from synagogue to synagogue. Before long there was an "official" rendering for many matters of law and belief. Unfortunately the oral law often made assured pronouncements on matters the Bible never even addressed. In some sense people even came to vest more authority in it than in the Bible itself. By the time Jesus walked the towns of Galilee and Judah, the oral law held unquestioned sway among religious persons. To oppose oral law and its expositors was to oppose God and his approved interpreters. Or so the people believed.

> *By the time Jesus walked the towns of Galilee and Judah, the oral law held unquestioned sway among religious persons.*

After Death, Life?

What did Jews of this era believe about afterlife? Taking some cues from the pessimistic Greek worldview and choosing to ignore biblical revelation outside the first five books (Gen through Deut), the Sadducees disbelieved in resurrection or any afterlife. They said death was the end, fully and finally.

The Pharisees opposed this view and insisted that God would bodily raise the dead in a great future judgment. Most common folk sided with the Pharisees.

The Old Testament itself has surprisingly little to say about resurrection. On this and many other topics of Christian interest, the Old Testament divulged only by shadow and innuendo what the New Testament later revealed by light and proclamation. Thus we should not expect the early teachings of the Bible to unfold a full doctrine of resur-

Daniel by Gustave Doré.

rection or afterlife. Most Old Testament references to death do not look beyond the grave. Nevertheless several passages settle things in favor of bodily resurrection and unending life. Chief among these is Daniel 12:2–3, where the prophet was given a vision of future tribulation and the final judgment. In terms that clearly vouch for a coming resurrection, he says: "Many of those who sleep in the dust of the earth will awake, some to eternal life, and some to shame and eternal contempt. Those who are wise will shine like the bright expanse of the heavens, and those who lead many to righteousness, like the stars forever and ever."

Messiah

Finally, what did Jews of this era believe about the promised Messiah? Looking back, we find that the picture was somewhat muddled. There are several reasons. First, as mentioned above, a growing portion of Hebrews in the centuries just before Christ were only nominally devoted to the God of their forefathers. Their  thoughts and hopes were not centered on Messiah, so it is doubtful that they held well-informed, closely examined views on what he would be like or what he would accomplish. They were just trying to get on with being citizens of this world and lacked firm conviction or interest in Messiah. Second, the majority of Hebrews at this time *did* fix their greatest hopes on a coming Messiah, but there were broad divisions over interpretation and theology. This split the pro-Messiah party into several factions, which helped ensure that no unified image of Messiah could be developed. Finally, most Old Testament prophecies and allusions to Messiah were by design somewhat cryptic. Certainly God never came out and announced something so specific as, "Messiah will be God in flesh and his name will be Jesus. He'll be born

Most Old Testament prophecies and allusions to Messiah were by design somewhat cryptic.

in a Bethlehem manger to a woman from Nazareth named Mary. This will happen during the waning years of Herod the Great's governorship." Later we will discuss God's wise purposes in simultaneously revealing and concealing Christ through Old Testament prophecies. For now we will simply note that God often does unexpected things even when fulfilling his promises. The key for devout followers of God is to walk in spiritual preparedness that enables them to recognize the will and works of God when they are revealed. When Messiah came, those Jews who walked in this preparedness recognized him not because he neatly fulfilled their finely developed expectations for Messiah but because the Spirit of God testified to their receptive hearts that Jesus was Messiah. In other words people came to faith in Jesus not because they had identified and memorized all

No one expected Messiah to be much of anything like Jesus.

the messianic prophecies and noticed that Jesus was systematically fulfilling them but rather because they recognized and received God's testimony about Jesus. Keeping these things in mind, you can understand that highly specific foreknowledge about Messiah's comings and doings was unattainable. No one expected Messiah to be much of anything like Jesus. God had made promises through the prophets to send a Messiah, and there were tantalizing hints as to what he would be like,

but all in all no one could be sure of Messiah's stat sheet or modus operandi until he was unveiled. Only in hindsight can we look at the Old Testament and see such "clear" prophecies and allusions as to who Messiah would be and what he would set out to accomplish. This includes even the stunning passages we examined at the end of chapter 4. In their original setting those passages would have been unlikely to deliver the conclusion: Messiah is God. Why? Because the Hebrew habit of mind was wholly unprepared to think of God's becoming a man. Extending this thought even closer to the heart of the matter, we can say that the chief trouble was spiritual: hearts and minds needed miraculous opening in order to perceive such high truths as the divinity of Messiah.

Given all these factors it is no surprise that views about Messiah varied widely. Very few people understood that he would be divine; most supposed he would merely be a human aided by God to do extraordinary things, much as had been the case with King David. The majority figured there would be only one Messiah, but some said more than one would come. People of secular persuasion believed Messiah was only a concept, an ideal around which the nation would rally in a bid to force change.[3] Given these variant opinions, it is safe to say that "Messiah is coming" meant different things to different people.

Despite the wide range of opinions about Messiah, there was one theme shared by everyone: Messiah would be King of Israel and a descendant of David. In this time between times, when God had gone silent and Israel was trampled by Gentiles, the Jews naturally longed for a conquering Messiah who would restore Israel's sovereignty. Thus they hoped Messiah would be political, persuasive,

Mistaken expectations form a vital backdrop for understanding why Jesus' teachings and mission were met with disbelief and hostility even among Israel's most dedicated religious groups.

and would rally an army of zealous warriors who would strike the earth to rid it of impurity. These mistaken expectations form a vital backdrop for understanding why Jesus' teachings and mission were met with disbelief and hostility even among Israel's most dedicated religious groups.

In a related matter, few people expected Messiah would suffer on behalf of the people. In fact most would have regarded the idea as an insult. From our vantage point it is initially difficult to see how they missed the importance of several Old Testament predictions. Consider Isaiah's teachings. In language which closely matches Jesus' experiences of death and resurrection, Isaiah 52:13–53:12 describes Messiah as suffering great pain and death on behalf of the people before rising triumphant over the grave. It goes down as the Bible's most vivid prophetic glimpse at the suffering and resurrection of Messiah, but it escaped the comprehension of Israel. In all fairness, however, a moment's reflection shows that this oversight is largely understandable. Keep in mind that the Jews had been told a great deal about the nature and power of God. Genesis says he is the Creator

Egyptians Drowning in the Red Sea (detail) by Bronzino.

of all. Exodus describes him sending plagues, parting seas, and descending on a quaking mountaintop in fire and smoke. The prophets extolled God as all-powerful, all-knowing, and ever-present. The psalmist said he counts the stars and names them all. Can such a God become a four-limbed, sandal-shod man? And even if that were possible, can such a God-man die on a cross? When judged by human standards of wisdom, these things seem impossible. Thus as the time between times came to a close, the Jews expected an altogether different sort of Messiah than the one who, unknown to them, stood ready to step from heaven into flesh and change the world.

Notes

1. See 1 Maccabees 4:46 and Josephus, *Against Apion* 1.8.

2. Scholars believe Jesus' birth may date to as early as 6 or 7 BC. More on this in chapter 6.

3. On the various views the Jews held about Messiah during the "silent years" (i.e., approximately 400–4 BC) see J. Julius Scott Jr., *Jewish Backgrounds of the New Testament* (Grand Rapids: Baker, 1995), 287.

Part II
Jesus' Life

A stone manger found at Megiddo.
Photo: HolyLandPhotos.org.

Chapter 6
Away in a Manger

Imagine a world in which the Creator is an all-mighty and eternal spirit being, immeasurable by instruments and undetectable by sight or sound. Further, imagine that this Creator has designed the natural order with such efficiency that everything carries on without any physically detectable involvement on his part. Finally, imagine that this Creator has created a race of beings who by design are uniquely capable of communication with him but who have set themselves against him and suffered great loss: loss of ready communication with him, loss of information about him, and loss of native capacity to please him. In such a world as this, what sorts of things might the Creator do to make his presence known? It seems logical that he might choose to "break the monotony" of the regular order by enacting events and signs that point outside this world. After all, events that supersede the laws of nature point to something that transcends nature itself.

This scenario is a simplified description of the Bible's teaching about God and his relations to our world after the fall of Adam and Eve. God is holy and invisible; we are at odds with him, and we languish under his curse, but he has not entirely walked away from us. Since the time he chose Abram and initiated his plan of redemption, God has occasionally chosen to wow us with his in-breaking power. One of his favored methods for doing this in biblical times was through the miraculous birth of children who were destined to play a vital part in his unfolding plan. Consider Sarah, whose aged body was incapable of bearing a child. God won renown and loyalty by giving her a child named Isaac. In turn Isaac prayed for his wife Rebekah. She was physically incapable of having children until God overcame natural barriers and gave her

Isaac, Jacob, and Joseph were all brought into the world by God's supernatural involvement in human reproduction.

twins, Jacob and Esau. As if seeking to complete the *tour de force,* God later performed the same work for Jacob's barren wife Rachel, with the result that a pivotal son named Joseph was born. Thus at key junctures God made clear that his work of redemption through Abraham's family was indeed *his* work. Isaac, Jacob, and Joseph—world-shaping figures without whom there would be no Israel, no Moses, no covenant at Sinai, no King David or promised Messiah—were all brought into the world by God's supernatural involvement in human reproduction.[1]

Into this sort of plotline a young girl named Mary once strayed quite unintentionally. She was not barren. She was not even married. For her, sexual intimacy and the quest for pregnancy belonged to the future time when she and her fiancé, Joseph, would be wed. Her attention was on chastity, planning, dreaming, and waiting patiently in her quaint hometown of Nazareth. But then God showed up.

Nazareth in 1877.

Breaking the Silence

After withholding his voice from the Hebrews for 400 years, God again struck up conversation by sending his chief angelic

The Annunciation by Caravaggio.

messenger to speak with two very different people in Israel. First was an aged priest named Zechariah. We will discuss his experience in chapter 8. Next was Mary, a teenage girl living in Galilee (Luke 1:26–38). On the surface a visit with a Galilean teen seems like a pretty inauspicious start to redemption's climactic campaign, but Gabriel had come to announce a special task that would change the world. Mary was probably no more than thirteen years old at the time, small in stature and worldly experience. Nothing in her brief life had prepared her to stand face-to-face with a spirit being whose origins reached back farther than earth itself. Long had this creature observed movement in God's universe. He had witnessed its creation, seen the origin and fall of humankind, and had walked among holy prophets to reveal secret visions (Dan 8:16–27; 9:21–27). Now he stood next to a simple peasant girl to whom no visions or ideas of grandeur had ever come.

Mary was probably no more than thirteen years old at the time, small in stature and worldly experience.

Judging from television shows, people today assume that angelic visits are accompanied by warm light, soft music, and deep feelings of peace. The reality is far different. According to the Bible *fear* is the standard response when angels draw near. Take the priest Zechariah, for example. He was overwhelmed with dread when Gabriel visited him (Luke 1:11–12). Why? Because angels are otherworldly and holy. They are untainted by sin, and they live in the presence of God. In our sinfulness we are not compatible with these qualities. In the presence of angels we see ourselves for who we really are, and like Adam and Eve we wish to duck behind a bush and cover our shame. Young Mary felt no differently, and Gabriel's first words only compounded her unease. "Rejoice, favored woman! The Lord is with you" (Luke 1:28). This greeting confused and alarmed Mary. She knew her unworthiness before holy God and felt it more deeply than ever in this moment. But Gabriel did not leave her to her fears. He assured her that she had "found favor with God." By this he meant that Mary was safe in the presence of holiness because God had seen faith in her heart and had placed his favor upon her.

Gabriel's greeting confused and alarmed Mary. She knew her unworthiness before holy God and felt it more deeply than ever in this moment.

Gabriel then got on with the business at hand. He told Mary that she would give birth to a son named Jesus and that the boy would be "Son of the Most High" and King over Israel forever. As staggering as this was, sharp-witted Mary immediately cut through her surprise and pointed out an obvious problem with Gabriel's announcement: she was a *virgin*. Now of course she was set to marry Joseph before long, but Mary understood that Gabriel was speaking of immediate pregnancy. There was another problem that must have troubled her as well: No son fathered by flesh-and-blood Joseph could rightly be called Son of the Most High. Joseph was a fine fellow, and Mary was fortunate to wed him, but in no case could he father a divine child!

Gabriel said to Mary, "Rejoice, favored woman! The Lord is with you" (Luke 1:28). *The Annunciation* by Da Vinci.

Gabriel appreciated this logic. He responded by saying: "The Holy Spirit will come upon you, and the power of the Most High will overshadow you. Therefore the holy One to be born will be called the Son of God" (Luke 1:35).

Before leaving Mary to ponder her whirlwind future, Gabriel added that God had also granted a pregnancy miracle to Mary's married relative Elizabeth, an unmistakable sign that

God was moving unilaterally to initiate the decisive phase of redemption history. To all of this, Mary humbly said: "I am the Lord's slave. May it be done to me according to your word" (Luke 1:38).

The Cost of Obedience

It is easy to underestimate how brave Mary was in the face of Gabriel's announcement. Her betrothal to Joseph was more than a verbal agreement between two persons in love; it was

a binding agreement that could not be broken except by divorce proceedings. Further, adultery (defined as sexual relations outside marriage) was strictly condemned in Jewish society, a reflection of God's own pronouncements through Moses. By becoming pregnant before her marriage to Joseph was consummated, Mary risked condemnation as an adulteress and possibly even death by mob justice. Joseph would not be obligated to defend her in that situation. He had not touched her and would assume she had been with another man. Thus

Adultery was often punished by stoning in ancient Jewish society.

by submitting to God's will, Mary put everything on the line. It is no exaggeration to say that her bravery in the midst of such uninvited threats is perhaps unparalleled in world history. This is Mary, servant of the Lord.

Though he did not spare her from shame, God did choose to blunt the blows that fell on his chosen servant. In mercy he sent an angel to inform Joseph of Mary's innocence and the supernatural origin of her

By becoming pregnant before her marriage to Joseph was consummated, Mary risked condemnation as an adulteress and possibly even death by mob justice.

pregnancy (Matt 1:18–21). He also told Joseph that the child would save his people from their sins. Joseph had decided to divorce Mary because of the pregnancy, but the angel's message put a stop to that. Like Mary, Joseph chose courageous faith in

God sent an angel to inform Joseph of Mary's innocence and the supernatural origin of her pregnancy.

spite of the high price he knew he would pay for obedience to God. Once they came together Mary and Joseph must have marveled at the path God called them to walk. Consider the irony of their situation. As the people of Nazareth turned against them for their presumed immorality, Mary and Joseph could not help but notice that those who censured them with the greatest zeal were those who most closely followed God's moral laws. Thus it was at the hands of the righteous that Mary and Joseph suffered the most. *Let good company part; the great God remains.* Perhaps this was the motto of the young couple as they huddled under God's wing. In any event their resolve was built on a fact no one else could believe: Mary was pregnant because the Holy Spirit had "come upon" her. The language reminds us of how God appeared in a cloudlike presence to the Hebrews as they trekked through the wilderness (Exod 40:34), but even this analogy stretches beyond the evidence Gabriel supplies. We simply are not given close details of Jesus' conception, and

Trinity by Previtali. Mary and Joseph naturally entertained visions of Jesus reestablishing Israel's long-defunct throne. Never would they have imagined that a cross would serve as his stairway to kingship.

like all miracles it is probably pointless to ask for details. God moved and the miracle was accomplished. This is knowledge enough.

And so a king grew in the womb of a virgin peasant girl. Jesus fell into the lineage of King David by virtue of the fact that Joseph, a distant son in that line, was his adoptive father. This meant everything was in line for the fulfillment of messianic prophecies that said Messiah would be a son of David (see for example Isa 11:1). With this in mind Mary and Joseph naturally entertained visions of Jesus reestablishing Israel's long-defunct throne. The whole nation had longed for this for hundreds of years, and Gabriel's grand announcements could only mean those longings would soon be fulfilled. Our son will be king! But the reality which followed left them confused and, for a season at least, *disillusioned*.

CLOSER LOOK

Did Israel Expect a Virgin-Born Messiah?

Christian preachers and theologians rightly teach that Jesus' virgin birth was foretold in the Old Testament by the prophet Isaiah. In Isaiah 7:14 the prophet said, "Therefore, the Lord Himself will give you a sign: The virgin will conceive, have a son, and name him Immanuel," a name meaning *God with us*. Would not the pious people of Nazareth think of this verse when unwed Mary turned up pregnant and speaking of angelic visits? Furthermore, when she and Joseph set out for Bethlehem, would this not have triggered memory of Micah's prophecy that Messiah would be born in that town (Mic 5:2)? Both questions must be answered in the negative. Christians have the benefit of hindsight when examining the Old Testament witness. We more readily discern the prophecies that refer to Christ because we know the details of his coming, and we have the testimony of the evangelists to guide us in seeing Christ in the Old Testament. Hence, while some few people before the time of Jesus' birth may have understood these prophecies, the vast majority did not.

A good way to sum up many of the messianic prophecies in the Old Testament is to say that they are examples of *sensus plenior*, a term Bible interpreters use to describe the fact that prophecies often have double or typological fulfillment. Such prophecies have an immediate application in the historical context of the prophet but then a fuller and more impactful fulfillment at a later date. This is particularly so in the case of Isaiah's prophecy. The immediate fulfillment of Isaiah 7:14 is described a few verses later in 8:3–4, and yet the language of 7:14 stretches beyond the rather mundane event described in 8:3–4. Thus attentive readers before the time of Christ had a shot at suspecting that a deeper prophecy was embedded here, but most likely very few readers made this connection. Furthermore, the great emphasis in the Old Testament is that Messiah would be a son of David. This sort of language would not lead one to expect virginity of Messiah's mother. So we must conclude that Messiah's virgin birth was unexpected by even the most pious Jews.

Counting Heads

While Messiah was being knitted together inside Mary's womb, the world outside continued in the standard way. Crops were sown and harvested, the faithful prayed for deliverance from sin, and kings collected their taxes. In view of this last concern, Caesar Augustus initiated in Galilee a census program that would eventually encompass his entire empire (Luke 2:1–3). This census seemed insignificant on the scale of world events. In fact there is no historical documentation for it outside the New Testament. Fitting, then, that God should use the mundane transactions of a pagan king to fulfill heaven's prophecies about the King of kings. Had there been no head count at Caesar's command, Jesus would have been born in Nazareth, home to Mary and Joseph, not the town named in Micah's prophecy.

Caesar Augustus initiated in Galilee a census program that would eventually encompass his entire empire. Photo: Euthman (CC License 2.0).

And so the decree came down from Caesar. In response Jewish heads of households all across the region journeyed to their original hometowns to be counted. This temporary migration was not commanded by Caesar. Rather it was a choice made by Jews who placed great emphasis on tribal identity. Every Jew could tell you which of the 12 tribes they hailed from, and they insisted on marking those distinctions in a general census. In Joseph's case he did not want to be known as Joseph of Nazareth, for that would have affiliated him with the northern tribe of Zebulun rather than King David's lineage, the southern tribe of Judah. Thus Joseph got up plans for a trip to Bethlehem when word came down about the census. It is doubtful that Mary was required by law to accompany him, but her stigma in Nazareth made the trip not only bearable but preferable.

Mary and Joseph arrived in Bethlehem just in time for Mary to duck into a stable and give birth. Photo: Bethlehem in 1877.

Bethlehem is well south of Nazareth, a journey of 85 miles over difficult country. In Jesus' era travelers could cover 15–20 miles per day, but in Mary's condition the holy family probably crept along, taking perhaps a full week to reach Bethlehem. Imagine Mary, heavy with child, propped atop a rocking donkey for mile after mile. Hers may have been history's first "induced" delivery! They arrived in Bethlehem just in time for Mary to duck into a stable and give birth. There was no room at the inn because the

They arrived in Bethlehem just in time for Mary to duck into a stable and give birth.

Church of the Nativity as it looks today. Photo: StormyDog (CC License 2.0).

town was packed for the census, and so an animal den became the staging ground for the birth of God's Son. Remarkably, this stable was probably nothing more than a cave opening, a rocky divot cut into the banked earth. At least as early as AD 150 Christian leaders identified a cave as Jesus' birthplace and in 330 Constantine built the Church of the Nativity atop the designated spot. You can visit the site today just five miles outside Jerusalem.

Shepherds Gaze

A few hillsides away from the place where Mary labored, shepherds were scattered high and low, huddled close to the ground as they kept watch over their sheep in the dark. Tending sheep was a low business; it typically fell to the outcasts and downtrodden of society. It was

The good news came first to outcasts, not the privileged.

considered an "unclean" occupation, and its practitioners were not trusted to give testimony in courts of law, but the Messiah born amid cattle and straw came to earth for people

Shepherds held low station in Jewish society, but God sent his Son especially for such people. Photo: Shepherds outside Bethlehem in 1869.

such as these. Thus God dignified men of low standing by sending an angel to disclose Messiah's birth to this group of shepherds. No announcement rang out in Herod's gilded halls. Wealthy merchants slept through this night undisturbed by heavenly visitors.

Scribes and Pharisees were not consulted as the angelic host gathered over the low hills outside Bethlehem. The good news came first to outcasts, not the privileged. Judging from God's past actions, this should not have surprised anyone. After all, it was on these same hills that an obscure boy from Bethlehem once tended his father's sheep. With a slingshot and a heart full of courage, that boy became David, king over Israel.

In the mouth of a cave lay a baby cradled by a trough stuffed with straw and blankets.

There were no Goliaths roaming the hills on the night of Jesus' birth, but something more terrifying than giants descended upon the unsuspecting shepherds. An angel appeared from nowhere and announced the birth of "a Savior, who is Messiah the Lord" (Luke 2:11). This Savior could be found in

The shepherds wowed everyone with their revelations. As for Mary, she "was treasuring up all these things in her heart and meditating on them" (Luke 2:19). Illustration from *Les Très Riches Heures du duc de Berry.*

David's city, "wrapped snugly in cloth and lying in a feeding trough." Just as the startled shepherds began to recover their footing, a multitude of angels took their stand with the original messenger and cried out, "Glory to God in the highest heaven, and peace on earth to people He favors!" (v. 14).

Brilliant light withdrew as the angels stepped back across their secret threshold, leaving the shepherds bunched together in breathless awe. It was completely dark again. The sheep remained there in need of shepherding, but these men spilled down from the hills to Bethlehem, searching for the subject of their revelation. They found things arranged just as the angel had reported. Picture the scene as they found it. In the mouth of a cave lay a baby cradled by a trough stuffed with straw and blankets. Mary and Joseph were there with dozens of townsfolk and stray visitors who had come for the big census only to find something far more newsworthy in Bethlehem. It is not every day that a woman tumbles into the edge of town and gives birth among livestock. It was a wonderful and touching scene, but initially no one besides Joseph and Mary knew the baby himself was special. The shepherds changed all that. They emerged from the outer darkness like guards slinking away from their posts. One or two people in the crowd must have thought it improper of them to leave their sheep, but then the men opened their mouths and told tales none there would ever forget. Messiah is born! He's lying right before your eyes!

After sharing other details of the angelic revelations, the shepherds turned back to their thankless task on the knolls above town. As for Mary, Luke says she "was treasuring up all these things in her heart and meditating on them" (Luke 2:19). Indeed, in the secrecy of her heart was the only place Mary could safely treasure the revelations of the past nine months. She could not understand them well enough to speak sensibly, and anything she spoke would only invite mockery and unbelief. And so in silence she contemplated the works of God as shepherds sprang joyously through the dark.

CLOSER LOOK

December Birth?

There is no compelling evidence that Jesus was born on December 25, and yet the majority of Christians throughout history have celebrated the birth of Christ on this date. This tradition was well established by the end of the fourth century. Today skeptics assert that the Christmas date is evidence that Christians blended several religious streams together and "compiled" the Christian faith piece by piece. The basis of this claim is the fact that December 25 was originally the date of a popular pagan festival that honored the so-called Unconquerable Sun. This festival was important to the Romans, and of course a great many of the early Christians lived in the Roman Empire. Hence, skeptics say that many Christians were also involved in the sun cult, and they eventually decided to fold

Christ's birth into the same celebration. At base this claim portrays early Christians as pluralists who did not devote themselves fully to Christ but instead participated in many different religious options. Importantly, the skeptics have no basis for such claims. The fact is, early Christians found it meaningful to celebrate Christ's birth at the same time as the pagan festivals because it sent a message: We worship the Unconquerable Son, not a supposed Unconquerable Sun. It was a strategic move that sought to highlight the fact that only Christ is worthy of worship. As for the exact date of Christ's birth, it is lost to history. That's just as well, for it is the *fact* of his coming, not the time or date, that calls for celebration.

Temple Rites and Revelations

Jesus was circumcised and named on his eighth day of life. His was a common name in that era. For this reason he was often referred to as Jesus *of Nazareth* once he was an adult. Thirty-three days after the circumcision Jesus and his mother went to the Jerusalem temple to perform dedication and purification rites before the Lord. We get a look into Mary and Joseph's empty pocketbooks at the temple, for their sacrifice of lowly birds (instead of a lamb) indicates that they had little money (Lev 12:8).

We get a look into Mary and Joseph's empty pocketbooks at the temple, for their sacrifice of lowly birds (instead of a lamb) indicates that they had little money.

While baby Jesus and his parents were at the temple, an elderly man named Simeon approached them (Luke 2:25–35). Simeon was a devout man whose hope was fixed on God's promises. The Holy Spirit had revealed to him that he would not die before seeing Messiah, and so on this day the Spirit led him to Jesus. He lifted the baby high and praised God for sending the Savior. He then told Mary, "Indeed, this child is destined to cause the fall and rise of many in Israel and to be a sign that will be opposed—and a sword will pierce your own soul—that the thoughts of many hearts may be revealed" (Luke 2:34–35).

Nearby, keeping a keen eye on Jesus and listening to Simeon's revelations, was a wizened old prophetess named Anna (Luke 2:36–38). Her husband had died in their seventh year of marriage, and since then she had lived 84 years as a widow. This means Anna was about 105 years old, almost certainly the oldest living person in Israel. Since her husband's death she had dedicated herself to serving God in the temple complex, all the while hoping for a moment like

Simeon by Yegorov. The Holy Spirit had revealed to Simeon that he would not die before seeing Messiah.

this. Her faith and patience paid off more grandly than she ever imagined possible. Now she joined Simeon in praising God and heralding the newborn boy who had come to save people from all over the world.

Once again God chose unlikely messengers to announce the coming and purposes of Christ. Like the shepherds, like Mary and Joseph, and like Mary's relative Elizabeth, Anna and Simeon were "invisible" to the big world outside. They had no standing in society. Kings did not consult them, and the wealthy passed them by without a glance. But here in the temple they were privy to high knowledge only God can give, knowledge of hope and judgment. As we repeatedly find throughout the New Testament, Messiah's coming brought a wide array of outcomes. He brought hope and forced division. He elicited both love and hatred from his audiences. His messages were cause for joy and sorrow. What his coming meant to people depended on their response to his teachings and his deeds. The same is true for you and me. As

What Messiah's coming meant to people depended on their response to his teachings and his deeds. The same is true for you and me.

we will see in the next chapter, from his earliest days Jesus was a polarizing figure in Israel.

Note

1. Other Old Testament examples of God's intervention in the conception and birth of key figures include Samson (Judg 13) and Samuel (1 Sam 1).

Adoration of the Magi by Mantegna.

Chapter 7
Visitations

The ancients knew the stars better than you or I do. Many of us live in cities or suburbs where manufactured light dims the night stars, but the people in Jesus' day had a full and open view of the starry heavens. They gazed at them nightly and used them to navigate their journeys. Learned men studied them, mapped them with stunning precision, and even searched them for signs. Many such men were engaged in the futile and forbidden practice of astrology, a cultic religion which held that stars control the fate of us all.[1] However, in another unexpected twist in the campaign to announce Messiah's arrival, God disclosed prophetic information to star-gazers from lands far away, lands where knowledge of the one true God was rare or nonexistent. All we know

In another unexpected twist in the campaign to announce Messiah's arrival, God disclosed prophetic information to star-gazers from lands far away.

about these men is encompassed in five words: they were "wise men from the east" (Matt 2:1). We do not know how many there were, though the three gifts they brought for Jesus lead many to assume there were three of them. We are not even sure what is meant by "wise" men. Were they magi in the

Babylonian sense, learned men who specialized in the interpretation of dreams and stars? If so they were something akin to astrologers. That they were granted a true sign from God as they craned their gaze into the cauldron of stars is most unexpected, for it entails that God accommodated himself to their false views in order to reveal truth. Perhaps this is so. Were they instead kings, as several early church leaders speculated? Not likely since their journey to Bethlehem would have taken them away from their duties for many months. Certainly history does not record anything about eastern kings abandoning their lands to trek after a Jewish toddler. Whatever they were, the wise men were granted special knowledge from God, knowledge that seemed so sweet and compelling that they set out on an epic journey to find the child Jesus.

Matthew and the Angel by Rembrandt. Matthew's inclusion of the wise men indicates that he and other authors of Scripture included even stories that seemed scandalous.

Matthew's decision to include this story in his Gospel indicates two things. First, the story of the wise men is certainly true, for no Jew would dare invent a story in which foreign men figure out the will of God by gazing at the stars! Such a tale would be fundamentally contrary to basic Jewish beliefs. Second, Matthew's inclusion of the story indicates that he and other authors of Scripture included even stories that seemed scandalous. Their chief concern was to tell the truth even if it seemed shocking or unbelievable.

> *The story of the wise men is certainly true, for no Jew would dare invent a story in which foreign men figure out the will of God by gazing at the stars!*

Visiting Herod

The wise men arrived in Jerusalem dust covered and adorned in strange clothes. They straightway proved their unfamiliarity with the political and religious context in Israel by asking openly, "Where is He who has been born King of the Jews? For we saw His star in the east and have come to worship Him" (Matt 2:2). One can imagine the hush that fell whenever

The Wise Men by James Tissot. The wise men told Herod they had come to worship the King of Israel (Matt 2:1–8).

they said such things. Herod's sword was quick to lash out at anyone who threatened his rule. Among those whom he had executed on suspicion of betrayal were his own sons and his beloved wife Mariamne. So renowned was Herod for his violent and paranoid temperament that the Romans often quipped, "Better to be Herod's swine (*hys*) than his son (*hyios*)." The pig, it seemed, was more likely to survive. And so the inquisitive wise men scattered whole crowds with their naïve questions.

When Herod caught wind that men from the east were inquiring after the King of the Jews, he called together the experts in Jewish Scripture and asked them where Messiah would be born. If anyone in Israel could discern the answer from Scripture, it would be these men. As a nominal Jew Herod had at least passing interest in the Jewish hope for Messiah, but as a king who believed his reign was under threat, this interest was driven not by piety but rather by a desire to protect his position against all comers, even

The wise men before Herod. From a 15th-century stained-glass window.

Messiah himself. The priests answered that the Messiah would be born in Bethlehem, as the prophet Micah had foretold (Matt 2:5–6).

Armed with this knowledge, Herod summoned the wise men. He learned that the star had ap-

The birth star appeared to the wise men two years before they came to Jerusalem.

peared to them two years previously and that it signified a birth event. A plan was shaping up in Herod's mind as the wise men unknowingly paved the way to the child's doom. In a cunning move Herod told them to go on to Bethlehem

by themselves, search out the child, and then report the child's precise location on their way back east. In this way Herod hoped to conceal his true intentions. Marching his armed forces to Bethlehem with the wise men would raise the alarm, sending Joseph and Mary into hiding. By letting the wise men go alone, however, Herod bought himself the chance to send a stealth strike force the next night. In this way the threat to his throne would be cut

The Wise Men Guided by the Star by Gustave Doré. By following God's sign, the wise men found Jesus and worshipped him.

off before he even grew out of his diapers. Suspecting none of this, the wise men became puppets in Herod's evil plot.

Visiting Jesus

Nightfall had come by the time the wise men left Herod's presence. Right away they noticed that the star had reappeared overhead (Matt 2:9). It had apparently been a long while since its last appearance, for they were overjoyed to see it. As they watched, the star moved and led them to the place where Jesus was living. Folks in Matthew's day knew full well that stars don't move or hover low over rooflines. For this reason it is almost certain that Matthew's language is figurative. He means something that appeared *like* a star led the wise men to Jesus. Does this mean the thing the wise men had seen two years previously was also just *like* a star? Maybe. Maybe not. We cannot be sure of our answers here though it is permissible to inquire and speculate if our conclusions are kept modest. In the final analysis it is best simply to say that God led the wise men to Jesus and did so using a method we cannot fully identify.

It is best simply to say that God led the wise men to Jesus and did so using a method we cannot fully identify.

Once the star pinpointed their destination, the wise men wasted no time getting to Jesus' house, which lay a mere five miles from Jerusalem. They fell to their knees and worshipped Jesus once they found him. Whatever confusion may attach to the identity and background of these men, here we see beyond all doubt that they have come to devote themselves to the one true God and his divine son, Jesus Christ. The wise men have proven their wisdom well.

Visiting Egypt

Jesus was approximately two years old when the wise men met him. We know this because the men told Herod that the birth star had appeared two years prior to their arrival in Jerusalem (Matt 2:7).[2] Furthermore, their questions presupposed that the birth had already happened and was widely known in Israel. This means the popular depiction of the wise men kneeling before a manger bathed in starlight misrepresents true history. By now Joseph and Mary were firmly settled in Bethlehem, and Jesus was a walking, talking toddler growing up in David's hometown.

Adoration of the Magi by El Greco. The popular depiction of the wise men kneeling before a manger bathed in starlight misrepresents true history.

The choice to settle here must have seemed appropriate to his parents as they considered Jesus' link to David and his future mission in Jerusalem. The wise men knew none of this. Their sole concern was to worship the child God had revealed, and they did so with offerings of gold, frankincense, and myrrh. Each of these was valuable and could quickly convert to cash, which turned out to be convenient only a few hours later.

Once everyone settled down for the night, God sent urgent dreams to Joseph and the wise men (Matt 2:13–15). For the easterners the message was simple: avoid Herod and ditch your plan to swing by Jerusalem on your way home. For Joseph the message was complicated, impossible even: grab Mary and Jesus and head out the door right this minute and don't stop until you reach Egypt. *Egypt!* Imagine the scene. Joseph awakened Mary and the boy, sacked some basic supplies along with the valuables the wise men had given them, slung it all over the back of his startled donkey; and together they all melted into the black Judean hills, hearts pounding and eyes wide with alarm.

Anno Domini by Edwin Longsden Long. God told Joseph to take his family and flee Herod's wrath. We know nothing of Jesus' stay in Egypt.

The shadows drew long the next day, and still the wise men had not reappeared in Jerusalem. By God's command they had evaded Herod. Realizing his loss, the enraged regent gave orders to kill all boys two years of age and younger in Bethlehem. Thankfully Bethlehem was a small village, and so the slaying involved no more than perhaps twenty households, but of course that is twenty too many. In a fulfillment that may never be fully understood, Matthew tells us that the slaying

Herod gave orders to kill all boys two years of age and younger in Bethlehem.

completed a dire word Jeremiah had spoken long ago (Matt 2:17–18). What is certain is this: the murder of the children highlights the sorry, sinful condition of the human heart. Herod's actions are unusually heinous, but *all* hearts harbor a similar sickness. It is well for you and me that, unlike Herod and every other despot in history, we lack the power to foster and indulge all our darkest thoughts. But on this day Herod's target eluded his blow. The child fled toward sunbaked Egypt, towed by parents whose expectations were turned upside down yet again. Jesus escaped Israel to save his life, but one day he would return with a plan to offer it once for all.

We know nothing of Jesus' stay in Egypt. It was home to a significant population of Jews in that day, likely more than half a million strong. Most of them lived in Alexandria, and so chances are good that this is where the holy family sheltered. Joseph probably got carpentry work as he could, but all the while he and Mary listened for the news they longed to hear: Herod the Great is dead. When Herod did finally die, an angel relayed the news to Joseph before word rippled through the community in Egypt. It was time to return home.

CLOSER LOOK

Jesus and the Fulfillment of Prophecies

If you read the Gospels carefully, you might notice that sometimes Jesus and the events surrounding his life are said to fulfill Old Testament passages that, when examined in their original context, do not seem to have any obvious reference to Messiah. One example is Matthew's reference to weeping in Ramah, which we noted above. Another example is Matthew's statement in 2:15 that Jesus' flight to Egypt was a fulfillment of Hosea 11:1, where the prophet says, "When Israel was a child, I loved him, and out of Egypt I called My son." In the original context Hosea has Israel in view and seems to make no intentional allusion to Messiah. So how can Matthew say Jesus fulfilled Hosea's words? The answer comes in two parts. First, Jesus the Messiah and Israel the nation are depicted as type and antitype, such that Jesus' experiences are in significant ways parallels or recapitulations (do-overs) of Israel's national history. For example, Israel is God's son and so is Jesus. Israel the nation existed due to a series of supernatural pregnancies; Jesus was born of a virgin. In Matthew's inspired perception Israel was exiled in Egypt and so was young Jesus. Israel was called out of Egypt and so was Jesus after Herod's death. Thus the Son relived the experiences of the nation, only he did so without sin and error. He got it right where Israel often got it wrong. Second, the New Testament authors rightly recognized that in some sense the entire Old Testament was building up to the coming of Christ, pointing to him at every turn as the culmination of God's plan. Thus Jesus can be called the fulfillment of the *entire* Old Testament. In summary, neither Matthew nor the other authors of the New Testament "invented" prophecies or fulfillments. Rather, they justifiably saw the Old Testament as prelude to the life of Christ.

The Forgotten (and Forgettable?) Years

Joseph apparently intended to settle his family in Bethlehem again as they returned from Egypt, but as he drew near, he learned that Herod had passed the governorship of the region to his son Herod Archelaus, a man known for brutality. God confirmed to Joseph in a dream that it would not be safe to settle in a Bethlehem overseen by Archelaus, so he made for Galilee instead. In a daring move that must have humbled them all, Joseph moved his family back to Nazareth, the scene where unwed Mary turned up pregnant a few years earlier. Most likely they had family there and a thin band of friends to support them, but certainly the rumors and stares would have dogged them for years to come.

In a daring move that must have humbled them all, Joseph moved his family back to Nazareth.

Matthew, ever mindful of Jesus' fulfillment of Old Testament themes and expectations, saw the move to Nazareth as

Nazareth, 1890.

a fulfillment of the prophets: "Then [Jesus] went and settled in a town called Nazareth to fulfill what was spoken through the prophets, that He will be called a Nazarene" (Matt 2:23). Though no specific prophet had said Messiah would be a Nazarene, the theme Matthew seems to have in mind fits with prophecies that Messiah would be despised and forsaken (Isa 52:13–53:12). Nazareth had a low reputation in Israel. Years later a young man named Nathaniel was told by a friend that Messiah had been revealed and that he hailed from Nazareth. To this Nathaniel replied, "Can anything good come out of Nazareth?" (John 1:46). Here then is yet another unexpected line in the scroll of Messiah's background: the King of kings is from a nowhere town, and in that nowhere town his family is blacklisted on suspicion of immorality.

Here then is yet another unexpected line in the scroll of Messiah's background: the King of kings is from a nowhere town, and in that nowhere town his family is blacklisted on suspicion of immorality.

Once Joseph and his family returned to Nazareth, they went off radar for a decade. None of the Gospel writers mentions a single thing about Jesus' life during this phase. It is not surprising that by the second and third centuries people were tempted to fill this void with stories of a miracle-working child Jesus. The *Infancy Gospel of Thomas* is one of the more fanciful examples. Among other things it concocts a tale of five-year-old Jesus fashioning 12 model sparrows out of moist clay on a Sabbath. The townsfolk (including Joseph) found him out and scolded him for doing "work" on the Sabbath. In response Jesus clapped his hands and commanded the sparrows to fly away. They promptly obeyed. Dirt became living bird at the command of Mary's boy, and the whole town was filled with wonder and awe.

Fictional stories such as Jesus and the clay sparrows were invented centuries after Jesus lived.

There are several reasons we know that such things never happened. First, we are told in John 2:11 that Jesus performed his *first* sign at Cana in Galilee during a wedding feast. He was at least thirty years old at that time, which means he had not worked miraculous signs as a child. Second, when Jesus went to the temple as a twelve-year-old boy, his parents were "astonished" to find him sitting among the elders holding forth on matters of theology and law (Luke 2:48). Would they have been astonished at this if he had strung together feats of supernatural power and knowledge as a child? Certainly not. Making live birds from clay is far more impressive than having a head for theology, and so their wonder at a lesser feat (his theological discourse) proves that the greater feat (creation of living birds from dirt) never happened. Third, in Luke 2:51–52 we are told that after Jesus' parents fetched him from the temple he "went down with them and came to Nazareth and was obedient to them . . . [and] increased in wisdom and stature, and in favor with God and with people." This describes an exemplary but nonmiraculous childhood. Finally, when Jesus kicked off his ministry, he went to his hometown synagogue in Nazareth and preached about himself from the prophet Isaiah. The home folks were so upset at Jesus' grand claims that they rose up and tried to throw him off a cliff. Would they have found his claims so absurd if he had wowed them with miracles during his childhood? Of course not. Their stunned reaction is yet another proof that Jesus' childhood was almost entirely normal.

Likely Chronology of Events in Christ's Early Life

Birth in 6 BC (calculated from Herod's death in 4 BC)

Temple presentation as an infant; prophecies by Simeon and Anna

After the temple presentation they returned to Bethlehem where they settled for approximately two years

The wise men visited Herod and toddler Jesus

Flight to Egypt before Herod murdered the toddler boys of Bethlehem

The holy family remained in Egypt for roughly a year

Returned to Nazareth after Herod died in spring of 4 BC

CLOSER LOOK

What Does the Silence Say?

One of the most outstanding proofs that the Gospels were written by men who earnestly sought to tell the truth about Jesus' life is the fact that they did not attempt to carbon copy the same exact story four times over. Matthew, Mark, Luke, and John differ from one another enough to ensure that fresh, unique elements appear in each Gospel while simultaneously disbarring any charge that they have colluded together in a conspiracy to promote a false biography. There is much similarity in their accounts as well, of course, but the differences are obvious and noteworthy. Some of the most outstanding differences occur when major events or facts in Jesus' life are mentioned by only one Gospel. For example, only Matthew tells us that Jesus and his family lived in Egypt for awhile. Matthew thought this was worth mentioning since he especially liked to point out the ways in which Jesus fulfilled Old Testament themes, and so he points out that Jesus, like Israel, came out of Egypt by God's hand. Mark, Luke, and John sought to make other emphases in their accounts, and so they left the Egyptian sojourn unmentioned. For instance, Luke chose to give a thorough accounting of Jesus' birth circumstances. By the time he tells about Jesus being presented at the temple as a baby he has spent 118 verses! No surprise then that Luke leaps from the temple presentation to Jesus' next big temple moment (as a 12-year-old boy) with only a lightning quick mention of the fourteen years in between. He skips the wise men, Herod's murderous wrath, the flight to Egypt, and the return trip when the family averted Bethlehem and settled in Nazareth instead. Nothing other than sheer unbelief on the part of the reader would suggest that Luke's silence on these issues indicates that he either knew nothing of them or disbelieved Matthew's account. Luke was not obligated to say all that he knew. No writer in history has been so obligated, in fact, for every book conveys only a thin slice of the author's knowledge. In the final analysis we can be grateful that all four Gospel authors emphasized different facts in Jesus' life. Because of that variety we have a much fuller picture of Jesus than we would have otherwise had; plus we have confirmation that all four authors set out to tell the truths that had revolutionized their lives.

Visiting the Temple

Jesus' visit to the temple when he was 12 years old is the only event narrated from his post-Egyptian childhood. It is a fascinating account full of hints at what Jesus might become (see Luke 2:41–52). The journey from Nazareth to Jerusalem covered approximately 90 miles. To get there Jesus' family traveled in family and friendship groups; these groups in turn were part of a larger caravan traveling from Nazareth and surrounding areas.

Caravan near Mount Carmel, 1900.

This method provided safety in numbers, plus the sharing of provisions helped ease the logistical burden on everyone.

Once the Passover festivities wound down, the caravan headed back toward Nazareth. Children clumped together and hung at the fringe of the procession, playing hero as they fended off imaginary attackers and shared tall tales of their experiences in the holy city. When it came time to halt and bed down, stray children found their parents and spent the night as a family unit. Mary and Joseph waited patiently, but Jesus never rallied to their side as night fell over their first day's journey.

Mary and Joseph waited patiently, but Jesus never rallied to their side as night fell over their first day's journey.

The boy was plenty old enough to know when the caravan was due to leave Jerusalem. Had he failed to join it? All day long Joseph and Mary had assumed he was walking with friends or his younger half brothers and half sisters. Now it felt like a fatal assumption. As soon as it was light the next day, they sped back to Jerusalem, but they were forced to delay their search till morning because night had fallen by the time they arrived. At sunup the next day they scanned streets and courtyards for Jesus. Eventually they found him in the temple complex sitting among the teachers. It was common for learned men to stay behind after the

"After three days, they found Him in the temple complex sitting among the teachers, listening to them and asking them questions. And all those who heard Him were astounded at His understanding and His answers" (Luke 2:46–47).

Passover throngs had thinned in order to hold discussions on Scripture, law, and regional politics. Many of them hailed from out-of-the-way towns where intellectually stimulating discussion was hard to come by. Here was their chance to hash out the big topics and trade verbal blows with proponents of opposing views. Amateurs who attended these meetings came to listen rather than speak, but here was Jesus, a mere *lad*, sitting in the midst of the experts and astounding them with his understanding and answers (Luke 2:47).

Mary scolded Jesus for his stunt. What mother wouldn't? Jesus seemed genuinely surprised by her reaction. "Didn't you know that I had to be in My Father's house?" Though his childhood had been routine (no feats of power), the fantastic revelations given before and after his birth remained unalterable. His decision to stay behind at the temple was in keeping with those revelations, and he supposed Mary would perceive this. At 12 Jesus was coming of age, and both Mary and Joseph needed to shift their thinking. For this reason Jesus flashed a hint of impatience in response to their anxiety. As we will see in later expositions, he was not typ-

Jesus was not typically sympathetic when people who had received revelation were slow on the uptake.

ically sympathetic when people who had received revelation were slow on the uptake. With revelation comes responsibility. Jesus expects much from those who have received much. In any case his explanation for his truancy was simple: I had to be in my Father's house. This claim of familial relations with God Almighty would have appalled the gathered teachers, so it is safe to assume that Jesus said this only to his parents as they pressed close in on him. Imagine Joseph and Mary clasping him by the hands and leading him off as the crowd looked on with great interest. Many of them would see Jesus again in about 20 years, whether here in the temple or out in the Galilean countryside. They had loved him as a boy. What would they think of him as a man?

Jesus' Family Life

The Bible gives few disclosures of what Jesus' life was like as a boy, teen, and young adult. We know his adoptive father, Joseph, was a carpenter. Jesus was grafted into this trade as a matter of course. He could have

Carpentry was a good way to meet basic economic needs, but wealth could not be carved from wood.

learned to build homes, fashion agricultural tools, and perhaps create fine cabinetry. Carpentry was a good way to meet basic economic needs, but wealth could not be carved from wood.

Christ in the House of His Parents by Millais. Following Joseph's example, Jesus became a carpenter.

Jesus probably plied his trade in Sepphoris, a thriving city fired with Greek culture that lay not more than four miles from Nazareth. This would have exposed him to many non-Jewish ideas, thus giving him a working man's education as he carried an open ear along with his hammer and saw. Jesus took avid interest in many topics and achieved a level of learning that was uncommon for working men. The episode with the teachers at the temple backs this conclusion. Assuming he kept building on this early store of knowledge, he would have been remarkably adept in biblical exposition by the time he was an adult. This fits with known facts, for the crowds would later remark with surprise that Jesus had never had a formal education (John 7:15).

Finally, Jesus' home growing up was crowded with half brothers and half sisters who were born to Mary and Joseph after Jesus' birth. Mark 6:3 names four of Jesus' brothers and mentions the fact that he also had sisters. Throughout history some have claimed that Mary remained a virgin her entire life and that Jesus' so-called siblings were in reality children Joseph brought into the marriage, but the Bible does not support this view. In fact the Bible supplies evidence against the theory of Mary's perpetual virginity. For instance, Matthew 1:25 reports that Joseph "did not know [Mary] intimately until she gave birth to a son." The most natural implication here is that once Jesus was born Joseph and Mary practiced marriage in the usual way, producing children through sexual intimacy. One additional note of interest regarding Jesus' siblings: they did not readily believe in him as Messiah (see, for instance, John 7:5). In fact it appears that none of them believed until after his resurrection. This confirms that Jesus' childhood was not filled with wondrous acts of divine power and knowledge, plus it also hints that Mary and Joseph were careful to let Jesus unfold his identity on his own terms and in his own time. Not even to their own family members did they say: this child is Messiah, the Son of God.

Jesus' home growing up was crowded with half brothers and half sisters who were born to Mary and Joseph after Jesus' birth.

Finally, evidence from silence leads us to suppose that Joseph died while Jesus was a

Many have supposed Mary remained a virgin all her life. Bible evidence shows this belief to be mistaken.

teen or young adult, for he is never mentioned as being present for any of Jesus' ministry experiences, nor does Jesus ever signify him when he discusses the members of his family (see Mark 3:35). There is also the fact that at his crucifixion Jesus assigned Mary's care to John, one of his followers. This duty would not have been Jesus' to discharge if Joseph had still been alive. It is also noteworthy that Jesus assigned Mary's care to someone outside his family. Obviously a rift had opened up within Jesus' family. Mary believed in Jesus because of the revelations given to her. Granted, she was deeply confused about how his life was turning out, but she stuck by his side even as he was crucified. The siblings did not share her faith. The revelations had not come to them, and Jesus' claims were just too much for them to accept. He was their brother after all! For these reasons Jesus entrusted his mother to a man who shared her faith, for such a man could better understand the difficult path Mary walked.

Evidence from silence leads us to suppose that Joseph died while Jesus was a teen or young adult.

Notes

1. Isaiah 47:13–15 speaks of the futility of looking to the stars for signs. Other passages that condemn astrology include: Deuteronomy 4:19; Jeremiah 10:2; and Daniel 2:2–17.

2. Matthew says the wise men told Herod the exact date on which the star first appeared to them. That Herod then sought to kill all boys two years of age and younger indicates that the star had appeared two years previously, give or take a few months.

Baptism of Christ by Patinir.

Chapter 8
Initiations

When God first broke his centuries of silence, it was to announce to a priest named Zechariah that his aged, barren wife would become pregnant and bear a son. They named him John in obedience to the angel's instructions, and he became one of the most celebrated men in Israel's history. John's purpose, said the angel, would be "to turn the hearts of fathers to their children, and the disobedient to the understanding of the righteous, to make ready for the Lord a prepared people" (Luke 1:17). Rather than having Messiah drop onto an inattentive scene, God sent John the Baptist to incite religious fervor and heighten the expectation that God would do great things for his people in the coming Messiah.

John was an enigmatic figure. He would have frightened most of us if we came across him in his element. After all, he was a raw and unkempt wilderness man who wore a camel-hair garment tied off

> *John was an enigmatic figure. He would have frightened most of us if we came across him in his element.*

with a leather belt. For meals he scrounged around the countryside for insects and honeycomb. Here is a man who struck the perfect pose for fiery end-times preaching, and that's exactly

John the Baptist by von Gracinica. John came to prepare the way for Messiah, who would complete God's work of salvation.

what he did. Mark 1:4 summarizes John's ministry as follows: "John came baptizing in the wilderness and preaching a baptism of repentance for the forgiveness of sins." John was also quick to say that his message was not complete. He was merely preparing the way for the one who would complete God's work of salvation. "Someone more powerful than I will come after me. I am not worthy to stoop down and untie the strap of His sandals. I have baptized you with water, but He will baptize you with the Holy Spirit." This means those who were baptized by John had not yet experienced the fullness of God's plan. Rather, they had identified themselves with the community of the faithful, a community whose ultimate hopes were pinned on the coming Messiah.

Those who were baptized by John had not yet experienced the fullness of God's plan.

Breaking Heaven's Door

Sometime after John stirred the populace to repentance, Jesus arrived and asked to be baptized. This goes down as the most shocking request recorded in the Bible. John sensibly refused Jesus. "I need to be baptized by You, and yet You come to me?" (Matt 3:14). It is not hard to understand John's stance here. He and Jesus were distant relatives; their mothers had even spent several months together during their coinciding pregnancies. Odds are good that John's mother shared some of Mary's remarkable story with him as he grew up. At the very least John had always known that Jesus was greater than he. But was Jesus the Messiah? John suspected so but awaited confirmation. If anything, Jesus' request to be baptized threatened to fill John with doubt. In response Jesus explained that he sought baptism to "fulfill all righteousness." This explanation proved that Jesus was not seeking to repent of any sins. Rather, he wanted to identify with God's holy work and God's people. Seeing this, John relented and lowered the Son of God under the murky waters of the Jordan River. This was the most unique dunk in history, and John must have been in fearful awe at his assignment! As Jesus broke back up through the waters, the heavens tore apart. Everyone looked on as the Holy Spirit descended on Jesus in the likeness of a dove. A voice boomed from heaven, announcing Jesus' divine sonship. Matthew records the voice as

The probable area of the Jordan River where John baptized Jesus. Jesus was baptized because he wanted to identify with God's holy work and God's people. Photo: HolyLandPhotos.org.

speaking to the crowd, saying, "This is My beloved Son. I take delight in Him!" (v. 17). Mark and Luke record it as if God had addressed Jesus instead, saying, "You are My beloved Son; I take delight in You!" (Mark 1:11 and Luke 3:22). The variation in wording here demonstrates that under the guidance of the Holy Spirit the evangelists took reasonable freedoms in how they recorded key statements. Importantly, the essential meaning is the same in both versions: God the Father is pleased with God the Son.

The variation in wording here demonstrates that the evangelists took reasonable freedoms in how they recorded key statements.

John would briefly be saddled with doubts a few years later when both his ministry and Jesus' took such unexpected, non-triumphant directions, but for now he was convinced that Jesus was Messiah. After all, God had told him previously: "The One you see the Spirit descending and resting on—He is the One who baptizes with the Holy Spirit" (John 1:33). Having witnessed this very thing, John now said of Jesus: "I have seen and testified that He is the Son of God" (v. 34).

Now that he had been empowered by the Spirit and identified to John the Baptist and others, what sort of Messiah would Jesus be? A date with the devil provides an early answer.

CLOSER LOOK

Do We Have the Exact Words of Jesus?

As we see in the example of God's voice at Jesus' baptism, under God's guidance the evangelists took reasonable liberties when conveying the statements and details surrounding events in Jesus' life. The biblical evidence proves they were not constricted by a requirement to give word-for-word recordings of everything they heard. Rather, their God-given task was to write accounts that conveyed the truth of world-changing events and teachings. Jesus himself promised that the Holy Spirit would "remind" the disciples of everything he had taught them (John 14:26). For the Christian reader this promise supplies confidence that the Gospel writings are fully reliable. It is no trouble that Matthew, Mark, Luke, and John sometimes state things differently. For a fuller explanation of this important issue, please see chapter 20.

Messiah's Choice

If the crowd gathered round Jesus' baptism expected him to towel off and make straight for Israel's vacant throne, they were sorely disappointed. As Mark tells it, "Immediately the Spirit drove Him into the wilderness" (Mark 1:12). The verb translated "drove" can also be translated "to hurl." There is immediacy and even something akin to violence in the Holy Spirit's action. Why the urgency? Surprisingly, the devil himself awaits Jesus in the barrens beyond the river. Why would God drive Jesus into the devil's trap? Having made public pronouncement on Jesus' identity, it was

The devil himself awaits Jesus in the barrens beyond the river.

urgent that the Father test his Son's fortitude. God does something similar with all of his followers. Though he himself never tempts anyone with evil, he does choose to loan us out

Satan Plaguing Job by William Blake. Job was getting on quite well in life when out from nowhere God invited Satan to take a run at him. "The Lᴏʀᴅ said to Satan, 'Have you considered My servant Job?'" (Job 1:8).

to the devil's schemes as a way of testing our commitments and growing us through trials. Remember Job? He was getting on quite well in life when out from nowhere God invited Satan to take a run at him. "The Lord said to Satan, 'Have you considered My servant Job?'" (Job 1:8). Now, immediately after christening Jesus in the sight of John and the crowds, God asked Satan to consider his own Son. To ensure that this was accomplished, the Spirit escorted Jesus into the wilderness where he would lack food, friendship, and all comforts for more than a month.

A second reason Jesus had to face the devil is that you and I must face him daily. As we will see more fully in later chapters, Jesus came to be our substitute. He could not be a true and adequate substitute if he moved through life in a holy bubble, cordoned off from the dirty reality of temptation. Thus the Son came to face our demons with the aim of coming out spotless on the other side. There was nowhere better to start this task than the harsh wilderness, a place which troubled the ancients. They took them to be the haunt of demons and other dark forces. Deserts and barren places are hostile to life and devoid of human companionship. You hurry through as best you can, keeping a wary eye out for wild beasts desperate for food. You conserve water, fighting repeated urges to satisfy your thirst. If you travel alone, your thoughts turn inward, eating at you with accusations and fears. You may die here. Are you ready to meet your Maker?

Jesus could not be our true and adequate substitute if he moved through life in a holy bubble, cordoned off from the dirty reality of temptation.

Of course Jesus was never victim to a guilt-ridden

conscience, but after fending off wild animals and going 40 days without food, he had reached a point of great vulnerability. He was a man after all. His body and strength were ebbing

away. Recognizing this deterioration in Jesus' condition, Satan launched his temptations. He approached Jesus and said, "If You are the Son of God, tell these stones to become bread" (Matt 4:3). Jesus was starved. Without doubt it lay within his power to command the entire desert floor to become a banquet tray filled with choice foods, and yet he knew there was a principle to uphold: "Man must not live on bread alone but on every word that comes from

The Temptation of Christ by Duccio. Satan approached Jesus and said, "If You are the Son of God, tell these stones to become bread" (Matt 4:3).

the mouth of God" (v. 4). Thus he chose discipline and suffering over relief through obedience to Satan's promptings.

Undaunted, the devil transported the emaciated Jesus to the pinnacle of the temple in Jerusalem. "If You are the Son of God, throw Yourself down" (Matt 4:6).

Jesus chose discipline and suffering over relief through obedience to Satan's promptings.

He then quoted from Psalm 91 where the psalmist describes the benefits of being under God's protection. Instead of calling Jesus to exercise his own power, Satan here tempted him to force the Father's hand by "naming and claiming" a Bible verse. Though each member of the Trinity is coequal, the presumptuous act Satan prescribed would reverse the lines of authority that are native to the godhead. The Son came to obey the Father and none other. Thus he replied, "It is also written: Do not test the Lord your God" (v. 7).

Finally, Satan again transported Jesus to a place where his temptations would have maximal force. This time they went atop a high mountain, and the devil paraded before Jesus a vision of the world's kingdoms: rivers of gold and gems spilling from the coffers of great nations, cityscapes that stretched long against blue-gray horizons and needled toward heaven, kingdoms whose powers reached from sea to valley and on to sea again. "I will give You all these things if You will fall down and worship me," he said to Jesus (Matt 4:9). Satan does not wield unchecked reign over the kingdoms of earth, but it is true that *his* spirit pervades the current age. Humans and their institutions of power are corrupted, recast in the marred image of a fallen angel. By working his influence over his devotees, Satan proposed to position Jesus at the pinnacle of worldly power. Satan reserved his greatest hope for this temptation, but Jesus turned him back with greater

Satan does not wield unchecked reign over the kingdoms of earth, but it is true that his spirit pervades the current age.

force than ever. "Go away, Satan! For it is written: Worship the Lord your God, and serve only Him" (v. 10).

By this response Jesus revealed a fact that was not apparent before: it had been within his power to banish Satan all along.

The Temptation of Christ by Gustave Doré. Jesus turned Satan away with a strong condemnation.

A spoken word or a wave of the hand could have ended the temptations. Entire legions of angelic warriors would have come had he ordered it (Matt 26:53). He chose not to avail himself of such privilege because he came to suffer with us and for us, not to triumph with a cheap show of power that sheltered him from genuine human experience. He was to live as a servant made low by rejections, mockings, and beatings. For this reason Jesus chose to endure Satan's enticements until he had proven his ability to withstand even the best arrows hell could loose. Then he humiliated the devil by sending him home.

Angels came to serve Jesus in the wake of Satan's departure. The text tells us nothing specific of their ministrations, but

Jesus required food and drink to break his long fast, and these were likely supplied to him at this time. Consider the significance of what had just passed. Jesus was no robotic Messiah. He had the power of choice, and certainly he was free to bow the knee to Satan and serve himself rather than the Father. What kind of Messiah Je-

Jesus came to suffer with us and for us, not to triumph with a cheap show of power that sheltered him from genuine human experience.

sus would be hinged on his choices, and each was made as he staggered along the knife edge of starvation and fatigue. Here in the first major crossroads he faced during his min-

istry, Jesus chose to be the Messiah his Father had appointed him to be—the Messiah who obeys, the Messiah who embraces humility, the Messiah who suffers and dies for you and me. In summary, Jesus chose to be Messiah for *you and me* rather than Messiah for himself alone. A single choice for himself would have made him useless for you, me, and every other sinner in history.

Angels Ministering to Christ in the Wilderness by Cole.

Hometown Prophet

The man who walked out of the wilderness after the devil left was stronger than before. He "returned to Galilee in the power of the Spirit" and won widespread acclaim as he kicked off his preaching campaign (Luke 4:14–30). This momentum hit a wall of opposition in his hometown, however. He entered the synagogue on a Sabbath and stood up to read from the scroll of Isaiah. He unfurled it and read selections from

Isaiah, saying, "The Spirit of the Lord is on Me, because He has anointed Me to preach good news to the poor. He has sent Me to proclaim freedom to the captives and recovery of sight to the blind, to set free the oppressed, to proclaim the year of the Lord's favor." (vv. 18–19). When he finished reading he handed the scroll back to the attendant and announced that he personally was the fulfillment of Isaiah's words. As was the custom, he then sat down and prepared to receive the crowd's response to his com-

mentary. It was hard for them to process Jesus' claim. He had spoken well and was gracious in tone and demeanor. No doubt many onlookers were proud of their native son for the amazing things that were being said of him in the sur-rounding towns. He

Nazareth market, 1894.

had overcome a tough start in life and had made something of himself. But inevitably the problem of familiarity arose: they *knew* this man. Some remarked that he was Joseph's son, repeating what was believed in Nazareth since the day

The citizens of Nazareth grumbled against Jesus as a pretender.

unwed Mary turned up pregnant. How could the illegitimate son of a mere carpenter stand in the synagogue and claim he is the fulfillment of messianic prophecies? And who did he think he was by traveling around with a retinue in tow? And so they grumbled against him as a pretender.

Having faced down the devil himself a short while ago, Jesus was unshaken by human opposition. He reminded the people that in former times God sent his faithful prophets to non-Jewish peoples when the Jews themselves turned stony ears against the prophetic utterances. When the crowd heard this, "They got up, drove Him out of town, and brought Him to the edge of the hill their town was built on, intending to hurl Him over the cliff" (Luke 4:29). Interestingly, this gave Jesus a chance to reconsider Satan's second temptation. Would he allow himself to be driven off the cliff on the presumption that the Father would break his fall a few inches above the ground? Such an outcome would wow the would-be murderers, but this was not the sort of Messiah Jesus had come to be, nor was it the kind of faith he had come to engender. Therefore, in a tantalizingly obscure statement that may imply some sort of supernatural stupefaction of the mob, Luke tells us that Jesus evaded death by simply passing "right through the crowd" (Luke 4:30). If this was indeed a miracle, it was one of the few Jesus performed in Nazareth. Mark says the Lord was "not able to do any miracles there, except that He laid His hands on a few sick people and healed

Nazareth in 1842, by David Roberts. "They got up, drove Him out of town, and brought Him to the edge of the hill their town was built on, intending to hurl Him over the cliff" (Luke 4:29).

them" (Mark 6:5). It is not that Jesus' hands were tied by unbelief; rather, as he says elsewhere, there is no sense in casting pearls before swine (Matt 7:6). Persistent unbelief earns unresponsiveness from God, and so Jesus left the folks in Nazareth and moved on to harvest in other fields.

He Gave Them Fish and a Purpose

Fishing can be dangerous when the Son of God takes interest in your efforts! One morning, as Jesus taught on the shores of Lake Gennesaret (Sea of Galilee), the crowds came out from the fishing villages and pressed close against him, muffling the sound of his voice and thus preventing folks on the fringe from catching his words. Sound carries much better over water, and so Jesus decided to board a nearby boat and teach while anchored offshore. Jesus had met several of the local fishermen at an earlier date, including Simon Peter (see John 1:35–51), and so he took the liberty to step into an empty boat

Sea of Galilee. Jesus asked Peter to put the boat out a ways so he could teach the people gathered ashore. Photo: HolyLandPhotos.org.

and ask Peter to come aboard and take them out a ways (Luke 5:3). Several of Peter's assistants joined them, and together they watched Jesus' teachings play across the eager faces of the crowd seated on the sloping banks of the lake.

When Jesus finished teaching, he told Peter to put out into deeper waters and let the nets down. The men had been washing their nets and wrapping up a futile night of fishing when Jesus first spotted them in the morning. They had been awake all night and then stayed with the boat longer than usual so Jesus could teach the people lakeside. By now the fishermen were thinking of their homes, warm meals, and soft beds from which none of them planned to rise anytime soon. But Jesus' hold on these men was already strong. Desiring to please him, they obeyed his wishes and shoved out into the depths. Just as soon as they slipped the nets overboard, fish filled them to the point of breaking. They had captured an entire school. A second boat plied the waters close by. They were partners to Peter and his crew, and so Peter hailed them, and they came to share the burden of the large catch. Soon both

Jesus and Peter. With Jesus directing their efforts, the disciples caught so many fish that their nets began to break (Luke 5:6).

boats were overwhelmed and began to sink. The flood of fish bewildered the men and threatened their lives. It is not clear exactly what the fishermen thought of this event. Did they see it as a work of power by Jesus? Did they instead think he had made use of omniscience? John tells us (2:11) that Jesus' first miracle was performed a few days later at the wedding at Cana. In this light it is probably best to say that Jesus did not perform a miracle here but rather that he simply made use of his supernatural knowledge. The fish had to be schooled together somewhere in the lake waters. Jesus did not coax them together.

The flood of fish bewildered the men and threatened their lives.

He just happened to know where they were. Thus he directed the ship to lower the nets to that exact spot. In any case Peter recognized the meaning of the event: Jesus had the sort of knowledge only God can have. He threw himself down where Jesus sat and cried out, "Go away from me, because I'm a sinful man, Lord!" (Luke 5:8).

Peter's response might strike us as odd at first glance. His boat was sinking in deep waters far from shore. A great store of fish fell all around him as they spilled from torn nets. He began to believe that God himself was sitting in the boat with him, and the first things out of his mouth were a confession of sin and a plea for Jesus to *go away* just when he was needed most! What was Peter thinking? Actually, his was pretty much the standard response to revelations of God's power. Moses hid his face in fear when God appeared in the burning bush (Exod 3:6), Gideon cried out in terror when he met God under an oak tree (Judg 6:22), and Isaiah lamented his unworthiness when in a vision he

Moses at the Burning Bush by Bouts. "Moses hid his face because he was afraid to look at God" (Exod 3:6).

was ushered into God's throne room (Isa 6:5). No sinner can bear God's holy presence unless God first makes him clean. Fortunately God is willing to cleanse those whom he calls (Isa

6:6–7). Therefore Peter's plea was appropriate, but God the Son was unwilling to depart from Peter simply because he was a sinner. "Don't be afraid," he told him. "From now on you will be catching people!" (Luke 5:10).

> *No sinner can bear God's holy presence unless God first makes him clean.*

Like the nets that broke all around him, human paradigms could not contain the teachings and actions Peter would be privy to in the coming years. This place of privilege was his not because he sought it but because against all odds God the Son chose him to have a founding role in history's greatest movement. Jesus also chose James and John, Peter's colaborers in the fishing business. All three men had probably considered this possibility for some time given their previous encounters with Jesus and the remarkable endorsement John the Baptist had given him (John 1:35–37). Now was the moment of truth. Would they follow Jesus into the unknown or remain lakemen, secure in a way of life they knew and loved? Sensing that the doors of heaven were opening right before their eyes, each of these men leaped at the chance to follow Jesus. They left family, employees, and all the benefits of a multiboat fishing business to follow a man who had given them fish and a purpose.

Christ and the Apostles by Schule.

By the time Jesus finished gathering them, 12 men had committed to following him as permanent students of his message. Why 12? Before suffering exiles and dispersions, there had been 12 tribes in Israel, all descendants of Jacob's 12 sons. By choosing 12 students, Jesus essentially said, "I am the fulfillment of Israel's hopes." Just by walking around with 12 disciples in tow, Jesus made a daring claim. As for the duties of these men, they were to memorize and comprehend Jesus' teachings, witness his deeds, and then go out and spread the news among the peoples. Jesus himself sent them out on trial runs during his ministry, and after his ascension to heaven this task became the consuming passion of all but one of the original disciples. For the rest of their lives, they fished the pools of humanity, saving forever any who believed.

> *By choosing 12 students, Jesus essentially said, "I am the fulfillment of Israel's hopes."*

He Gave Them Wine and Good Cheer

Three days after calling Nathanael to join his retinue, Jesus and his disciples were invited to a wedding in Nathanael's hometown of Cana, an obscure Galilean city whose location is now lost from all memory. But what is lost geographically has lived on in one of the most poignant stories from Jesus' life. Jesus' mother was at the wedding as well. Joseph had presumably died by now, so Mary tracked with her eldest son now that he was head of the household and chief steward of her well-being. This means Mary had journeyed over to the wedding from Capernaum, the newly adopted home base of Jesus. Like any woman Mary was no passive observer of the wedding

festivities. She paid close attention and noticed the details. Wedding celebrations in this culture could last up to a week long, and the groom's good name was on the line the entire time because it was his duty to honor his bride and guests by providing

Possible site of Cana, 1869.

first-rate dining and fellowship. When Mary overheard from alarmed servants that the wine had given out, she alerted Jesus, thus initiating a remarkable exchange. "What has this concern of yours to do with Me, woman?" he replied (John 2:4). He went on to say that his hour (his time of widespread unveiling through forthright preaching and miraculous acts) had not yet come.

The first thing that springs to mind when we read this passage is the question: Was Jesus being rude to his mother? Nearly so. His response was abrupt and pointed, but the underlying Greek word for *woman* in this verse is not a derogatory term. What Jesus has done here is signal to Mary that she must not attempt to direct his actions to suit her perception of priorities, nor can she goad him into untimely action. This does not mean he was unconcerned about the groom's reputation. Jesus cares for people. He would not allow the groom to be shamed or the bride to be hurt because the guests had consumed more wine than was expected. Mary understood this even as she recognized that her son had given her a mild rebuke. "Do whatever He tells you," she told the nervous servants.

> *Jesus cares for people. He would not allow the groom to be shamed or the bride to be hurt.*

Nearby stood six stone jars capable of holding up to 30 gallons of water. They were empty, so Jesus instructed the servants to fill them with water. The servants would assume that Jesus planned on passing water off on the guests now that the wine was gone. Disaster was nearer now than before, but what else could be done? The groom's shame would soon be revealed, and the whole household would share in the blame. At Jesus' command the servants dutifully transferred water from well to jar, well to jar dozens of times until all six stood

Wedding at Cana by de Vos. Jesus told the servants to fill six large jars with water. He then turned it all into choice wine (John 2:1–11).

full. This makes 180 gallons of sweet, aromatic, merry-making *water*. Then came the moment when the shortfall would be revealed: Jesus told the servants to dip some out and give it to the chief servant. To this point the underservants had kept the shortage secret. Of course Mary had discovered their troubles, but the chief servant (who acts as master of ceremonies) had been kept in the dark out of fear. They watched as the chief servant tipped the cup to his lips and then immediately set out to find the groom. I imagine that the servants started for the doors at this point, as well they should have had Jesus not been there. The wine had dried up, but today was a day for ascension, not downfall. Once he found the groom, the chief waiter gushed, "Everybody sets out the fine wine first, then, after people have drunk freely, the inferior. But you have kept the fine wine until now" (John 2:10). The chief servant was referring to the fact that once the guests' senses were dulled a bit by the drinking of fine wine, the cheaper fare was generally brought forward without anyone noticing the switch. The mark of a really fine feast, he told the flushed groom, is when the best is saved for last. The groom was surely puzzled by this acclamation, and we cannot help but be tickled at the fact that he and his ser-

Jesus provided abundance when a need arose.

vants won undeserved renown. As for Jesus, he has delivered up a discrete revelation. Outside of Mary, the servants, and the watchful disciples, no one at the party learned of his miraculous deed until it was recounted widely by sermon and book in the coming years. For now Jesus' chief purpose was fulfilled: his disciples, who had already seen shades of his glory, were strengthened in their commitment to him (v. 11). And they could not help but wonder: If Jesus can transform water into wine and fetch fish by the boatful, what else can he do? For some of them, the answer came quicker than they might have expected.

Christ at Emmaus by Rembrandt.

Chapter 9
Transformations

The question of identity is the paramount issue facing anyone who examines the life of Christ. Who was Jesus, really? Jesus himself said *everything* hangs in the balance of your answer. Once, when he and his disciples were near Caesarea Philippi (the regal city rebuilt by Herod Philip early in Jesus' lifetime), Jesus asked, "Who do people say that the Son of Man is?" (Matt 16:13). This is what is known as a loaded question. After all, to attentive ears Jesus' adoption of the title "Son of Man" was an unmistakable allusion to the messianic prophecy of Daniel 7:13–14. The disciples certainly did not miss this point, but first they set out to tell Jesus what others were saying of him. "Some say John the Baptist; others, Elijah; still others, Jeremiah or one of the prophets" (Matt 16:14). Since we are more than 2,500 years removed from these great men, it is difficult to understand how much honor and praise these identifications attributed to Jesus. John, Elijah, Jeremiah, and the host of prophets were all highly esteemed by faithful followers of God; anyone who drew favorable comparisons to them was a person of high reputation indeed. But when it came to iden-

> *The question of identity is the paramount issue facing anyone who examines the life of Christ.*

tifying Jesus, these comparisons are inadequate, and so Jesus prodded his disciples into confessing their take on his identity. Quick-tongued Peter, who most often could not keep an utterance down even when it threatened to expose his folly, answered well for once: "You are the Messiah, the Son of the living God!" (v. 16).

Near Caesarea Philippi Peter confessed to Jesus, "You are the Messiah, the Son of the living God!" (Matt 1:16).

Peter got it exactly right, but Jesus warned them all to keep quiet about it for now. Running throughout the Gospels is a tension between disclosure and concealment. Jesus was often forthright about who he was, but on the flip side of that token was his patient, disciplined plan to unfold his identity and purpose in a timely manner. He hinted at the reason for this tactic immediately after Peter's confession. He told the disciples that he would be rejected and killed by Israel's religious leaders in the near future but that his death would be reversed after three days. This kind of talk prompted another one of Peter's upwellings, only this time it was the sort he should have kept down. "Oh no, Lord! This will never happen to You!" (Matt 16:22). It was an understandable response. For Peter or any other pious Jew, talk of Messiah's rejection and execution was unthinkable. As sensible as Peter's admonition seemed, he only earned a sharp re-

> *Running throughout the Gospels there is a tension between disclosure and concealment.*

buke from Jesus. "Get behind Me, Satan! You are an offense to Me because you're not thinking about God's concerns, but man's" (v. 23). Pretty stern words from Peter's Savior, wouldn't you say? But bear this in mind: the cross was Jesus' central purpose from the outset. Even before time itself began, God had a plan to send his Son to die on behalf of sinners (see Rev 13:8; Eph 1:4; Acts 2:23). This means Peter sought to wreck a plan whose Designer was God. As guardian of that design, Jesus was warranted in his strong rebuke of Peter, but there is more. Jesus not only knew the Father's cross-centered plan; he also knew what deep faults had caused Peter to misjudge that plan. What Peter had done was to fix Jesus within a messianic paradigm drafted solely on human priorities. Peter sought to make Jesus a palatable, crowd-pleasing Messiah of renown rather than a Messiah of sorrows and rejection who came to die on a cursed tree. Earth would lead heaven if Peter were in charge of the messianic campaign, but he never realized this was

Even before time itself began, God had a plan to send his Son to die on behalf of sinners.

the trajectory of his thoughts until Jesus pointed it out in this raw moment of confrontation. What Jesus gave Peter was a diagnosis of his heart and mind. They are too much of this world, said Jesus. Raise them to heaven if you wish to see the wisdom of God in Messiah's difficult path.

The rest of the disciples could have taken this diagnosis as their own. They were just as confused as Peter. Jesus' death prediction (following a confession of his deity!) and his rebuke of Peter fit neither their desires nor their expectations. Just what kind of Messiah was Jesus going to be? Many of his

Jesus and the apostles.

followers dropped off when his teachings went down narrow, unforeseen paths. Would the Twelve now do the same? Sensing the need to throw them a lifeline, Jesus explained that his disciples must be willing to follow him in suffering and that if they did so there will be great reward on a future day when Messiah comes in glory with his angels to close out the current age and usher in God's eternal kingdom. To back this promise with tangible evidence, Jesus said he would soon give a preview of that day's glory: "I assure you: There are some standing here who will not taste death until they see the

Son of Man coming in His kingdom" (Matt 16:28).

Clothed in Whitest White

Six days after Peter's rise and fall near Caesarea Philippi, Jesus took Peter, James, and John (his inner circle, so to speak) up onto a mountain for a private screening of his future glory. Night fell. Jesus began praying. Seeing this, the disciples elect-

ed to fall asleep rather than join Jesus in prayer. This indiscretion nearly cost them the experience of a lifetime. The hillside was quiet and still as Jesus prayed alone, but heaven bent down and transformed the kneeling Lord so that his face shone like the sun and his clothes

The Transfiguration (detail) by Raphael. Heaven bent down and transformed the kneeling Lord so that his face shone like the sun and his clothes emanated a blinding whiteness such as is never seen on earth (Matt 17:1–9).

emanated a blinding whiteness such as is never seen on earth (Matt 17:1–9). Peter and the other two slept on, bathing unawares in the light cast from Jesus' form, but they awoke soon after Moses and Elijah appeared and began speaking aloud with Jesus. On cue sleepy Peter decided it was time to speak up. "Lord, it's good for us to be here! If You want, I will make three tabernacles here: one for You, one for Moses, and one for Elijah" (v. 4). Peter's aim was to put up tentlike structures that would shelter the holy visitors and allow them to remain with Jesus indefinitely, but before he could finish explaining himself, the cloud of God's presence enveloped the disciples. A voice from its midst said, "This is My beloved Son. I take delight in Him. Listen to Him!" (v. 5). Terrified, the disciples dove facedown against the ground. Peter was no longer thinking of tabernacles and protracted visits from saints; he was thinking of bare survival under the threat of God's overwhelmingly holy presence. But then his Mediator came. Jesus reached down and touched each of them re-assuringly and told them not to fear. When they looked up, they saw that Jesus was alone again. Heaven had retracted from earth, leaving only its Son to stand on a darkened mountaintop.

Jesus was alone again. Heaven had retracted from earth, leaving only its Son to stand on a darkened mountaintop.

When they later picked their way down from the heights, Jesus shared the details of his conversation with Moses and Elijah. Peter later passed this information on to Luke, and Luke in turn recorded it in his Gospel. In particular Luke says Jesus spoke to the heavenly visitors about "His death, which He was about to accomplish in Jerusalem" (Luke 9:31). That this would be an "accomplishment" shows that Jesus' death was not the result of world forces he could not control. Rather, he was in charge of his own execution even though it came at the hands of Israel's religious hierarchy. Continuing their descent, Jesus told the three that they must keep the mountaintop experience to themselves until after he had risen from the dead. By Jesus'

Jesus was in charge of his own execution even though it came at the hands of Israel's religious hierarchy.

choice these three men were the leaders among the disciples. He knew that if they kept strong in the face of mounting challenges the others would follow their example. Furthermore, after the resurrection they would point back to Jesus' mountaintop transfiguration and recognize it as a promissory note on his ultimate destiny. They also saw it as a disclosure of his supernatural identity. For example, Peter points back to this occasion and says of himself and the other two disciples: "For we did not follow cleverly contrived myths when we made known to you the power and coming of our Lord Jesus Christ; instead, we were eye-witnesses of His majesty. For when He received honor and

Jesus' transfiguration served as confirmatory evidence of his divinity.

glory from God the Father, a voice came to Him from the Majestic Glory: 'This is My beloved Son. I take delight in Him!' And we heard this voice when it came from heaven while we were with Him on the holy mountain" (2 Pet 1:16–18).

Thus for Peter, James, John, and all the people who were eventually touched by the retelling of their experience, Jesus' transfiguration served as confirmatory evidence of his divinity.

Messiah's War Horse

A few days before Jesus' death predictions came true, he and his disciples journeyed toward Jerusalem to celebrate the Passover. The disciples were in a festive mood, for despite Jesus' warnings they had yet to grasp that the end was near. To hear them tell it, in fact, they were on the cusp of a great triumph. Giving themselves over to the euphoria, they even debated their rank in the coming kingdom and jockeyed for favored positions alongside Jesus' throne.

Mere days before Jesus' death, the disciples debated their rank in the coming kingdom and jockeyed for favored positions alongside Jesus' throne.

They approached a village called Bethphage. A crowd of followers kept close on Jesus' heels the whole way. They had seen him raise Lazarus from the dead (John 11:1–44) and, like the Twelve, they were sure something even grander was due to happen in Jerusalem during the festival. Jesus knew better. Keeping his focus on the steps that would lead him to Calvary, Jesus told two disciples to run ahead and fetch a donkey and her colt which they would find tied up alongside the street. "Untie them and bring them to Me. If anyone says anything to you, you should say that the Lord needs them, and immediately he will send them" (Matt

Grave of Lazarus, 1893.

Entry of Jesus into Jerusalem by Gustave Doré. Jesus' choice to ride a juvenile donkey into Jerusalem was equal to a confession: I am Israel's king.

21:2–3). Did Jesus make a prior arrangement with the owner, or was this an exercise of divine knowledge and privilege? The text is vague enough to make either view seem possible. In any case this event is cited as a fulfillment of something the prophet Zechariah had written centuries beforehand. "Rejoice greatly, Daughter Zion! Shout in triumph, Daughter Jerusalem! See, your King is coming to you; He is righteous and victorious, humble and riding on a donkey, on a colt, the foal of a donkey" (Zech 9:9).

As with virtually all messianic prophecies, the disciples did not recognize Zechariah's words as having reference to Jesus until they reflected carefully on the Old Testament writings in the weeks, months, and years after Jesus had risen from the dead (John 12:16). But certainly Jesus knew in advance which prophecies pertained to him. For this reason his choice to ride a juvenile donkey into Jerusalem was equal to a confession: I am Israel's king.

The disciples did not recognize Zechariah's words as having reference to Jesus until they reflected carefully on the Old Testament writings in the weeks, months, and years after Jesus had risen from the dead.

The foal that was brought forth had not yet been trained to seat a rider, yet Jesus mastered it without effort. This is impressive given the fact that crowds gathered on either side of the road outside Jerusalem shouted acclamations, waved noisy palm branches from side to side, and cast palms and cloaks onto the roadway at the donkey's feet. Left to its instincts the beast would have bolted, but the Master of all nature rode its back and kept its instinct at bay.

One more fact about the donkey bears mentioning: Jesus is Israel's long-hoped-for king. The fact that he would ride into town on a donkey rather than a war stallion showed that his kingdom is peaceable, otherworldly even. His victory is assured, but it will not come by force of arms.

Jerusalem's Golden Gate, the entrance Jesus probably used on Palm Sunday.
Photo: HolyLandPhotos.org.

Jerusalem was packed with pilgrims who had come for Passover. Many of them had heard about Jesus. Some had even seen his miracles firsthand and wished to follow him as disciples. When these crowds heard that Jesus was on his way, they flooded out and lined both sides of the road. Many of them shouted out confessions of faith: "Hosanna to the Son of David! Blessed is He who comes in the name of the Lord! Hosanna in the highest heaven!" (Matt 21:9). This is a rough citation of Psalm 118:26, which was commonly recited during the Passover festival, but in this case the crowds wedded it to their faith in Jesus and transformed it into a messianic pronouncement. And as mentioned above, the crowds also paved the road before Jesus with their cloaks and palm branches, an honorific service reserved for kings.[1] No Jew could watch these proceedings and fail to grasp what Jesus and the crowds were getting at. Some Pharisees had

Mute stones of earth would cry out praises if the people failed to do so, for Messiah cannot march to war without herald.

come out to see the spectacle. They could not believe their eyes or the blasphemies that fell on their ears. "Teacher, rebuke your disciples," they urged him (Luke 19:39). But Jesus would do no such thing. Mute stones of earth would cry out praises if the people failed to do so, for Messiah cannot march to war without herald. As Jesus passed them, the confounded Phari-

Though the crowd was hyped up on either side of him, Jesus knew that this day's praise would be the next day's curse.

sees erupted with accusations against one another: "You see? You've accomplished nothing. Look—the whole world has gone after Him!" (John 12:19). The reality was far different, however.

Though the crowd was hyped up on either side of him, Jesus knew that this day's praise would be the next day's curse. Human hearts are fickle, twisted at root and ever shifting. As Jesus rounded a corner, he looked at Jerusalem and wept for the city that did not recognize her hour of divine visitation. She had waited long for this moment, but in the zero hour her leaders looked out and saw only a rebel riding into town, a harbinger of threat rather than hope.

Expulsion and Curse

In waning daylight the holy temple sat like a gilded sentinel high over Jerusalem as Jesus and his disciples entered town. All around them eager pilgrims vied for attention, but the Lord made for the temple grounds so he could survey the scene there. He wished to know if anything had changed since he had stormed its courts a few years back (John 2:13–23). He had taken decisive action then because the sanctity of the temple was being polluted by men who crowded circus-

Jerusalem at sunset. Photo by Mockstar (CC License 2.0).

like into hallowed courts to sell sacrificial animals at elevated prices. Animals bleated and bellowed all around and spread their filth across pave stones. Vendors shouted, pilgrims protested, and a sea of voices lapped one over the other, creating a melee. The temple's holy purposes had become commercialized, secularized, *vandalized.* Corrupt money changers lurked in nearby booths. Most coins of the region were engraved with images of idols. Pious Jews would not dare pay their annual temple tax with such unholy currency,

The temple's holy purposes had become commercialized, secularized, vandalized.

but of necessity their pockets were full of such coins. The money changers ostensibly set up shop to solve this problem by supplying pilgrims with half-shekel pieces that did not bear idols. Trouble is the exchange rates they charged proved that their true purpose was to get rich. They were ripping the people off in the name of religion and convenience.

Christ Cleansing the Temple by El Greco.

Seeing these outrages, Jesus had made a whip of cords and driven everyone out. Bystanders asked him why he did this and on whose authority he acted. Jesus' answer lived on in the memory of Jerusalem and would soon come back against him in his trial: "Destroy this sanctuary, and I will raise it up in three days" (John 2:19). This cryptic answer was an early reference to events that would later unfold at Calvary and a nearby tomb. The destroyed sanctuary to which he referred was his own body and thus prefigured his coming execution. His mention of rising on the third day was a reference to his resurrection, a miracle that would demonstrate that he had the authority to do such daring things as clear the temple, heal the sick, and forgive sins. Jesus' meaning boiled down to: "I clear this temple of its corruption by my own divine authority."

Now, mere days before the fulfillment of the promise given in John 2:19, Jesus again beheld the same unholy scene at the temple. Nothing had changed. His prophetic voice had gone unheeded. Since it was already late in the day, he withdrew, taking no action for the time being. But when the next day dawned, he journeyed back to the temple and duplicated his action from a few years before. He tossed out buyers and sellers, turned over the tables of the moneychangers, and accused everyone of turning the house of prayer into a den of thieves (Matt 21:13).

It is difficult to overstate the magnitude of Jesus' action. The Passover festival was the most sacred event on the Jewish calendar. Pilgrims from hundreds of miles away came every year, having counted the days till the holy week arrived. Further, the temple was the heart of Jewish identity and religious practice. What Jesus did by clearing the temple was hand down an indictment against the core of Jewish life. If that was somehow lost on anyone, he provided further clarification by cursing a nearby fig tree, the symbolic representation of Israel (see Hos 9:10; Nah 3:12; Zech 10:2). Jesus came across the tree at about the same time that he cleansed the temple. It was in leaf, but it was not the proper time of year for it to produce edible fruit. Jesus, being hungry, cursed the tree for its inability to provide for his needs. "May no one ever eat fruit from you again!" (Mark 11:14). The tree wasted away almost immediately, dead

The Passover festival was the most sacred event on the Jewish calendar.

from root to limb. Why did Jesus do this? It had nothing to do with the tree itself or its inability to produce fruit in the wrong season. Rather, Jesus purposefully chose a barren tree and used its condition to provide

Judean fig tree. Photo: HolyLandPhotos.org.

a shocking illustration of God's judgment against Israel's religious institutions: the temple and priesthood had proven unable to meet the needs of the people. They were barren, corrupt, and unfamiliar to the God who had instituted them. Rather than reforming them yet again, God was now finished with both. No more temple. No more priesthood. Both were on the cusp of final destruction.

Body and Blood

The Passover meal was a somber celebration of the fact that God makes distinctions when passing out death and judgment. The celebration originated when God instructed every Hebrew

The Passover meal was a somber celebration of the fact that God makes distinctions when passing out death and judgment.

household enslaved in Egypt to smear lamb's blood on the doorposts of their home. The lambs served as substitutes for the firstborn sons of each household. Homes whose doorposts lacked the mercy symbol were robbed of sons when night fell. Thus the Egyptians suffered great loss while the Hebrews escaped unharmed.

Now, nearly 1,500 years later, the ultimate Passover substitute came and stood looking at Jerusalem from without, disciples by his side. To Peter and John he said, "Go and prepare the Passover meal for us, so we can eat it" (Luke 22:8). He explained that they would find a man in the city carrying a water jug, a most unusual sight. When they found the man, they followed him into a house and asked the owner to show them a room where Jesus and his disciples could eat the Passover. They discovered that a room was already prepared for them, just as Jesus had said. The stage was set for a climactic meal that has been reenacted millions of times over the past 2,000 years.

When Jesus and the disciples gathered for the meal that night, the Lord said it would be his last Passover meal "until it is fulfilled in the kingdom of God" (Luke 22:16).

When Jesus and the disciples gathered for the meal that night, the Lord said it would be his last Passover meal "until it is fulfilled in the kingdom of God" (Luke 22:16). Silence fell over the room at this kind of talk, but the clamor in Judas's heart must have been deafening. He had yet to reveal his hand openly, but both he and Jesus knew that the plot was in motion. While they were eating, Jesus announced, "I assure you: One of you will betray Me" (Matt 26:21). Each man protested, "Surely not I, Lord?" (v. 22).

While they were eating, Jesus announced, "I assure you: One of you will betray Me."

Ignoring them, Jesus continued, "He's the one I give the piece of bread to after I have dipped it" (John 13:26). He then dipped the bread into a bowl of herbs and fruit puree and handed the sop to Judas. "The Son of Man will go just as it is written about Him, but woe to that man by whom the Son of Man is betrayed! It would have been better for that man if he had not been born" (Matt 26:24). Holding the morsel Judas then had the gall to say, "Surely not I, Rabbi?" (v. 25). Then he passed the bread through his deceitful lips and sealed his doom as Satan entered in (John 13:27).

Jesus knows all and sees all. He was in charge even of his betrayal, and so to Judas he said, "You have said it. . . . What you're doing, do quickly" (Matt 26:25 and John 13:27). What Judas was doing, of course, was betraying Jesus into the hands of Roman and Jewish authorities who would kill him 12 hours later. It is not clear whether Judas expected Jesus to be executed, but then again Jesus had predicted his own execution many times by now in the presence of Judas. Certainly Jesus was sure of what was coming. His hour was drawing near, and by his side sat the man who had set the clock in motion. That man had no excuse for his betrayal. Even now the expectation of judgment grew heavy over his head.

Before sending Judas off on his dark task, Jesus instituted a sacred tradition known as the Lord's Supper. Taking bread, he broke it and passed it around among the disciples. "Take and eat it; this is My body," he said (Matt 26:26). Jesus next passed around a cup of wine, saying, "Drink from it, all of

you. For this is My blood that establishes the covenant; it is shed for many for the forgiveness of sins" (Matt 26:27–28). Some have thought that Jesus literally meant the bread and

By infusing symbolism into the taking of bread and wine, Jesus established a meal memorializing a sacrificial death in which he offered up his body and blood to God on behalf of the world.

wine became his body and blood in this meal, but of course none of the disciples thought that since Jesus was sitting there clearly distinct from the bread and wine that he passed around. The disciples took Jesus' words as he meant them: symbolically. He previously called himself a door, a vine, and the way. Certainly no one took those ascriptions literally. Rather, they recognized them as the sort of imagery tools all effective teachers use. By infusing symbolism into the taking of bread and wine, Jesus established a meal memorializing a sacrificial death in which he offered up his body and blood to God on behalf of the world. Like the Passover lambs that were being eaten all across town, Jesus would be "consumed" by the people for whom he died. Once he had risen from the dead and ascended to heaven, this memorial meal served as a celebration of the sacrifice he made for us.

By saying that his sacrifice represents a "new covenant," Jesus meant that he is the fulfillment of the pacts God made with Abraham, Moses, and David. Moreover he is the full and final mediator between God and humankind, a fact the disciples had yet to fully grasp. Given these credentials and all he was set to do for humanity, we might

Christ Washing the Feet of the Disciples by Duccio. Jesus again evaded all expectations by standing up and wrapping a towel around his waist. He then poured water into a basin and washed the feet of his stunned disciples.

expect Jesus to demand that the disciples serve him hand and foot on this his final evening, but Jesus again evaded all expectations by standing up and wrapping a towel around his waist. He then poured water into a basin and washed the feet of his stunned disciples. Leave it to Peter to voice the thought everyone else kept secret. "You will never wash my feet—ever!" he protested (John 13:8). Also keeping true to form, Jesus came back with a stark answer that sobered Peter. "If I don't wash you, you have no part with Me." Hearing this, Peter essentially requested a full bath! He had bounced from one extreme to another, but Jesus let him down gently by saying that foot-washing was enough (John 13:10). Jesus did this as an example for them to follow. The disciples were privileged unlike anyone else in history, but far from allowing this to breed arrogance, they were commanded to serve all people with utter humility.

The disciples were privileged unlike anyone else in history, but they were commanded to serve all people with utter humility.

The Lord himself set the example by washing their sweaty, dirty feet.

This 12th-century structure is built on the traditional site of the upper room where the Last Supper took place.

As they left the house and headed into the night, Jesus led his disciples in the tradition of singing Psalms 114–118. "Tremble, earth, at the presence of the Lord, at the presence of the God of Jacob," they sang as God's own feet trod the streets of Jerusalem. "Our God is in heaven and does whatever He pleases," they shouted as Jesus chose to walk into the trap laid for him. "The Lord is gracious and righteous; our God is compassionate," they sang as Jesus marched forward to purchase righteousness and compassion for humankind. "Praise the Lord, all nations! Glorify Him, all peoples!" rang out as

Jesus thought of all who would come to him for eternal life. "I called to the LORD in distress; the LORD answered me," sang Jesus even as he knew the Father would momentarily abandon him on the tree of execution. Even so, "The LORD is for me," sang Jesus, "I will not be afraid. What can man do to me?"

CLOSER LOOK

Was the Last Supper a Passover Meal?

The authors of the Gospels did not aim to give us exact chronological accounts of Jesus' life. We might expect otherwise when we read Luke's purpose statement in Luke 1:3, where he says he set out to write "in orderly sequence" the things done by Jesus. However, it is clear from the Gospel evidence that Luke means logical sequence rather than chronological sequence. For instance, the Gospels are in many cases arranged around topical or geographical concerns, not a linear time line. The result of this approach is that we are left unsure about many chronological issues in Jesus' life. The Last Supper is a case in point. Matthew, Mark, and Luke (the Synoptic Gospels) teach that the Last Supper was the official Passover meal, which fell on a Thursday night. Jesus was then crucified the next day, post-Passover, on Friday. His resurrection occurred on Sunday morning. John's Gospel agrees that Jesus was crucified on Friday and raised from the dead on Sunday, but he seems to differ from the other Gospels by placing the Passover on Friday rather than Thursday. This could mean John is saying that the Last Supper was not strictly a Passover meal; it could also mean that Jesus was crucified on the day of Passover rather than the day after, as the Synoptics have it. Do we have a contradiction between John and the other Gospels? Some critics have answered yes. Defenders of the Bible have countered by pointing out several possible solutions.

First, if one bears in mind that the authors were not primarily concerned with chronology, the importance of chronological differences between various Gospel accounts is minimized. Their emphasis was on telling the truth about the person and work of Jesus Christ, not providing a precise calendar of events. We are in danger of over reading the Gospel accounts if we do not bear this point in mind.

Second, some scholars suggest that John is correct to say that Passover fell on a Friday the year Jesus was executed. This would mean that the Last Supper in all four Gospel accounts was not a standard Passover meal but was instead an early Passover celebrated only by Jesus and his disciples. Knowing he would die the next day, Jesus moved the meal up by 24 hours so he and his disciples would not miss this last chance to celebrate Passover together. The difficulty with this view is that the Synoptic Gospels give no hints that the Last Supper on Thursday night was anything other than the standard, citywide Passover event.

Third, it is possible that John agrees with the Synoptic Gospels on the Last Supper after all even though his language can lead to the opposite conclusion. John depicts the Jewish priests as wishing to avoid ritual impurity on the Friday morning of Jesus' crucifixion so they can be fit to eat the Passover later in the day (John 18:28). This seems to indicate that John depicts the Passover as falling on Friday rather than Thursday, but since the whole week was part of the sacred festival package (so to speak), it is possible that the priests had already eaten Passover proper on Thursday night but wished to remain ritually pure for some of the ancillary meals that fell on Friday. This line of argument persuades many scholars.

Fourth, some observers prefer to suggest that John has consciously departed from the exact dating of events in order to paint a theologically true portrait of Jesus as the Passover Lamb. In order to do this with maximum impact he shifts the Passover date so that Jesus' execution coincides with the hour that Passover lambs were slain throughout the city of Jerusalem (John 19:36). If this solution is correct John is indeed depicting the Passover as falling on Friday rather than Thursday. On this reading John has not changed the ultimate meaning or truthfulness of vital events. Whether or not the Last Supper was an official Passover meal, it is the meal at which Jesus instituted the Lord's Supper. And whether or not Jesus died at the same hour the Passover lambs were being slain, he died for the sins of the world.

Which of these solutions is best? It is difficult to say. Each enjoys at least modest plausibility. I suggest you start your quest for resolution by appreciating the importance of the first point given above.

Note

1. See a similar act performed for King Jehu in 2 Kings 9:13.

Christ in Gethsemane by El Greco.

Chapter 10
Night Shifts

While wealthy pilgrims all across Jerusalem settled down in the homes of well-positioned friends or select inns after the Passover meal, Jesus and his band of brothers spilled out of the city gates, skipped down through the Kidron Valley, and then ascended onto the western slopes across from Jerusalem. The area was called Mount Olivet. On its hillside was located a thick grove of olive trees and an oil press which collectively were known as the garden of Gethsemane. This was their regular haunt during Passover week. When they arrived, Jesus once again pared the group down to his inner circle of Peter, James, and John. These he took deeper into the grove to pray while the remaining eight were asked to wait without.

As he picked his way into the heart of dark Gethsemane, Jesus felt his task more keenly than ever before. Waves of horror and stress broke over him. To his trusted trio he said, "My soul is swallowed up in sorrow—to the point of death. Remain here and stay awake"

The garden of Gethsemane. Jesus and his disciples spent their nights here during the festival week.

(Mark 14:34). He wanted them to be watchful and prayerful. Even now a mob was forming in the city; Jesus' name was on the lips of hostile men. Knowing this and a thousand other factors that were beginning to merge, Jesus went on a few paces and dropped like a stone to the ground. He was alone with the Father, facedown on the precipice of a great chasm. Hate, filth, lies, murder, adulteries, pride—the bottomless reach of world evil would soon open wide to receive him. After that would come the judgment of holy God. Catching a glimpse

Jesus in Prayer in the Garden of Gethsemane by Mantegna.

of this, the sinless Son cried out, "Abba, Father! All things are possible for You. Take this cup away from Me" (Mark 14:36). But the Father would not do this. Jesus knew this full well, and so he conceded, "Nevertheless, not what I will, but what You will." By choosing to submit to the Father's will, Jesus showed that he was in full command of his journey to the cross. None of his steps were mislaid, and even his enemies—the devil, the religious elite, the Romans—gave him chances to change his tune and escape execution. The unavoidable truth is that Jesus sought out the cross.

The unavoidable truth is that Jesus sought out the cross. But this was no suicide; it was sacrifice.

But this was no suicide; it was sacrifice. He had come willingly to lay down his life, but now that the moment of offering approached, he needed his Father's hand to steady him.

After an hour with his Father, Jesus arose from prayer and returned to the three. During the Passover meal a few hours previously, Jesus had foretold that Peter would deny him three times before morning. With fervent avowal Peter had denied this would happen. He said he would be faithful to the end even if all others fell away. Morning was now just a handful of hours away. Dawn would prove whose prediction was right. Of all men, then, Peter had cause to beat back fatigue and remain watchful. Nevertheless Jesus found him sleeping the night away along with the other two. "Couldn't you stay awake one hour? Stay awake and pray so that you won't enter into temptation. The spirit is willing, but the flesh is weak" (Mark 14:37–38). Jesus then turned back to prayer, repeating much of what he had previously said. "My Father, if this cannot pass

Jesus said, "My Father, if this cannot pass unless I drink it, Your will be done"

unless I drink it, Your will be done" (Matt 26:42). After this he again found Peter and his fellows sleeping on watch. These men had been Jesus' companions for more than three years. They had seen more wonders than any of the other disciples. When Jesus raised Jarius's cold, limp daughter from the dead, Peter, James, and John were there to witness it. When Jesus was transformed on a mountaintop as Moses and Elijah visited from the unseen realm, God the Father enveloped these same three men in a cloud of glory and spoke revelations of his Son. These and a hundred other miraculous acts they had seen, and yet now, in the hour of Jesus' most critical need, they chose

sleep over wakefulness, self-service over aid to the Lord. Seeing this, Jesus wandered off to pray alone once more. When he finished, he knew time was up. He returned to the sleeping disciples and said, "Enough! The time has come. Look, the Son of Man is being betrayed into the hands of sinners. Get up; let's go! See— My betrayer is near" (Mark 14:41-42).

Christ on the Mount of Olives by Goya.

Kiss the Son

Judas knew the way. After all, he had been here with Jesus many times. As he picked his way up through the moonlit grove, he was following a familiar path. The mob slinking up at his back trusted this was so. Too much was on the line for mistakes. Jesus' popularity had reached critical mass. If the present course held, the whole city would soon be in the grip of messianic craze. For this reason the religious leaders requested Rome's aid. Rome assented and gave over 200 troops from the temporary barracks located at the Castle of Antonia. These men, trained to keep down riots during emotion-packed Jewish festivals, were joined

Jesus' popularity had reached critical mass. If the present course held, the whole city would soon be in the grip of messianic craze.

to a group of Jews that had been rousted from their police duties at the temple. Together they were given a command: find the Nazarene now and be quiet about it.

This is why Judas was useful to them. Rather than marching all over the hillside stirring all the other pilgrims that were camped in the vicinity, with Judas's aid they could zero in on the supposed blasphemer and drag him away without much commotion. And so the soldiers together with temple police and club-toting priestly affiliates crept along, torches held aloft as they watched Judas's every signal. And then he paused. He had spied the Son of Man with his band of revolutionaries.

Judas broke in on Jesus while he was still rousing his sleepy disciples. The soldiers and police were still filing into view when Judas rushed up and gave Jesus a kiss of greeting. "Judas, are you betraying the Son of Man with a kiss?" Jesus asked (Luke 22:48). For a moment no one moved or spoke. Jesus stood with Judas and the rest of the disciples in a knot that con-

The Taking of Christ by Caravaggio. A great number of those in the mob had not gotten a clear view of Judas's kiss, which was the signal by which he had agreed to identify Jesus.

stricted ever tighter as several hundred men formed up around them. A great number of those in the mob had not gotten a clear view of Judas's kiss, which was the signal by which he had agreed to identify Jesus. No action could be taken until they knew for sure which one was Jesus. Finally, Jesus stepped through his clotted disciples and offered himself up by asking, "Who is it you're looking for?" (John 18:7). "Jesus the Nazarene," they answered. To this Jesus replied, "I am He." More literally, Jesus' words are translated as simply, "I am." To the Jews gathered there this response called to mind the words by which God had identified himself to Moses: "I AM WHO I AM. This is what you are to say to the Israelites: I AM has sent me to you" (Exod 3:14).

Here, under the gnarled boughs of an olive tree, God himself stepped forward and surrendered to an arrest party.

Here, under the gnarled boughs of an olive tree, God himself stepped forward and surrendered to an arrest party. This was more than they could handle. En masse they lurched backwards and fell to the ground when Jesus said, "I am." God the Son had spoken, and though none of his assailants came to worship, they were forced to bow at the unveiling of divine identity.

Kiss of Judas by Giotto.

Once they recovered their senses, Jesus again asked who they were looking for. They answered the same as before, and Jesus replied, "I told you I am" (John 18:8). They came forward now and seized him. He asked, "Have you come out with swords and clubs, as if I were a criminal, to capture Me? Every day I used to sit, teaching in the temple complex, and you didn't arrest Me" (Matt 26:55). Jesus' actions had been public and well received by many people, but in response the religious leaders deployed a night mob to do in secret what they feared to attempt in daylight. In a world turned upside down, cowardice trumped innocence and integrity, but Jesus was unfazed. The divine plan was right on track. "All this has happened so that the prophetic Scriptures would be fulfilled," he said (Matt 26:56).

God ordained this night's troubles, but this was too high for Peter's mind to grasp. What he *could* grasp was his need for redemption. Already he had failed Jesus by sleeping on watch. Predictions of his denial were now foremost in his mind. He felt that all eyes were on him, watching for his downfall. Now was the time to act.

Cowardice trumped innocence and integrity, but Jesus was unfazed.

Nearby stood another man who felt that he was being watched. He was Malchus, slave of the high priest. With several chief priests present, Malchus was likely the first to grab Jesus, making a show of his loyalty to the priesthood by placing himself front and center in the arrest of the Galilean troublemaker. Malchus's enthusiasm and Peter's desperation inevitably came crashing together. Peter, trained to wield nets rather than swords, drew out his blade and made a wild stabbing motion that sliced off Malchus's ear. The disciples possessed one other sword among themselves. We are not told who held it, but heaven itself must have frozen it to its sheath to prevent disaster in this critical moment. The tensed soldiers ringed Peter but kept their cool because Jesus diverted their attention. He retrieved Malchus's severed ear and touched his head, restoring what had been robbed from him. He also sternly rebuked Peter:

Christ in Gethsemane by Fra Angelico.

"All who take up a sword will perish by a sword" (Matt 26:52). Jesus reminded them that if he wished it he could call 72,000 angelic warriors down to the hillside and end his troubles instantly. Could such a man really need an assortment of fishermen and tax collectors to brandish swords for his protection?

Besides, the Scriptures foretold these events. Nothing could stand in the way of their fulfillment (v. 54).

Jesus said to Peter, "All who take up a sword will perish by a sword." The disciples escaped into darkness as the soldiers led Jesus away. As men often do when things go horribly wrong, they simply ran. What about Judas? He had forsaken his teacher and the men with whom he traveled for several years. To the priests and soldiers he was only a tool whose one use had now come and gone. They discarded him without so much as a second glance. Scripture does not tell us what Judas did as everyone else emptied off the hillside, but I imagine him standing a long while at the spot where he kissed the Lord, watching to one side the disciples disappear uphill and to the other the soldiers as they led downhill by torchlight the Rabbi whom he had forsaken. There Judas stood alone in the dark, belonging nowhere and to no one.

Judas by Nikolaj Nikolajewitsch.

Questions in the Dark

As the disciples fled, the soldiers tied Jesus up and escorted him to a meeting with Annas. Annas had been high priest nearly 20 years earlier and had given way to his son-in-law, Caiaphas. As with any living priest who had once presided as high priest, Annas had ongoing influence in Israel. He was like a wise old sage perched atop the mountain path. People came to him for advice in a pinch. Here was a pinch if ever there was one. Jesus—miracle worker, preacher, prophet, troubler of the religious order—had been arrested in the middle of the night. What should be done? Had the point of no return come and gone? Wisdom must show the way forward in such hours, and so as Caiaphas and the ruling priests of the Sanhedrin were mustered from their beds, wise old Annas took the first crack at lighting the way (John 18:12–14, 19–23). Since this was not an official proceeding, Annas was informal in his approach. He plied Jesus with basic questions about his teachings and his disciples. It was as if he had never heard of the Nazarene before (18:19). Jesus apparently found the questions obtuse. His response amounted to: Why do you ask this? My teachings have been public, not clandestine (vv. 20–21). Hearing Jesus' modestly curt response, one of the temple policemen reached out and slapped him. "Is this the way you answer the high priest?" (v. 22). Undaunted, Jesus stood his ground. "If I have spoken wrongly, give evidence about the wrong; but if rightly, why do you hit Me?" (v. 23). Annas realized that nothing more could be done here except give in to the tension and foolishly beat Jesus before he even reached trial. Thus Annas saved face and sent the prisoner on to Caiaphas, fettered and forewarned that justice would be hard to find on this night.

Annas saved face and sent the prisoner on to Caiaphas, fettered and forewarned that justice would be hard to find on this night.

While Jesus' trial before Caiaphas was kicking off, Peter faced his own round of hostile questions. He and another Christ follower (almost certainly John) had dared to circle back from their initial flight to follow the arrest party at a distance. Peter's companion knew Caiaphas personally, and so he was admitted to the courtyard straightaway and got to within earshot of the room where Jesus was being questioned. No doubt he listened carefully and was thus able to record the trial for posterity at a later date. As for Peter, he was initially left standing outside where the doorkeeper peppered him with questions. "You aren't one of this man's disciples too, are you?" (John 18:17). Peter denied this hotly as he was finally allowed into the courtyard. Once inside he moved to warm himself at a fire, round which stood slaves and temple policemen who were eavesdropping on Jesus' trial and discussing the night's remarkable events. By venturing fireside, Peter leaped from frying pan to fire. The attentive crowd soon identified him as a disciple of Jesus. Again he swore otherwise, but to no avail. One of those standing there had been at Gethsemane when the night's events began to unfold. He

took special notice of what happened there because his relative, the slave Malchus, had been both wounded and healed in the span of a few moments. This man was able to place Peter at Jesus' side beyond all doubt (v. 26). On top of all this, there was Peter's

Peter's Denial by Rembrandt.

accent. Clearly he was a Galilean, not an urbanite! Pressed now for a third time, Peter unleashed his customary passion. With curses and oaths he swore that he did not know Jesus (Matt 26:74). Outside the city walls a rooster greeted the oncoming day. The sound of it pierced Peter's soul and brought back to him the words Jesus had spoken earlier that night (Mark 14:30). He fled out of sight and wept as few men have ever wept.

CLOSER LOOK

Order and Sequence in Jesus' Trials

It is neither possible nor necessary to lay out an absolutely assured sequence of events for Jesus' trials. Each evangelist wrote in accordance with his own angles and interests. Things John found significant go entirely unmentioned by the Synoptic Gospels and vice versa. As we have said before, the Gospel writers were not obligated to write everything they knew. All writers enjoy the liberty of writing down selected events. This is true today, and it was just as true 2,000 years ago. And so for instance Matthew may justifiably say, "Those who had arrested Jesus led Him away [from Gethsemane] to Caiaphas the high priest" (Matt 26:57). He entirely skips the intervening event mentioned by John, which is the trip to see Annas (John 18:12–13). Apparently Matthew wanted to zip straight to the scene with Caiaphas, a man of greater gravity since he was the reigning high priest. The fact that Matthew leaves Annas unmentioned doesn't mean he knew nothing about Annas's involvement and much less that he denied it ever happened! Additionally, the night of Jesus' trials was chaotic, and he was not tried in the typical way by either Jewish or Roman authorities. The whole series of events was haphazard and improvised as the Jewish leaders rushed to shove Jesus under the wheels of injustice before his sizable body of followers could swing momentum back in his favor. The sooner they could get him charged, humiliated, and convicted, the greater their chances of snuffing out his movement. The irregularities and flash-bang abruptness of Jesus' experiences are mirrored in the Gospel accounts. While this makes it difficult to bring all four Gospels together seamlessly, it also gives us four separate visions of the same reality: Jesus was unjustly charged, unjustly tried, and unjustly condemned to die.

Under Oath Before the Living God

When gathered in full strength, the priests and scribes who composed the Sanhedrin numbered 70 strong. Now, in the small hours of a Friday morning, they gathered to pass judgment on Jesus. Matthew and Mark explain that from the outset the Sanhedrin planned to condemn Jesus to death. Justice they cast aside. They only wanted incendiary evidence that would justify their purpose, and so they hosted a string of witnesses who came telling tales on Jesus, but their words would not match up. They couldn't even sync up when recounting Jesus' scandalous statement about tearing down and rebuilding the temple (John 2:19–21; Mark 14:59).

Frustrated with the ineptitude of his own kangaroo court, Caiaphas took command and tried to hang Jesus by his own words. First he asked, "Don't You have an answer to what these men are testifying against You?" (Mark 14:60). Jesus refused to answer, and so Caiaphas cut straight to the heart of the matter: "By the living God I place You under oath: tell us if You are the Messiah, the Son of God!" (Matt 26:63). Unwilling to dishonor God, Jesus acknowledged that he

From the outset the Sanhedrin planned to condemn Jesus to death. Justice they cast aside.

was Messiah. "You have said it . . . I am" (combining Matt 26:64a; Mark 14:62). Jesus then went on to say, "In the future you will see the Son of Man seated at the right hand of the Power and coming on the clouds of heaven" (Matt 26:64b). In this response Jesus has melded Daniel 7:13–14 and Psalm 110:1, resulting in a clear claim to divinity. The point certainly wasn't lost on Caiaphas. He bolted upright and tore his clothes in demonstration of anger. "He has blasphemed!" he shouted. "Why do we still need witnesses?" (Matt 26:65). Caiaphas's ploy had worked. Under oath before God, Jesus spoke honestly and thus "incriminated" himself by confessing his deity. The assembly shouted their verdict: death to the blasphemer. Some of them began abusing Jesus with blows, slaps, and spittle. Traditional Jewish views about Messiah included the expectation that he would pass judgment by the sense

Christ Before Caiaphas by Giotto.

of smell alone (a belief which stemmed from a misreading of Isa 11:3). And so they blindfolded Jesus and beat him some more. "Prophesy to us, Messiah! Who hit You?" (Matt 26:68).

The abuses and mockery continued till dawn when the Sanhedrin passed their official judgment. As a nation subject to the will of Roman occupiers, Israel did not have the right to impose the death sentence against its citizens. Thus Jesus was sent to stand trial before Pilate, the Roman governor.

Silence and Confession

Pilate's glance was forever straying outside the walls of his compound, not just after women or gold but after other civic posts. Pilate was not fond of the Jews or Jerusalem and would *As a nation subject to the will of Roman occupiers, Israel did not have the right to impose the death sentence against its citizens.* have preferred an assignment among freewheeling Gentiles. Earlier in his career he allowed his angst to translate into open cruelty and insensitivity toward his subjects. This sort of behavior won him some enemies among Jews and Romans alike with the result that he was forced to tone down his suppressions and walk with greater caution by the time Jesus stood trial before him. This does not mean he was a genuinely reformed man. Rather, he learned to express his cruelty by subtle measures that would not risk his faltering position as governor. He could no longer flaunt his rule over the Jews, but neither would he accommodate their every whim.

Christ Before Pilate by Munkácsy.

These tensions came to the surface when the Jews dragged Jesus to Pilate's headquarters that morning. The priests and elders refused to come in to Pilate, John tells us, because they did not wish to become ritually impure by entering the dwelling place of a Gentile (John 18:28). No doubt this set Pilate on edge, for because of Jewish peculiarities, he had to come out to them. Who is master and who is subject here? When he arrived among them, he asked what charges were being brought against Jesus. They answered, "If this man weren't a criminal, we wouldn't have handed Him over to you" (John 18:30). The Jews were hoping Pilate would simply vouch for their decision and pass Jesus on to execution. "Don't bother us with questions," they essentially said. "We just want the man dead." But it would not be that simple. Lacking the power to execute criminals, the Jews were forced to make their case there at the entry to Pilate's headquarters. They hit upon a winning tactic

by arguing that the kingship element of Jesus' messianic claims presented a threat to Roman sovereignty and national security. When Jesus refused to answer this charge, Pilate left the Jews stand-

A model of the Fortress Antonia, where Jesus was tried by Pilate. Photo: HolyLandPhotos.org.

ing outside and called Jesus to come into his quarters where he could put the question to him privately: "Are You the King of the Jews?" (Matt 27:11). "You have said it," Jesus answered (Luke 23:3). Realizing that Pilate would not understand the nature of his kingship, Jesus then explained, "My kingdom is not of this world. If My kingdom were of this world, My servants would fight, so that I wouldn't be handed over to the Jews" (John 18:36). Furthermore, Jesus said he came into the world to tell the truth. "Everyone who is of

Today a school stands on the site of the Fortress Antonia. Photo: HolyLandPhotos.org.

the truth listens to My voice" (v. 37). This prompted Pilate's famous retort, "What is truth?" The Jews outside certainly didn't know. Neither did Pilate as he strode back to where the priests were gathered. He asked them if Jesus was from Galilee.

The accent must have suggested this.

Learning that Jesus was indeed Galilean, Pilate decided to send him to the attention of Herod Antipas, a son of Herod the Great. This Herod was prefect over the Galilean territory, and he happened to be in town for the festival.

> *The Jews hit upon a winning tactic by arguing that the kingship element of Jesus' messianic claims presented a threat to Roman sovereignty and national security.*

He was no friend of Pilate's. Sending Jesus was a dig in Herod's side, a passing of the trash if you will. Let Herod sort this mess out! Ironically, however, Pilate's maneuver ended up forging a friendship bond between him and Herod (Luke 23:12). It turns out that Herod had long wanted to meet Jesus. Pilate inadvertently sent him a gift! Herod's motives for welcoming Jesus were less than impressive, however. What he wanted was

What Is Truth? by Nikolajewitsch.

a show of magic (v. 8). He kept waiting for Jesus to perform, but he only stood there mutely as Herod tried to tease power out of him. The Jews were there also, continuing their campaign of slander. Finally Herod and his soldiers grew bored and devolved into the same kind of base behavior Caiaphas and the Sanhedrin had displayed. They mocked Jesus and dressed him in a royal robe for his journey back to Pilate.

Rebel's Freedom

Having received Jesus back from Herod, Pilate offered him

up to the crowd which had gathered outside the headquarters. It was still early morning at this point. Most of Jerusalem had no idea that Jesus had been arrested and was standing trial. For this reason the crowd outside consisted almost entirely of Jesus' enemies. Members of the Sanhedrin, temple police, an assortment of elders and scribes, citizens supporting the religious establishment—these types were packed together at the gate, urging Pilate to ratify the death sentence for Jesus. To this crowd Pilate said, "I find no grounds for charging Him. You have a custom

Christ Before Pilate and Herod by Duccio.

that I release one prisoner to you at the Passover. So, do you want me to release to you the King of the Jews?" (John 18:39). It was never a reasonable offer, as you can see. The piranhas had gathered to feed, not pardon.

Meanwhile, Pilate's wife sent an urgent message by courier. It reached Pilate as he sat on the judgment seat which was positioned in the courtyard, allowing him to hold audience with the Jews. "Have nothing to do with that righteous man," said the note, "for today I've suffered terribly in a dream because of Him!" (Matt 27:19). As Pilate read the note, the chief priests and elders of the Jews were working the crowd in an effort to champion an imprisoned revolutionary named Barabbas. They persuaded the doubters, and soon the whole crowd cried out to Pilate, "Release for us Barabbas!" (Luke 23:18). Pilate, unnerved by his wife's note and convinced that Jesus was innocent, asked what he should do with Jesus. "Crucify Him!" they shouted over and over, drowning out Pilate's objections. The crowd wanted blood. Pilate sized up the situation in a flash. Innocent though Jesus might be, Pilate judged it better to condemn the innocent than cause a full-scale riot by his pardon. Besides, Pilate knew that such a disturbance would spell the end of his reign. Seeing that the crowd was on the cusp of violence, Pilate had his servants fetch a bowl of water. In full view of the crowd he dipped his hands into the bowl and made like he was washing away the filth. "I am innocent of this man's blood," he said. "See to it yourself" (Matt 27:24). He gave the rebel Barabbas his freedom, but in concession to the Jews he handed Jesus over to be flogged by the soldiers.

"Release for us Barabbas!" shouted the crowd.

The flogging consisted of 40 lashes with a flagellum, a whip whose leather cords were loaded with shards of jagged bone and metal. The soldier manning the whip would sling it in such a way as to wrap the cords around the victim's torso, allowing the shards to dig into the flesh. He would then yank backwards violently, unwinding the cords and causing the flesh to tear as the shards tore away from the places in which they had become embedded. So severe were the wounds from flogging that victims sometimes died before further punishments could be administered. Jesus lived through his lashings, but the soldiers were not satisfied with the damage done. They twisted crown-shape a vine of

Christ and Pilate by Maes. Pilate had his servants fetch a bowl of water. In full view of the crowd he dipped his hands into the bowl and made like he was washing away the filth.

thorns, possibly from date palms that produce barbs up to 12 inches long. This they shoved down into the flesh of Jesus' head. "Hail, King of the Jews!" they said as they bowed before

Flagellation of Christ by Rubens. The flagellum was a whip whose leather cords were loaded with shards of jagged bone and metal.

him and roughed him up (John 19:3). They draped over his shoulders the robe Herod had given him and then paraded him before his accusers. Perhaps Pilate believed this vision of suffering would mollify the crowd and prompt them to rethink their call for death, but it seems only to have incited their hatred further. Pilate then suggested they should crucify Jesus themselves, though he knew they hadn't the right to do so (John 18:31).

The Jews answered that according to their law Jesus must die since he made himself out to be the Son of God (John 19:7). This kind of talk alarmed Pilate and reminded him of his wife's warning. All ancient peoples believed that God spoke through dreams. Had Pilate's wife heard from God regarding the Nazarene? With these thoughts in mind, Pilate again held a private interview with Jesus. "Where are you from?" he asked. He had to know, was *desperate* to know. He was now nearer to releasing Jesus than ever before. He only needed some satisfactory answers, but Jesus wouldn't give them. The Bible does not explain why Jesus kept silent here, but most likely he sensed that everything had come down to a needle-thin point. If Pilate balked here, the mob would storm the

So severe were the wounds from flogging that victims sometimes died before further punishments could be administered.

citadel and tear Jesus apart, thus circumventing several prophecies that foretold a different sort of ending. Jesus must die on the tree (Deut 21:22–23), must be pierced for the world's transgressions (Isa 53:5), must be led away to formal execution (Isa

53:7–8), must spill his blood for the nations (Isa 52:15), must keep his mouth shut in the moments where a misplaced word could win his freedom (Isa 53:7), must die by official religious decree rather than mob action (Isa 53:4), must be the victim of biased judicial proceedings (Isa 53:8), must be killed alongside criminals (Isa 53:9), and must be buried in the grave of a rich man (Isa 53:9).

Ecce Homo by Ciseri.

None of these would have been fulfilled had Jesus died in Pilate's courtyard, and so the Son of Man remained silent when it mattered most. He did let Pilate know one thing, however: you have no power that is not given by heaven (John 19:11). All thrones are gifted to men by heaven itself, and all earthly authority is second order. There is a Greater than Pilate, and it is to him that everyone involved in this fiasco will someday answer.

Pilate understandably came away from this interview in a near panic. He made "every effort" to release Jesus but the Jews shouted back that he was a traitor to Caesar for entertaining such desires (John 19:12). If Caesar heard that a so-called King of Jews was let off by Pilate, he would swiftly depose the governor. Pilate's head was swimming at this point. His morning had gone wrong from the very start. Now an enigmatic and possibly supernatural man stood before him condemned to die for made-up offenses. Pilate's choice was between justice and expedience. True to character he chose expedience. "Here is your king!" he announced, giving in to the mood that played out before him. To the satisfaction of the crowd, he handed Jesus over to be executed.

By now Barabbas had probably been released to the crowd. Picture him milling about, asking and answering questions while blinking hard in the light of a freedom he had not foreseen. He deserved only death, but Jesus won him his freedom. Now consider that you and I walked with Barabbas that day, freed from chains whose bonds we could never break. In the freeing of this rebel, all rebels for all time are freed.

Pilate's choice was between justice and expedience. True to character he chose expedience.

Or at least they are offered that chance. More on this later. For now Jesus was being led off to a God-forsaken hill outside the city gates. What happened there and in a nearby tomb is the concern of part III of our book.

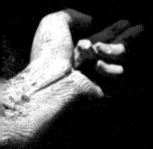

Part III
Jesus' Cross

Chapter 11
Cursing Tree

Somewhere back in the fog of ancient history, a forlorn and forgotten man, guilty of some heinous crime or possibly the *victim* of one, became the first subject of crucifixion. He might yet have been alive and panic-stricken when grappling hands posted him to the tree. Or perhaps he was already bloodied and dead, erected on high for post-mortem mockery rather than execution. However it began, the world-traveling Greek historian Herodotus stumbled across the specter of crucifixion in fifth-century Persia where he learned that it had been practiced at least as far back as the sixth century BC when King Darius executed 3,000 Babylonians in this manner. We also know that the Celtic Barbarians of Ireland and Britain practiced crucifixion as early as 100 BC, for another restless Greek savant, Posidonius,

Meeting Scythian Emissaries by Smuglewicz. Five hundred years before Jesus, King Darius of Persia crucified thousands of his enemies.

roamed among them and observed that it was used as a means of sacrificing humans to flesh-hungry gods. If the full history of crucifixion were known, most likely we would find that it reaches farther back than roving Celts or famed Persian kings; possibly it appeared in rudimentary form near the dawn of history itself when men first pondered how they could best shame their enemies.

The purposes and methods of crucifixion varied greatly. The common themes were wood, elevation, humiliation, suffering, and death. Sometimes living trees were used while in *The purposes and methods of crucifixion varied greatly.* other cases posts with crossbeams were stabbed into the earth, providing a rack on which stretched bodies could hang aloft like panting scarecrows. If the victim was killed before he was fastened to the beams, he was left to rot beneath the probing sun as a symbol of his shame and as a warning to other would-be offenders. If on the other hand he was still alive when affixed to the tree, he was likely to remain so for *days.* At first his cries would be vigorous as he searched for mercy in every upturned face. Then, as hours passed into days, only meager pleas would escape his cracked lips. Life could linger in this way because the wounds of crucifixion were painful but not fatal. Death came in slow degrees by dehydration, fatigue, and respiratory distress. In some cases the victims were literally nailed in place with iron spikes measuring as much as nine inches in length. This promoted a round of free bleeding but not the sort that

Nine-inch nails were often used to pin victims to a cross.

drained a man dry. In other instances the victim's arms and feet were simply tied fast against posts or a tree trunk with rope or vine. Since this entailed little or no bleeding, it ensured that death would not come until long after the victim's will to live had passed. Whether by tree or post, nail or rope, every victim would agree that death did not come soon enough.

Crucifixion among the Greeks and Romans

If the Jews remained mostly unaware of crucifixion through their early centuries, Alexander the Great provided for their education in the fourth century BC when he swept down Is-

rael's coastline and made a stop at Tyre. Tyre was uniquely situated. One-half of the city was hunched down on the coastline while the other half rose up from the waters a mile out to sea, forming what amounted to a separate island kingdom. This unique geography posed a real challenge to Alexander's war efforts, and so the citizens were able to hold him off for a remarkable seven months. In the end Alexander scraped the coastal portion of Tyre flat as a floor and pushed the rubble out into the waters, forming a narrow, jagged gangway across which his soldiers tramped to set up siege against the island. Realizing that ruin was upon them, the surviving Tyrinians eventually surrendered to Alexander in hopes of escaping with their lives. The tactic failed.

Siege of Tyre by Castiagne. Alexander the Great lay siege against Tyre for many months before breaking through and crucifying 2,000 male survivors.

Fuming mad at having been stalled by a nation of fishermen and sea merchants, Alexander made an example of Tyre by crucifying 2,000 of her male survivors and hoisting them aloft as trophies of war.

The Romans, students of all things Greek, would not be outdone by Alexander. When in 73 BC a gladiator-slave named Spartacus sparked off a slave revolt that nearly toppled the empire, Roman leadership perceived that they needed to set an example which demonstrated that class revolt led to devastation, not freedom and life. Thus when Spartacus and his pack of 70,000 ill-equipped slaves were finally trounced by 10 legions of Roman soldiers, the final 6,000 rebels were spared long enough to be fastened to posts (one for each slave) that were erected all up and down the length of Rome's famous 130-mile

The Appian Way was the world's first major highway system.

road, the Appian Way. For months to come, travelers were hemmed in by sun-blackened corpses as they rolled, rode, or strode along the length of Italy's boot, nostrils clenched tightly shut.

By the first century AD this ancient Persian art was regularly practiced on a hill outside Jerusalem—a craggy knoll called Calvary or Golgotha, which means "place of the skull." Here, over soil stained with criminal blood, Roman soldiers in league with Jesus' Jewish enemies lifted high the marred body of history's lone innocent man.

Six thousand slaves were crucified up and down the path of the Appian Way.

The Tree Foreknown

There is no evidence that the Jews of Moses' day knew about the sort of crucifixion Jesus suffered, and yet Deuteronomy 21:22–23 says: "If anyone is found guilty of an offense deserving the death penalty and is executed, and you hang his body on a tree, you are not to leave his corpse on the tree overnight but are to bury him that day, for anyone hung on a tree is under God's curse. You must not defile the land the LORD your God is giving you as an inheritance." Perhaps the Jews crossed paths with early practitioners of crucifixion after they spilled out of Egypt, but most likely the verse has a broader purpose than addressing crucifixion:

God insisted that human death must be dignified even in the event of justifiable execution.

God is insisting that human death must be dignified even in the event of justifiable execution. To drape a corpse across the span of a tree and leave it exposed to weather, beasts, and rapt eyes for days on end is to denigrate the value of life. Slain animals lie on the ground until they are consumed or rot to nothingness. Shall humans, even the worst of them, suffer similar shame? God forbade this, and so as the Jews encountered cultures whose values differed, they were to hold forth a holy witness to the importance of human dignity. Thus from their earliest times the Jews frowned upon the use of crucifixion or related means of execution. For those among them who did part life in this way, it was taken to be the ultimate sign that God had singled them out for condemnation. The cross was seen as a cursing tree; death by crucifixion implied that death had come down as a punishment by God's own hand.

> *The cross was seen as a cursing tree; death by crucifixion implied that death had come down as a punishment by God's own hand.*

Cicero Denounces Catiline by Maccari. Famed Roman orator Cicero said, "The very word 'cross' should be far removed not only from the person of a Roman citizen but from his thoughts, his eyes and his ears."

The Romans felt little different. In fact, they refused to execute their own citizens on a cross. Quicker, more dignified means (like beheading!) were preferred. The Roman orator Cicero (first century BC) labeled crucifixion "the most cruel and disgusting penalty," and further stated that "The very word 'cross' should be far removed not only from the person of a Roman citizen but from his thoughts, his eyes and his ears."[1]

Remarkably, the Son of God came to earth and fixed not only his thoughts, eyes, and ears on the bloody spectacle that the Romans averred, but he *spoke* openly of it as well. The cross rose ever higher on Jesus' horizon as he approached the terminus of his mission. Early in the Gospel of John, he explained his purpose to a religious teacher. He strongly hinted at crucifixion when he said, "Just as Moses lifted up the snake in the wilderness, so the Son of Man must be lifted up, so that everyone who believes in Him will have eternal life" (John 3:14–15). Few standing there would have guessed it at this early juncture, but hindsight would later reveal that the lifting up came via the erection of wooden beams, not ascension to a golden throne. In a similar episode which fell soon after Peter confessed Jesus as Messiah, Jesus explained to the disciples that he "must suffer many things, and be rejected by the elders, the chief priests, and the scribes, be killed, and rise after three days" (Mark 8:31).

Jesus said that in fulfillment of the prophetic Scriptures he must be "counted among the outlaws."

Peter found this so objectionable that he scolded Jesus sharply. A dying Messiah was the last thing he was prepared to accept! Then, perhaps most clearly of all, in Luke 22:37 Jesus said that in fulfillment of the prophetic Scriptures he must be "counted among the outlaws." The disciples (and Jews generally) were not looking for a Messiah who would suffer, let alone die, and least of all die *on a cross*. Thus they could not foresee the cross even when Jesus repeatedly set it before them as the cursing tree which loomed broad and high over the path ahead.

Note

1. For these and other ancient statements on crucifixion, see Martin Hengel's excellent book, *Crucifixion in the Ancient World and the Folly of the Message of the Cross* (Grand Rapids: Fortress Press, 1977).

Chapter 12
Divisions

After he was beaten, mocked, and whipped by the soldiers under Pilate's command, Jesus was fitted with a crossbeam in preparation for his crucifixion. The beam weighed 40 pounds or so; it was placed across his shoulders and neck and then tied at either end to his wrists. This was a routine practice during crucifixion. The victim was made to tote the beam from the site of his sentencing to the site of his execution. The beam would be tiresome cargo for any doomed man as he picked his way through city streets lined with hecklers, past the gates, and on to the fell hillside beyond, but it was especially burdensome for Jesus because he had been severely beaten across his back and shoulders. Somewhere along the way he began to fail under the beam's weight. He had gone without sleep the night before. No food had come to him during his trials. Blood loss, betrayal, and the wooden beam now combined with fatigue, hunger, and an unseen spiritual weight to bend him low to earth.

At the city gates it became clear that Jesus could go no farther, and so the soldiers passed the beam onto the back of a bystander who had just come into town from the countryside. Simon was his name. He was a Jew from the northern coast of Africa. Chances are Simon knew little or nothing about Jesus

Simon and Jesus by Astorga. Simon was a Jew from the northern coast of Africa. The soldiers made him shoulder the crossbeam and follow close behind Jesus.

before this moment. But that mattered little. Recognizing him as an able-bodied man, the soldiers made him shoulder the crossbeam and follow close behind Jesus as the procession continued on toward Golgotha. From this vantage point Simon must have become captivated by the man whose fate was unexpectedly commingled with his own. Judging by the shouting crowds, he would have seen that Jesus was loved and hated and that his life's message was both peaceable and divisive. No doubt Simon also stayed on for the crucifixion event after the beam was lifted from his back. There he listened to the mockery as well as the defenses that were uttered on Jesus' behalf. Signs in the sky and earth soon followed. A few days later Simon would have heard of Christ's resurrection. Perhaps he even saw the risen Lord for himself. In any event faith seems to have dawned in Simon's heart at some point after he hauled Jesus' crossbeam, for his sons (Alexander and Rufus) later became somewhat prominent in the burgeoning Christian movement (Mark 15:21; Rom 16:13).

A number of women also trailed behind Jesus, weeping and lamenting what was happening to their beloved teacher. Despite his obvious troubles, Jesus was more mindful of the judgment that would someday befall the people of Jerusalem. To the mourning women he said, "Do not weep for me, but weep for yourselves and your children" (Luke 23:28). He foretold them that the city that rejected Messiah would suffer a future retribution so severe that her citizens would invite nearby

> *Despite his obvious troubles Jesus was more mindful of the judgment that would someday befall the people of Jerusalem.*

mountains to topple down and cover their heads in shadow and ruin. But that day was yet 40 years future. This day's judgment was against the sins of the world and the Son who would bear them. In keeping with these bitter dealings, someone offered Jesus a drink of soured wine as he reached Golgotha. Jesus took a nip but turned it away once he realized it was wretched. It is not clear whether the drink was offered in mercy or mockery. Possibly it was a makeshift narcotic which could dull the searing waves of pain that washed over him. We know that these sorts of drinks were sometimes offered to crucifixion victims. If this was the nature of the drink, Jesus rejected it out of principle. He had come to suffer and die for the world; any lessening of pain or sorrow would dilute his offering on our behalf. Thus came one of many divisions that played out atop Golgotha this day. Any other man facing crucifixion would down the numbing draught greedily, seeking to kill off all sensation before the piercing nails found flesh and bone. Certainly the men with whom Jesus was executed would have taken advantage of this. Not Jesus. He turned away the cup of comfort and instead put to his lips the broad chalice of divine wrath. Let the pain come full-on.

> *This day's judgment was against the sins of the world and the Son who would bear them.*

Wine Mixed with Myrrh by James Tissot. Crucifixion victims were sometimes offered narcotic-laced drinks to dull their pain.

Dividing Garments

At 9:00 in the morning Jesus was lowered down atop the cross, which initially lay flush against the ground for staging purposes. While soldiers pressed his arms down, his wrists were nailed to each end of the crossbeam that had been fastened onto the vertical post. Next a single spike was driven through his crossed legs at the ankles. Spikes could easily be turned

Crucifixion by Rembrandt.

left or right as they struck bone, and so the hammer blows fell heavy and true to ensure that both legs were secured tightly. After this the whole apparatus—vertical post and crossbeam—was hoisted up into the air with the base being fixed into a hole in the ground. So was hung Jesus of Nazareth, doer of good.

We mentioned earlier that crucifixion was done in a variety of ways. Some crosses were shaped like a capital T. On these the crucified's head crested the crossbeam. Above this there was nothing. Others were shaped like a capital X. These typically sat close to the ground and positioned the victim in such a way as to match the X-shaped cross. Here too nothing could be placed above the victim's head. Neither of these was the sort of cross which was used in Jesus' execution. His was shaped more like a tall lower-case t, such that the vertical pole extended well above the crossbeam. This offered the executioners a place on which to hang a tablet stating the victim's crime. On Pilate's orders the tablet that was placed above Jesus' head said he was charged with being King of the Jews. For Pilate this was a final stab at the Jewish leaders, for such a charge demeaned their nation by reminding them of their subjection to Rome. Claiming to be a Jewish king was

Crucifixion (detail) by Zurabaranz. "Pilate also had a sign lettered and put on the cross. The inscription was 'Jesus the Nazarene, The King of the Jews.' Many of the Jews read this sign, because the place where Jesus was crucified was near the city, and it was written in Hebrew, Latin, and Greek" (John 19:19–20).

literally a crime punishable by death. Initially the chief priests complained to Pilate about the tablet. They wished for it to say something like, "Jesus *claimed* he was King of the Jews." Pilate dismissed their complaint and no doubt reveled in the fact that he had riled his enemies. After a while the chief priests eased up with their objections and actually started a mocking chant in

Claiming to be a Jewish king was literally a crime punishable by death.

which they hailed Jesus as King of the Jews. They took Jesus to be a pretend Messiah; in the final analysis they saw that this was much the same thing as a pretend king.

Crucifixion victims were ordinarily stripped of all their clothes before they were fixed to the cross. Clothes were harder to come by in those days, and there was no sense in ruining whatever garb the victims wore to their final hour. For this reason the soldiers had a custom of bargaining among themselves

to see who would claim the deceased's garments. A good robe or belt might be had, or possibly some sandals that still had a bit of life in them. Jesus was allowed to retain his loincloth since the Jews placed great value on modesty. Everything else he had worn was piled at the foot of the cross. Thus as Jesus hung above them, the soldiers who guarded him picked through his things, unknowingly fulfilling a prophecy found in Psalm 22. This psalm was written by King David. As with all messianic prophecies, the

Erection of the Cross by Doré. As Jesus hung above them, the soldiers who guarded him picked through his things, unknowingly fulfilling a prophecy found in Psalm 22.

human author wrote more than he knew, for the divine hand was upon him to reveal higher knowledge. Added to this is the fact that King David was seen as a prefiguration of the coming Messiah. Or perhaps more accurately the coming Messiah was expected to be the fullness of everything David had been only in pale shadow. Thus throughout Psalm 22 David's recollection of his sufferings count as allusions to the suffering Jesus would undergo on a climactic future day. Some of the allusions are strikingly clear, as for instance in verses 16b–18: "They pierced my hands and my feet. I can count all my bones; people look and stare at me. They divided my garments among themselves, and they cast lots for my clothing." Now the soldiers freely did

> *The coming Messiah was expected to be the fullness of everything David had been only in pale shadow.*

exactly this, playing a game of chance to win from Christ garments of cotton and leather when so much more was on offer had they only looked up in faith (Matt 27:35). Some of them found faith a little while later, but not yet. For now they cast lots and edged in on one another for a look at the outcome. The Son of God looked down upon all their cruel works and spoke to heaven: "Father, forgive them, because they do not know what they are doing" (Luke 23:34).

Dividing Rebels

Few things satisfy the public more than seeing a hardened criminal fall underneath the stone wheels of justice. Think of how media from around the world gathered to televise the hanging of Saddam Hussein on December 30, 2006. For years we all watched as Saddam suppressed and murdered opposition groups in Iraq. When his actions caught up to him, the watching world was satisfied that justice was done. People in ancient times were no different. Troublemakers and murderers drew crowds on their dying day, and for this reason the execution

> *Jesus' cross was propped up beside a roadway atop Golgotha, allowing passersby to goggle at his misery.*

grounds were always situated in such a way as to allow easy public access. Thus Jesus' cross was propped up beside a roadway atop Golgotha, allowing passersby to goggle at his misery. Some wagged their heads in derision; others shouted for Jesus to come down from his cross and save himself. "Let God rescue Him now—if He wants Him!" (Matt 27:43).

Two men took particular interest in such talk. They were hanging next to Jesus on the left and the right. The Bible describes them by using a Greek word that is equivalent to *rebel* or *revolutionary*, with a connotation that the men were violent and perhaps even murderous. In short, these were the sort of men for whom crucifixion was invented. This was *their* hill on which to die and *their* way of dying. How did Jesus come to be mixed up in this? It was all part of the Father's master plan. God the Son, perfect in all his ways, was sentenced to die amid outlaws as a symbol of every sinner's ruin (Isa 53:8–9).

> *God the Son, perfect in all his ways, was sentenced to die amid outlaws as a symbol of every sinner's ruin.*

Once the initial fog of pain and horror lifted a little, clearing their senses, Jesus' rebel companions became aware of the crowds and the things they were shouting at Jesus. Soon they joined their voices to the chorus of hatred. Eventually one of them seized upon the idea that Jesus should deliver all three of them from execution if he was really God's Son. "Aren't You the Messiah? Save Yourself and us!" (Luke 23:39). Not for a second did he believe Jesus was really Messiah. He only wished to vent anger at all goodness as he hung there dying justly for his crimes. The other criminal initially shouted similar insults at Jesus but then ceased because faith dawned in his heart. Watching Jesus endure unjust insults, hearing perhaps some praiseworthy stories recounted from his life, seeing the devotion of the women

Crucifixion by Rubens. The rebels hanging on either side of Jesus were the very sort of men for whom crucifixion was invented.

who had followed Jesus to this awful hillside—these forces and others eventually beat down his unbelief and convinced him that Jesus really was Messiah. And so he rebuked his companion, calling on him to fear God and keep silent. Whether the man heeded this admonition is unknown, but we do know that the repentant rebel turned to Jesus and pleaded not for his bodily life but for his eternal soul. "Jesus, remember me when You come into Your kingdom!" (v. 42). Here the heart of the Savior is most clearly revealed. He, God in flesh and innocent of all wrongdoing, hangs filthy and bleeding next to a

Detail of the *Bockstorfer Altar*. The repentant rebel asked, "Jesus, remember me when You come into Your kingdom!"

The repentant rebel turned to Jesus and pleaded not for his bodily life but for his eternal soul.

man whose life works have justly earned death on a cross. Shall such a man find mercy at death's door? One occasionally hears that deathbed confessions are bogus and that God has no regard for the frightened latecomer who pleads mercy only because he's looking death in the face. Not so according to Jesus. To the sin-wracked man stretched out beside him, Jesus said, "I assure you: Today you will be with Me in paradise" (v. 43).

Dividing Mother and Son

It is hard to comprehend what Jesus' mother must have felt on this day. For more than 30 years now, Mary had rested her hope and her heart on the promises Gabriel made when she was an unwed peasant girl. The conception miracle followed shortly after his visit. God moved and Mary bore new life. To her Jesus had never been anything less than a miracle child, the Promised One from God. Her expectations eclipsed even the highest stars. In that light how could it all end on a cursing tree? Can God curse his own Son? Something had gone terribly wrong, and Mary could not see where it first began. No soul in history has felt as deeply betrayed and confused as Mary did on this day.

No soul in history has felt as deeply betrayed and confused as Mary did on this day.

Mary had come along with several other women to see Jesus' execution. She was drawn to his cross and repulsed by it in equal measures, and thus in the four Gospels we sometimes read that she is close by the cross while at other times it is said that she stood at a distance, unable to bear the grief

of a near pass. The Synoptic Gospels depict her strictly at a distance while John gives a glimpse of one of her close approaches. She was right by the foot of the cross in this scene; John can share the story with us because he was by her side. Recognizing the pair as he looked down, Jesus motioned to John and said to his mother, "Woman, here is your son." He then looked to John and said, "Here is your mother" (John 19:26–27). By uniting John to his mother, Jesus ensured that Mary would be taken care of in her elder years. John was obedient to this calling, for he says he

Crucifixion by Vouet. Nothing Gabriel told Mary all those years ago prepared her to see Jesus crucified.

took her into his household that very hour (v. 27). The cross divided mother from son through death, but Jesus ensured that Mary's ongoing life was guarded and guided by a trustworthy man.

It is sometimes asked why Jesus passed Mary into John's care when Jesus' surviving brothers would have legally (and morally) been in line to receive her. We know that Jesus' brothers did not yet believe he was God's Son, and so most likely

Jesus passed Mary to John because John shared her faith, thin and tremulous though it may have been as they stood before the cross. Had Mary gone on that day and joined the household of one of her unbelieving children, her faith would have been under assault as Jesus' siblings tried to "talk sense into her" about Jesus' true identity. Jesus knew that her soul could not bear

> *Jesus arranged for Mary to shelter under the faith of noble young John.*

such a burden even through the three-day passage from his death to his resurrection, and so he arranged for Mary to shelter under the faith of noble young John during those stormy days. After Jesus was raised and his siblings were converted, no one thought to revoke the stewardship Jesus had assigned to John even though Mary's faith was now shared by all of her children. What was given by the Lord was given for keeps.

Dividing Father and Son

At noon, three hours into Jesus' ordeal on the cross, the sky fell black and remained thus until three o'clock that afternoon. This was not merely a local weather phenomenon. A broad bank of storm clouds blowing in from the sea might darken Golgotha and the surrounding hills for a while, but historical reports depict this event as widespread and enduring. More than a hundred years later in AD 137, a Greek historian known as Phlegon of Tralles wrote that one day in AD 33, the year of Christ's crucifixion, the noontime sky went so dark that stars could be seen. This means the skies remained clear and unobstructed during the darkness. No storm could produce such an effect. Phlegon instinctively

Darkness at the Crucifixion by Doré. Records outside the Bible report that the noontime sky went so dark that stars became visible.

Christ on the Cross by Lievens.

called the event the "greatest eclipse" known to history, but it could not have been a natural eclipse since Jesus was executed during Passover week, a time when the moon waxes full and thus cannot obstruct the sun. Tertullian, a Christian writing at about the same time as Phlegon, similarly reported that at the time of Christ's crucifixion the light went out over Rome, Athens, and other Mediterranean cities far removed from Jerusalem. Possibly the darkness covered the whole half of the globe that would normally be lighted at that hour. No natural phenomenon can account for such an event; it can only have been a miraculous act of God, a sign of judgment against sin.

It is safe to assume that the darkness was greeted by fear and awe over all the waking world, especially among those gathered for the events at Golgotha, but the Gospel authors skip over the obvious and fix instead on a series of events that were loaded with mystery and meaning. At three o'clock Jesus cried out with a loud voice saying, "My God, My God, why have You forsaken Me?" (Matt 27:46). For anyone who has read the Gospel accounts closely up to this point, this is a shocking and deeply disturbing statement. Is Jesus not one with the Father? Do they not share for all eternity the same indivisible, unchangeable divine essence? It

Elizabeth Barrett Browning wrote, "Adam's sins swept between the righteous Son and Father."

seems impossible that the Son could be forsaken by the Father. What has happened here? Pondering this question, Elizabeth Barrett Browning wrote a poem in which she reflected on the life and salvation of William Cowper, the great hymnist. Of Christ's cry of dereliction to the Father, Browning suggests that the Son was abandoned because "Adam's sins swept between the righteous Son and Father." This is as good an explanation as any. We will explore this theme further in the next chapter. For now we note what extraordinary things were set in motion by Jesus' forlorn cry.

When the people standing nearby heard Jesus, they mistakenly thought he was calling for the prophet Elijah, for in the original language Jesus' words were, "*Eli, Eli, lemá sabachtháni.*" Mistaking "Eli" for "Elijah," Jesus' detractors took this as final proof that the famed Nazarene was nothing more than a charlatan who cried out for a *true* prophet to save him once his own ploys had failed. Elijah seemed a fitting prophet to call upon because the Jews had long expected that he would return to earth someday and lead heaven's deliverance of the righteous. These sorts of expectations built up around Elijah because he was long ago taken up from earth in a fiery angelic chariot before the watching eyes of Elisha, his successor in the prophetic ministry (2 Kgs 2:11–12). He was never seen among men again. From that day on the nation venerated Elijah as a man especially beloved of God, and they looked for him to return in a time of final crisis. As Jesus hung on the cusp of death, the crowd assumed he was calling for Elijah's work of deliverance. "Let's see if Elijah comes to save Him!" they shouted (Matt 27:49). But Elijah never came. It was not his

Elijah and the Chariot of Fire by Cifrondi. Elijha seemed a fitting prophet to call upon because the Jews had long expected that he would return to earth someday and lead heaven's deliverance of the righteous.

purpose to do so, and Jesus never asked otherwise. What Jesus voiced was not a beckoning for Elijah but a confession to God of deep suffering, and he chose these words purposefully as yet another fulfillment of Psalm 22. In the opening verse of that psalm, King David reflected on a time when he was oppressed and hounded nearly to death. "My God, my God, why have You forsaken me? Why are You so far from my deliverance and from my words of groaning?" (v. 1). Here, as in many other

The sufferings of David etched patterns and themes that Jesus filled to completeness as the perfect mediator between God and humankind.

places, David's experiences presaged those of Messiah himself. The sufferings of David, though minor compared to the blows that fell on Christ, etched patterns and themes that Jesus filled to completeness as the perfect mediator between God and humankind. And so the Son cried out as a man most forsaken by God.

Shortly after his cry of dereliction, Jesus said he was thirsty. One of the soldiers standing nearby went and soaked a sponge with the same sort of sour mash that had been offered hours earlier. Soldiers and laborers drank wine vinegar because it was cheap and gave a spike to trodden spirits. Truth be known the drink was probably foul enough to wake the dead! The laden sponge was fixed onto the end of a long reed and offered up to Jesus so that he might suck on it and wet his throat. It is doubtful that he bothered much with it. It is the offering itself that was important, for this too was a fulfillment of King David's sufferings. Psalm 69:21 records that in his hour of desperation David's enemies gave him vinegar rather than wine to drink. Having retraced this last Davidic step, Jesus prepared for his end. Combining the records of John and Luke,

Crucifixion by Ferrari. The offering of wine vinegar was a fulfillment of King David's sufferings (see Ps 69:21).

we learn that Jesus said, "It is finished! Father, into Your hands I entrust My spirit" (John 19:30; Luke 23:46). Having said these things, Jesus bowed his bloodied head and gave up his spirit. The greatest human life ever lived had come to an end.

Dividing Stone and Veil

The death of God the Son could not go unnoticed in the world he himself made. Jesus once said that if people did not shout praises to him the rocks of earth would be made to cry out in their stead. Seemingly in answer to this, stone and earth shook at the news of Jesus' passing while the world only reckoned it had killed a criminal. Rocks sheered and split; the shelters of men trembled; the earth was disturbed at its foundations (Matt 27:51). As with the darkness that unnaturally enveloped the land, Jesus' enemies would interpret the quake as another sign that God was passing judgment on a heretic, a messianic pretender

Jesus' enemies would interpret the quake as another sign that God was passing judgment on a heretic, a messianic pretender who threatened true religion.

who threatened true religion. Jesus' friends and family may have entertained the same disturbing thoughts. What could the signs mean but that heaven's doom had fallen over Jesus? The answer would become known in the following days, but for now the world itself tilted toward destruction as God poured out his judgments.

A model of the Jerusalem temple. The curtain that separated the most holy place from the outer holy place in the Jerusalem temple was supernaturally torn down its length. Photo: Deror Avi.

As earth rumbled and shook in shadow, the curtain that separated the most holy place from the outer holy place in the Jerusalem temple was supernaturally torn down its length, beginning high at its top and running to the floor. The quake could not have caused this unless the temple's foundation was split and pulled apart, an action that would have made the whole complex thunder down in pieces. One can imagine how frightened the attending priest became as the fabric divided right before his eyes. That we know anything at all about this event indicates that he described his experience to others. The story justifiably became a key evidence for interpreting the death of Christ and its significance in redemption. For instance, the author of Hebrews says the torn curtain showed that Christ won for us unobstructed access to God's presence (see, for instance, Heb 10:19–20).

> *The torn curtain showed that Christ won for us unobstructed access to God's presence.*

At the same time the curtain was tearing top to bottom, select tombs around Jerusalem shook loose their stone doors and opened wide as their saintly dead awakened to new life (Matt 27:52). Three days later, once Jesus himself was raised from death, these revived persons crept out from their cracked catacombs and strolled into town. To modern readers this reads like the largest "spookfest" in history, but to Christian eyes it was a holy sampling of the future resurrection in which all the earth's dead will be raised, some to face punishment and others to enter God's presence forever. We do not know specific identities or what became of these people in the days and weeks that followed. Most likely they were just ordinary believers. After all, a resurrected prophet or king of old would have created a stir, and no such stir is reported in the Bible or elsewhere. Assuming they were regular folks, did they hunt down their relatives and hold reunion? Did any living person even recognize them? How long had they been dead? Was the Roman occupation news to them? Did they die again or simply ascend to heaven? On the lighter side, did they have to pay back taxes? Did their relatives hand over the properties they had inherited? We can think of a

Apparition of the Dead in Jerusalem by Tissot. To modern readers this reads like the largest "spookfest" in history, but to Christian eyes it was a holy sampling of the future resurrection.

thousand questions ranging from serious to seriously humorous, but neither history nor Scripture answers us. With the early Christians we should count this event as a "strange but true" preview of the coming day when all the dead will rise. Messiah's death cracked open tombs; his resurrection emptied them; his future return will raise us all.

Crucifixion by Grunewald. Seeing the manner of Jesus' death, the centurion called out, "This man really was God's Son!"

The crowd gathered at the cross could not have known that the temple's curtain tore when Jesus cried out or that sealed tombs opened all around them when he gave up his spirit. What they did know was that darkness continued to hold fast above their heads and that the earth revolted underneath their feet when Messiah passed on to the other side. These things struck fear in their hearts, but the centurion's reaction proves that the most impressive event of all was the manner of Jesus' death (Mark 15:39). A close look at Jesus' final utterances reveals that he was *in command* of his own death. He died at exactly the moment he willed to die. This was no suicide. A leap off a bluff is fundamentally different from the command Jesus wielded

A close look at Jesus' final utterances reveals that he was in command of his own death. He died at exactly the moment he willed to die.

over death. By His spoken words ("It is finished! Father, into Your hands I entrust My spirit") Jesus ceased basic life processes. His heart ceased pumping. His lungs inhaled no more. Consciousness blinked out, and spirit escaped the tethers of bodily life. Taking note of this as well as the eerie timing of the earthquake, the impressed centurion cried out, "This man really was God's Son!" (Mark 15:39).

Dividing Water from Blood

Many in the crowd agreed with the soldier's abrupt confession of faith. They spilled down off the troubled hillside and went home striking their chests in expression of grief and shame (Luke 23:48). They had witnessed the death of God's Son! Some of them had even shouted approval of his execution. Now they slinked away fearing heaven itself. Several of the paths leading from Golgotha would have passed the nearby tombs. Might the dispersing crowds have spied the cloven entrances as daylight returned to earth? Were the witnesses of Christ's death also witnesses of its immediate result: the resurrection preview? It is a tantalizing possibility to consider. If so, no other group of people in history has gained rights to see the whole sum of God's redemptive plan condensed into such a swift series of events. The death of the Son and the death of death itself played out before their eyes in the span of a few moments.

Back atop the hill strengthening sunlight fell on Jesus' limp form, revealing ragged wounds the preternatural darkness had obscured. Perhaps this surging visibility is why Mary and the other women retreated some distance away, watching to see what would become of their Beloved's spent body. John was still with them as well. Perhaps he instinctively led them away from the unveiling of carnage. As they kept their vigil, the Jewish leaders back in town were closing in on finality with Pilate. Against Roman custom they wanted the bodies hauled down from the crosses as soon as possible because the Sabbath was quickly approaching. If the bodies hung there for three hours longer, it would be a violation of the Sabbath's sanctity. A riot might result if the mass of Jews gathered for Passover saw corpses breaking the horizon on Golgotha during Sabbath. Realizing

Against Roman custom the Jews wanted the bodies hauled down from the crosses as soon as possible because the Sabbath was quickly approaching.

this, Pilate granted the request. He dispatched soldiers to finish off the victims and pull them down from the crosses. The standard procedure for hastening death was to smash the leg bones of the condemned so that they could no longer breathe. The legs were vital in the breathing process because the victim needed to push himself upwards in order to open up his collapsing diaphragm and lungs. For this reason broken legs led to eventual suffocation as arm muscles fatigued, cramped, and failed in the task of heaving the torso upward.

When the soldiers sent by Pilate arrived, they took up an iron mallet and smashed the shin bones of the rebels who hung on either side of Jesus. We can imagine their cries as fresh pain surged through their bodies. Death was galloping forward now. In the distance Mary and her companions must have shuddered and covered their tearchapped faces. Jesus is next. Will the horror never end? None could watch as the soldiers moved to hobble Jesus in the same way. Had the soldiers asked the centurion and his fellows who had attended the entire crucifixion event, they would have known

Crucifixion of Christ by Oberrheinischer. Unconvinced that Jesus was really dead, a soldier stabbed him with a spear.

that it was unnecessary. They knew the Nazarene was already dead. Perhaps the centurion even moved to stop the soldiers. But what is a centurion's word against Pilate's command? A soldier raised the mallet to land his blows, but he hesitated. He perceived the truth: Jesus really was dead already. One of his companions remained skeptical, however, and so he raised his spear and drove it upward through Jesus' side, piercing the lining around his heart and lungs. Hemorrhagic fluid, which is dominated by water, naturally divides from blood in certain kinds of chest wounds. The soldier's spear pierced the cavities where blood and hemorrhagic fluid had pooled, and thus water and blood issued

Many Bible interpreters have searched for deeper meaning in the division of water and blood. Probably there is none to be found.

from the wound when the spear was withdrawn. Many Bible interpreters have searched for deeper meaning in the division of water and blood. Probably there is none to be found. The simplest meaning and likely the *only* meaning is this: there could be no doubt that Jesus of Nazareth had really, truly died on the cross of Calvary.

Breaking the Thieves' Legs by Tissot. In a practice known as crurifragium, soldiers broke the legs of crucifixion victims in order to hasten death.

John looked on as these things happened. Years later he wrote of them in his Gospel and took special care to note that the piercing spear and disused mallet had not been chance elements of the crucifixion. Rather, they were fulfillments of the divine plan. Like the Passover lamb, Messiah (who was the ultimate Passover Lamb) was not to have any of his bones broken (John 19:36; Exod 12:46). Further, through the prophet Zechariah God the Father had said: "Then I will pour out a spirit of grace and prayer on the house of David and the residents of Jerusalem, and they will look at Me whom they pierced. They will mourn for Him as one mourns for an only child and weep bitterly for Him as one weeps for a firstborn" (Zech 12:10). According to God's design these stipulations were fulfilled by the hands of men who knew nothing of their part in the great plan.

Dividing Secret from Public

As evening approached, a secret follower of Jesus made a decision that would thrust him into the middle of the most controversial burial in history. Joseph of Arimathea was actually a prominent member of the Sanhedrin, the body of religious leaders that had condemned Jesus to death. Luke tells us that Joseph had "not agreed with their plan and action,"

but out of fear he had kept his commitments to Jesus a secret (Luke 23:51; John 19:38). If this tragic day had revealed anything, it was that the time for secrets had passed. Jesus was now dead. In some sense it had ended this way because his many followers had not risen to the occasion and made their will known to the Jewish elite and their Roman overlords. They kept quiet when boisterous protest might

Joseph of Arimathea by Perugino. Joseph of Arimathea was a prominent member of the Sanhedrin, the body of religious leaders that condemned Jesus to death.

have turned the tide back out to sea. Joseph may have felt especially responsible as a member of the committee that finalized Jesus' fate. Now he realized that he had kept his secret too long. Emboldened and resolved, he stepped into the light as darkness fell.

If this tragic day had revealed anything, it was that the time for secrets had passed.

Joseph approached Pilate and asked that Jesus' body be released to him for burial. He was able to access Pilate in this way because he was a wealthy man and a respected member of the most powerful Jewish lobby. Ironically, Pilate and Joseph shared much common ground in regards to Jesus. Both believed him to be innocent of wrongdoing; both knew that out of jealousy the religious leaders had trumped up charges that led to Jesus' execution. Now they met and discussed what should be done with the body of the man neither of them had wanted to see killed. Discussing the gruesome business, Pilate expressed to Joseph his surprise that Jesus had died so quickly. Holding onto a last sliver of skepticism, he checked with the centurion to be absolutely sure that Jesus was already dead. It seemed too quick. Pilate had ordered that Jesus' legs be smashed shortly after three that afternoon. To this point he had no reason to think

The last thing Pilate wanted was to prolong the controversy by accidentally handing over a still-living Jesus to one of his disciples

this order had not been carried out. So, assuming the legs were broken just after three, Pilate calculated from experience that Jesus should have lived on for a while longer as he labored for every scrap of breath. The last thing Pilate wanted was to prolong the controversy by accidentally handing over a still-living Jesus to one of his disciples. The Jews would see him ousted from office immediately for such a blunder! And so Pilate looked to his trusted centurion for a sure answer. When the centurion confirmed the reality of Jesus' premature death,

Descent from the Cross by Rembrandt.

Pilate let slip his final reservations and authorized Joseph to take possession of the corpse. It was over at last. And we imagine Pilate heading off to console his dream-troubled wife.

As for Joseph, he left Pilate and bought some linen from a nearby vendor before hurrying back to Golgotha where the women were still waiting to see what would be done to Jesus' body. Out of respect for Jewish morals, the Romans would neither let the bodies hang and rot nor dump them right there on the killing grounds for vultures and dogs to consume, as was practiced elsewhere in the empire. Here, in the shadow of David's city, even the lowliest of crucified criminals was dignified with an interment, though in a common and unmarked grave that lay in the wastes. The women held out hope that Jesus would escape this fate. Joseph came to ensure that their hopes were fulfilled. Somewhere along the way a man named Nicodemus joined Joseph in the grim task. Like Joseph, Nicodemus was a prominent Jewish leader and probably a man

A first-century tomb, sometimes called the Tomb of Joseph of Arimathea, in the Church of the Holy Sepulcher. Joseph would have placed Jesus in a tomb like this. Photo: HolyLandPhotos.org.

of wealth. He was also a stealth disciple, apparently sharing Joseph's fear of repercussion for openly following Jesus. He had first come to Jesus under cover of darkness a few years earlier and plied him with questions about the need for spiritual rebirth. Jesus had emphasized this in his preaching, and Nicodemus was not too shy to admit that he could not understand Jesus' meaning (we will examine Jesus' meaning closely in chapter 16). Now that the Teacher was dead, the secretive pupil broke from

Now that the Teacher was dead, the secretive pupil broke from his fears and aided Joseph in easing Jesus' body down from the cross.

his fears and aided Joseph in easing Jesus' body down from the cross. Together they wrapped him in fine linen cloth and enfolded about 75 pounds of myrrh and aloes. Nicodemus brought these to keep true to Jewish burial customs. Additionally, Joseph decided to give Jesus a noble burial by placing him in a new tomb he owned, thus ensuring that no common grave would open to receive Messiah into anonymity.

The tomb was located close by in a garden which adjoined Golgotha (John 19:41). Joseph had recently cut and fitted this for his own future use. Probably it was part of the ancient stone quarry that wound its way under the earth outside Jerusalem. The women followed at a distance as Joseph and Nicodemus transferred Jesus' body to the tomb. Most likely one or both of these men had servants with them to aid in the transfer, for altogether the body, the cloth, and the aloes must have weighed close to 300 pounds. When they reached the tomb, they laid Jesus on a shelf which had been hewn out from the stone walls. Having placed him there, they then rolled a great disklike stone into place over the entrance, ensuring that the tomb would remain sealed unless a handful of able men rolled the sealing stone back up its track. The women watched this as they sat directly across from the tomb. They were shaping up a plan to take a Sabbath rest (on Saturday, the Jewish day of Sabbath) and then come back to this spot in approximately 36 hours (on Sunday morning) so they could render additional funerary services to their deceased Lord. Spices and perfumes they planned to bring; and they would pray that stout men would be present upon their return so the guardian stone could be rolled away.

The Tomb of Jesus in the Church of the Holy Sepulcher, the traditional tomb site for Jesus.

As will become more obvious later, it is important to note that Jesus' burial site was a matter of public knowledge. Two men who had previously kept quiet about their belief in Jesus stepped boldly into his plotline and ensured

Jesus' burial site was a matter of public knowledge.

that his corpse would not fall anonymously into the earth alongside unnamed rebels. It was instead placed inside a new tomb which lay near the site of Jesus' execution. It is impossible to think that

Entrance to a first-century tomb with a rolling stone.
Photo: HolyLandPhotos.org.

Joseph would forget the location of his own tomb, nor is it feasible to suppose that Nicodemus would assist in the burial and then lose all track of where Jesus' body lay. Further, the women from Galilee marked the tomb's location and planned a return trip for Sunday morning. Finally, as we will see below, a host of guards came to surround the tomb and keep out any would-be thieves. Jesus' death had been public; his place of burial was no less so.

Dividing Plot from Plotters

Matthew tells us in his Gospel that the chief priests and Pharisees gathered before Pilate the next day in hopes of heading off a plot they suspected Jesus' disciples were set to pull off (Matt 27:62). By "the next day" Matthew means the Sabbath, which began at 6 PM by Jewish reckoning. Hence, this meeting took place just three short hours after Jesus died. Most likely these men arrived to speak with Pilate shortly after Joseph of Arimathea, whom they now recognized as a turncoat, left with permission to bury Jesus' body. Following hot on the traitor's heels, these men pleaded with Pilate that they would be granted the use of Roman soldiers to guard the tomb. Joseph, they suspected, might be at the center of a plot to steal Jesus' body. Why did the Jews fear such a plot? They explained to

Joseph, the Jews suspected, might be at the center of a plot to steal Jesus' body.

Pilate that since Jesus had openly predicted that he would rise from the dead the stage was set for a master deception if the disciples could manage to steal and hide the body. A fabricated resurrection! If that were to happen, "Then the last deception will be worse than the first," they told Pilate (v. 64).

As recorded by Matthew, Pilate's response is worded in such a way as to leave interpreters divided about exactly what followed. Did Pilate grant the Jews the use of Roman soldiers, as he had done when Jesus was routed out of the garden the previous night? Or did he instead send the Jews packing, with the result that the tomb was manned by Jewish temple police rather than a phalanx of Rome's finest? Here is what Matthew writes: "'You have a guard of soldiers,' Pilate told them. 'Go and make it as secure as you know how.' Then they went and made the tomb secure by sealing the stone and setting the guard" (Matt 27:65–66). The most important thing to note is that the Jews, with or without the aid of foreign soldiers, sealed the tomb and set a guard outside it so no one could tamper with the site, much less haul away Jesus' body. Barring an unmistakable miracle, the dead Jesus would remain locked away behind silent stone for the rest of history.

> *Barring an unmistakable miracle, the dead Jesus would remain locked away behind silent stone for the rest of history.*

Chapter 13
Substitution

What exactly happened as Christ suffered and died on the cross? We know about the piercing nails, the waves of pain, the driving thirst, and the public scorn. Anyone who reads the Gospels and the scattered historical records of crucifixion can guess what kind of physical and emotional suffering these caused, but was there something more to the crucifixion of Jesus? Something intangible yet substantial? Something spiritual and eternal that has direct bearing on you and me? For two thousand years now Christians have answered yes. In fact, they have said it was the most important transaction in history. We shall devote this entire chapter to exploring the invisible, sacred actions that transpired when Messiah died on the cross.

What exactly happened as Christ suffered and died on the cross?

Place and Replacement

The first humans enjoyed a place of unparalleled privilege in the universe. They were made for relationship with God, and since nothing about them displeased him, they walked and talked with him as one does with a close friend. With

Adam and Eve were made for relationship with God, and since nothing about them displeased him, they walked and talked with him as one does with a close friend.

minds and hearts unclouded by sin, they could apprehend God's love for them and all the knowledge he wished to reveal about himself and his world. Alas, all of this changed when Adam and Eve misused the power of choice by seeking what they thought was a better life apart from God's revealed will. Since that time all humans have languished under a spiritual curse, banished from the place of unbroken privilege and access to God. Comparatively ours is now a journey through spiritual wasteland. We are lost in the dark and troubled by unseen assailants who are more real than we know. The Bible says we are all spiritually dead in our sins and transgressions (Eph 2:1). This is the human condition. Barring a far-reaching change of status, we are each doomed to God's final wrath.

Is it really as bad as this? One often hears the suggestion that God is not so angry at sin and sinners after all. He is love, we are told, and a God of love will choose free pardon over punishment. To this we must answer that though God is indeed love (1 John 4:8) he is equally a God of holiness and justice. Love that is not guided by holiness and justice becomes permissive and indulgent of evil. Think of the lenient parent whose unchecked children set up reigns of terror wherever they go. Civility, restraint, and moral aptitude are lost on such kids. Do

Although God is indeed love, he is equally a God of holiness and justice.

we call their parents *loving*? Are they flesh-and-blood models of the divine nature, presages of the final judgment in which God counts all behaviors equal? Of course not. Far from spying God's nature in such parents, we catch a glimpse of ruin. Their "love" is seen for what it really is: moral laxity. They wink at evil rather than doing the work to correct it. God cannot do this sort of thing because evil is a strike against his own nature. The moral laws that we have broken are not merely items on a list of do's and don'ts; rather, moral law is a close reflection of God's own eternal nature. God is holiness itself, and anything *unholy* is *anti*-God. To break a moral law is to assault God's being. The moral fabric of the entire universe would be torn to pieces if God were to let such rebellion go unpunished.

God is holiness itself, and anything unholy is anti-God.

For this reason humans need atonement. To *atone* means "to make right on a broken relationship or to repair a wrong." The terms or stipulations for atonement must be defined by God, not humans, for it is God who is offended. Just as no criminal is permitted to approach his victim and lay down the conditions for reparation, no human can set the agenda for appeasing the God whom he or she has angered. Early in history God revealed through panged human conscience that sacrifices should be made to him

Love without justice and holiness is mere indulgence. It leads only to ruin. True love holds high moral standards and corrects wrongdoing.

as expressions of sorrow for sin and gratitude for daily provisions. Thus it was a universal practice among the ancients to offer animals and vegetation as they blindly groped for the fringes of the Maker's robe. Not surprisingly they suffered under many misconceptions about God (or the gods, as they usually imagined) and struck out in many contradictory directions in hopes of landing on the right approach. The Hebrews, however, enjoyed unique knowledge of God. This knowledge came

To atone means to make right on a broken relationship or to repair a wrong.

An altar used for animal sacrifice in Megiddo.
Photo: HolyLandPhotos.org.

to them not because they were innately wise or morally superior to other nations but simply because God chose to pierce their darkness. Hence, they presented sacrifices with the assurance that they were in relationship with the one true God and that their sacrifices were offered in a way that was pleasing to him.

The lifeblood of sinless bulls and goats was spilled over Hebrew altars in expression of sinful humanity's need for pardon from God. But the question must be asked: Can the blood of sacrificial *animals* secure full and final atonement for *human* sins? Can a slain bull or goat serve as an adequate replacement for the errant humans to whom the wrath is due? The answer is no. In the New Testament we learn that animal sacrifices were not adequate for this task (see Heb 10:4). They were part of a provisional system that held back the tide until the fullness of time when God would send the once-for-all replacement sacrifice.

To serve as an adequate substitute in God's reparation program, the sacrificial victim needed to be sinless, truly representative of humanity, and able to bear on his lone moral frame the debt owed by millions upon millions of sinners. Obviously this means we are describing the need for a human sacrifice. More

To serve as an adequate substitute in God's reparation program, the sacrificial victim needed to be sinless, truly representative of humanity, and able to bear on his lone moral frame the debt owed by millions upon millions of sinners.

to the point: a *superhuman* sacrifice. This is one of the most breathtaking realities of the Bible. The holy God who made humans in his own image would someday require that one of his image bearers, a morally perfect human, stand in the place of his fellows and give satisfaction for the boundless sin debt. What man could be adequate for such a task? Only one: Jesus the divine Messiah, sent from heaven to be a human and a stand-in for Adam's children. In the remainder of this chapter, we will examine the ways in which Jesus satisfied God as our substitute.

Substitute in Life

Humans are acceptable to holy God for eternal fellowship only when they are spiritually unstained. We have not owned such native purity since our original innocence was wrecked in the fall. If we are to be made acceptable to God, it is required that a substitute stand in for humanity at the judgment seat and give account for a life that has been genuinely human and genuinely sinless. Let us take a moment to describe these requirements more fully.

If we are to be made acceptable to God, it is required that a substitute stand in for humanity at the judgment seat and give account for a life that has been genuinely human and genuinely sinless.

In order for Jesus to substitute capably for fallen humanity before the throne of God, he needed to be human in every way that is essential to the human condition. No hybrid human would do, for humans are not hybrid. Either a genuine and wholly righteous human stands in our place to be judged by God, or else we are left to stand there ourselves, filthy and doomed. But if all humans are sinful, in what sense can sinless Jesus truly represent us in God's judgment? The answer is simple: sinfulness is not essential to the human condition. We were originally good. Our fallen state is a tragic add-on that Jesus was not required to

If not for Jesus we would await judgment with dread and hopelessness.

adopt when he became incarnate. Hence Jesus can truly represent humans even though he was miraculously conceived and therefore does not share in our corrupted spiritual condition. In fact, Jesus *must not* share in this condition if he is to be a worthy substitute. Further, such things as finitude of knowledge are true but inessential conditions of the human nature, and so Jesus can bear divine qualities such as omniscience (to know all things)

Not even the smoke of sin can cling to the one who aims to stand unblemished before God.

and still be genuinely human. Finally, Jesus needed to live a full-orbed human life in order to count as the one who "passed through the fire" and came out on the other side unscathed and unscented. Not even the smoke of sin can cling to the one who aims to stand unblemished before God.

Christ in the Desert by Kramskoi. Jesus languished under heat and famine in the wilderness and faced the devil's onslaught, yet resisted all temptations.

Did Jesus meet all these conditions? The New Testament is clear that he did. In Hebrews 2:14–17 we are told that Jesus "shared" in our human conditions and was made "like His brothers in every way so that He could become a merciful and faithful high priest in service to God, to make propitiation for the sins of the people."

We humans are tempted, tested, and made to suffer in diverse ways. So was Jesus, and yet he was ever without sin (Heb 4:15). He languished under heat and famine in the wilderness and faced the devil's onslaught yet resisted all temptations (Matt 4:1–11). He suffered the loss of his earthly adoptive father, Joseph, and he wept openly when his friend Lazarus died (John 11:35). He stood before an assemblage of religious men and asked, "Who among you can convict Me of sin?" (John 8:46). When all was said and done, Jesus had walked through the fire of our world and come out pristine and pure. For this reason "He is able to help those who are tested" (Heb 2:18).

Additionally, even though Jesus was sinless, he needed to identify fully with God's righteous reign among humans. For this reason he chose to do such things as exercise the various purification rites given to the Jews by God. Had he rebuffed these things, it would have seemed to the people that he was a godless brigand who despised God's holiness. Jesus was far from being this sort of person, and so he intentionally walked in the path of righteousness as a demonstration of his allegiance to God. Probably the best example of this is his baptism by John the Baptist, as relayed in Matthew 3:13–15.

> Then Jesus came from Galilee to John at the Jordan, to be baptized by him. But John tried to stop Him, saying, "I need to be baptized by You, and yet You come to me?" Jesus answered him, "Allow it for now, because this is the way for us to fulfill all righteousness."

By this Jesus made it clear that he did not seek baptism because he needed to repent of any sin. Instead, he came to be passed beneath the waters because he intended to live a human life that was fully submitted to God the Father. This he achieved, and

Jesus came to Golgotha prepared to accomplish in death the same thing he accomplished in life: the offering of himself as the lone adequate substitute for sinful humanity.

for this reason he came to Golgotha prepared to accomplish in death the same thing he accomplished in life: the offering of himself as the lone adequate substitute for sinful humanity.

Substitute in Death

Having lived a sinless life and having fulfilled all righteousness, Jesus came to the cross prepared to offer himself as our substitute. But what exactly did that entail? A good place for starting our answer is to review the events detailed in Leviticus 16. On the annual Day of Atonement, the Hebrews gathered en masse before the priests and by faith participated in the reparation ceremony that was enacted before them. In this ceremony a bull and a goat were slain because God had chosen to symbolically substitute these animals for sinful humans. The blood was used to cleanse the officiating priests and the altar. Then, in the climactic event of the day, the high priest (Aaron) brought forth another goat and in God's presence placed his hands on its

Substitution involves two key responsibilities: bearing the sin of sinners and receiving God's just wrath on their behalf.

head and confessed over it "all the Israelites' wrongdoings and rebellious acts—all their sins" (Lev 16:21). The goat was then led away on a one-way trip into the outlying desolation. In this way the Israelites who looked on with faith in God's provision saw that God's wrath had fallen on doomed substitutes and that their sins had been borne far away by a goat. From these actions we see that substitution involves two key responsibilities: bearing the sin of sinners and receiving God's just wrath on their behalf.

This is exactly the role Jesus played on our behalf when he was jeered by an assembly of enemies and then pinned to the cross of Calvary. Peter says of him, "He Himself bore our sins in His body on the tree" (1 Pet 2:24). Imagine God the Father placing his hand on the head of his innocent

By the Father's decree our sin and shame were invisibly transferred to Jesus on the cross.

and beloved Son, with whom he had enjoyed unbroken eternal fellowship, and passing our sins onto him just as Aaron had done with the scapegoat long ago. By the Father's decree our sin and shame were invisibly transferred to Jesus on the cross. Paul speaks of this transaction in the following way: "He [God the Father] made the One who did not know sin [Jesus] to be sin for us, so that we might become the righteousness of God in Him" (2 Cor 5:21). Elsewhere Paul clearly spells out that this involved Jesus "becoming a curse for us" (Gal 3:13).

The cross is a sign of hope because it was first a sign of condemnation.

What was this experience like for Jesus? When you and I sin, we almost invariably feel the pangs of a guilty conscience. We duck our heads, mute our voices, and remain subdued and moody until we make good on our sin or else manage to bury it under excuses. If we sinners can feel so badly about our sins, imagine what it must have been like for Jesus when he became sin on our behalf! Not only had he never sinned in his human lifetime; as the eternal and divine Son of God, he was by nature the *antithesis* of sin and evil. The mental and spiritual anguish he experienced when our sins were heaped upon him are beyond our guessing.

Having become a curse for us, Jesus received God's wrath under a sky that was untimely black. The prophet Isaiah foretold this venting of wrath hundreds of years earlier as he wrote under the Holy Spirit's direction: "We all went astray like sheep; we all have turned to our own way; and the LORD has punished Him for the iniquity of us all" (Isa 53:6). Theologian Wayne Grudem describes it this way: "Jesus became the object of the intense hatred of sin . . .

It was then, in full comprehension of sins past, present, and future, that God the Father released his pent-up anger on the Son who had become sin.

. which God had patiently stored up since the beginning of the world."[1] Every abusive word, every base indulgence, every haughty look, every crime and murder and hurtful thought that ever dawned over the sullen world of men since the time of Adam's fall and on unto the final future day came crashing down on Jesus. It was then, in full comprehension of sins past, present, and future, that God the Father released his pent-up anger on the Son who had become sin, and he did not relent until his holy justice was satisfied.

As the bowl of wrath spilled out over Messiah, he fought not just revulsion and shame but utter despair. In a way we cannot understand, he was separated from the Father as sin troubled their fellowship. At the climax of his sufferings he let loose the famous cry of dereliction: "My God, My God, why have You forsaken Me?" (Matt 27:46). Jesus knew from

We must not mute or dilute the desolation Jesus felt as he was crushed by the Father whom he eternally loved, nor must we ever forget it was on our account that he suffered these things.

the beginning of his mission that he was to die for sins and that after this he would be with the Father forever, resurrected in victory over death. For these reasons it would be wrong to assume that his cry of despair indicates that he had lost sight of his hope in the Father. Nevertheless we must not mute or dilute the desolation Jesus felt as he was crushed by the Father whom he eternally loved, nor must we ever forget it was on our account that he suffered these things.

CLOSER LOOK

Did Jesus Descend into Hell after He Died?

Many Christians have believed that Jesus descended into hell between the time of his death and resurrection. Often it is said that he had to go there to pay a debt to Satan, as if it were Satan rather than God who demanded punishment for sins. More often it is said that Jesus went to hell not to pay the devil's ransom but to preach repentance and salvation to the generations of humanity that died before he was born. Are these beliefs biblical? If not, how did they arise?

To begin with we should note that the Bible never says Jesus went to hell, that he paid a debt to Satan, or that he offered the dead a chance to repent and be saved. The closest the Bible comes to laying such claims is found in 1 Peter 3:19–20. Speaking of Christ's death, Peter says, "In that state He also went and made a proclamation to the spirits in prison who in the past were disobedient, when God patiently waited in the days of Noah while an ark was being prepared." This passage is the ultimate origin of the mistaken views listed above, but none of these teachings are reasonable interpretations of what Peter said. Hell goes unmentioned; nothing is said of Satan or a debt he supposedly extracted from Jesus; and there is no evidence that the "proclamation" Jesus made had anything to do with repentance or post-mortem salvation. There is also the persistent witness of Luke 23:43, where Jesus tells the repentant rebel dying next to him, "I assure you: Today you will be with Me in paradise." If Jesus was in paradise immediately after his death, set to receive the rebel that very day, it is obvious that he did not first descend into hell to preach or pay a debt.

Given that the biblical evidence is squarely against Jesus' descent into hell, how did the belief come to be popular among Christians? The answer is found in the famed Apostle's Creed, an early confession of basic Christian beliefs that were handed down by the Lord's apostles. A key phrase in the Creed says Jesus "was crucified, dead, and buried, he descended into hell; the third day he rose again from the dead." All except the middle phrase is based on solid biblical evidence. Where then did the apostles get the idea that Jesus descended into hell? Answer: they didn't. The phrase that says Jesus descended into hell was added to the Creed many years after the apostles died. It first appeared in a copy of the Creed dating from AD 390, a firm 300 years after the apostles. The man who obtained this copy of the Creed was a monk named Rufinus. He took the phrase to be a metaphorical way of reiterating the fact that Jesus truly died, not that he went to hell. Aside from Rufinus's copy the phrase does not appear in another copy of the Creed until 650. Some time after that it found its way into all freshly made copies, such that the vast majority of recipients lost track of the fact that the phrase was not original to the Creed. By this arose the mistaken belief that the apostles and early Christians held that Jesus descended into hell after his death.

Substitution Summarized

We close with a brief summation of Jesus' substitutionary work in life and on the cross. In life Jesus lived as the ideal human. He loved God above all else, obeyed him always, and loved his neighbors (including his enemies!) as himself. This means Jesus was the ideal substitute for God's requirement that a man acceptable to him should live in complete righteousness from beginning to end. Due to this perfect righteousness and his divine capacities to endure the Father's infinite wrath against sins, Jesus presented himself as the lone sufficient substitute for our death penalty. Therefore on the cross Jesus endured not just man's punishment in the form of piercings, lashings, and mockery but also *God's* infinite punishment against sin as the divine holy nature struck the curse Jesus had become. Jesus *became sin* so that God could judge sin in human flesh and thereby satisfy the requirements of his justice. By faith we can enjoy full pardon from God not because God just let us off the hook but because Jesus Christ fully satisfied God's wrath against sin by enduring the blows that were due us. We can live because he died in our place.

> *Jesus became sin so that God could judge sin in human flesh and thereby satisfy the requirements of his justice.*

Note

1. Wayne Grudem, *Systematic Theology* (Grand Rapids: Zondervan, 1994), 575.

The Appearance to Thomas by Rembrandt.

Chapter 14
Up from Death

Dead men do not come back from beyond the grave. The ancients knew this just as surely as we do in the twenty-first century. Sure, rarely a person will set foot into the borderlands and then come rushing back to life when a failed heart restarts or when air-starved lungs are emptied of drowning waters. But once a body has been mourned over, ceremonially cleaned and clothed, committed to silent earth, stone chamber, or consuming fire, there is no hope for reversal except for that which comes at the faraway end of time. Jesus' disciples knew this. That is why they scattered at the start of Jesus' demise in the garden. That is also why they stayed away from the execution. Only the women and John came that day. They watched their Lord die and gave no thought to the possibility of his return from the grave. This was the end . . . the end of life for a man in whom they had placed all their best hopes.

The few followers of Christ who gathered at the cross gave no thought to the possibility of his return from the grave.

As with many other stories of Jesus' life, it is neither possible nor necessary to discern the exact sequence of events surrounding the Lord's resurrection and the visitations that followed.

Matthew and the Angel by Reni. The Gospel writers were commissioned to write truth about Jesus' identity and works so readers like you and I would be encouraged to place our faith in him.

This should not trouble us. The Gospel writers were commissioned to write truth about Jesus' identity and works so readers like you and I would be encouraged to place our faith in him. They have fulfilled this commission nobly, as 2,000 years of vibrant Christian faith demonstrate. Each writer wrote from his particular perspective, which means he locked in on the facts that helped achieve his specific aims and excluded those that did not. The authors typically organized their materials thematically rather than chronologically. For them questions of the *meaning* of what happened and *why* it was so were far more important than questions of *when* or *in what sequence*. Finally, from the earliest days of church history, scholars have known that each of the writers drew from different authoritative informants. For instance, early experts such as Papias, Irenaeus, Clement, Origen, and Jerome taught that Mark drew heavily upon the experiences and teachings of Peter. Conversely, John drew on his own experiences, not Peter's. Hence it is natural that the Gospels of John and Mark would regularly take different angles on the same story. The same is true with the other Gospels. As a result we have a good deal of variety across the four Gospel accounts, but ultimately everything fits within a master story whose unified message can be summarized in one brief phrase: Jesus rose from the dead on the

Each writer wrote from his particular perspective, which means he locked in on the facts that helped achieve his specific aims and excluded those that did not.

third day after his execution and showed himself to many witnesses. Cobbling together the different story angles recorded by the four Gospels, we may reasonably suggest that events unfolded in roughly the sequence presented in this chapter.[1]

The Quick and the Dead

The Sabbath ended at 6:00 in the evening when by Jewish reckoning Saturday gave way to Sunday. Jesus had been dead for a little over 24 hours, but already this counted as a three-day period since any portion of a day was considered as a whole when calculating the passage of days. Hence Jesus was dead and buried late on Friday, stayed in the tomb all day Saturday, and entered his third day of death and entombment as Sunday began.

Jesus was dead and buried late on Friday, stayed in the tomb all day Saturday, and entered his third day of death and entombment as Sunday began.

Since the time they had watched Joseph and Nicodemus place Jesus in the tomb, the women had been nestled indoors, resting and keeping to themselves as they observed the Sabbath restrictions. When the Sabbath ended as darkness fell on Saturday, three of them—Mary Magdalene, Salome, and Mary the mother of James—briefly left the home where they had gathered and went to purchase additional spices. Joseph and Nicodemus had included 75 pounds of aloes within Jesus' wrappings. The women could not have missed this fact as they watched on Friday, but as with so many things in life a woman's touch is the *finishing* touch. They sought to supplement and perfect the services Joseph and Nicodemus had performed, with the hope of making sure Jesus' body did not suffer the indignity of producing foul odor. Having purchased the goods in early

Mary at the Tomb (detail) by Schedoni.

evening, the women returned to their lodging and planned a daybreak trip to the tomb.

They set out when morning drew near. Theirs was a daring move and perhaps a little foolhardy. After all, how did they expect to gain entrance to the tomb? The sealing stone was heavy and would not yield to the efforts of three women. They pondered this difficulty as they walked along in the dying dark (Mark 16:3). They had no way of knowing that the tomb was guarded by the temple police since they had kept indoors for the duration of the Sabbath. Neither news nor rumor flies when sparrows stay nested. If the women had known about the guard, they would have stayed home, for there could be no thought of asking such men to open a tomb that they were supposed to shield from Jesus' disciples. It is best to conclude that the women were walking in faith—not faith in Jesus' resurrection but faith that something good would come of their desires to serve their fallen Lord.

A first-century tomb with a sealing stone.

As the women neared the tomb, the earth around them began to heave and revolt. Angels descended. They looked like ordinary men, Mark and Luke tell us, but their clothes were dazzling white in the fashion of heavenly raiment. One of the angels rolled back the sealing stone of Jesus' tomb as the earth shook; he then sat atop the stone like a battlefield victor astride his slain foe. Death was dead, but it was not the angel's doing. All he had done was open the door to show the way to a freshly vacated tomb. The resurrection event had already occurred, unseen and unmarked by the temple guardsmen or any human eye. The Lord was gone, but the dumbfounded guards remained. They were outfitted to rebuff Jesus' disciples should they at-

Death was dead, but it was not the angel's doing. All he had done was open the door to show the way to a freshly vacated tomb.

tempt to snatch away the body; now they watched frozen in fear as an altogether different sort of invader appeared. Most likely the guards fled soon after this, for nothing more is said of them at the gravesite.

What of the women? Mark, who is noticeably brief in many of his recollections, simply says they walked straight into the tomb and found an angel sitting there in the guise of

a young man. Noticing their fear, the angel bid them be calm and explained that Jesus had risen from the dead, just as he said he would (Luke 24:6–7). Why are you looking for the quick among the dead, he wanted to know. He then told them that they should run back and tell the disciples to go on to Galilee where Jesus would meet them. At once fearful and joyful, the women ran to carry out the angel's orders. Before getting

The Women at the Tomb by Fra Angelico. One of the angels rolled back the sealing stone of Jesus' tomb as the earth shook; he then sat atop the stone like a battlefield victor.

very far they came across the risen Lord, who greeted them with a simple, "Good morning!" (Matt 28:9). The women dove at Jesus' feet and worshipped in awe and fear. Looking down, Jesus told them, "Do not be afraid. Go and tell My brothers to leave for Galilee, and they will see Me there" (Matt 28:10).

From John we get the impression that Mary Magdalene must have peeled away and headed back toward Jerusalem immediately upon discovering the opened tomb. This would mean that she departed before hearing from the angel. It also means she was not with the group of women who encountered Jesus

It was with a troubled heart that Mary Magdalene raced back alone to tell the men that Jesus' tomb had been robbed.

on the pathway to Jerusalem. No hopeful words had yet come to her. Thus it was with a troubled heart that she raced back alone to tell the men that Jesus' tomb had been robbed.

Reports from the Grave

As the women were heading back for Jerusalem a number of the temple guardsmen reported the morning's incredible events to the chief priests (Matt 28:11-15). Keep in mind that none of the guards had seen Jesus rise from the dead. They knew that the earth had been shaken and that angels had come to breach the tomb. They also watched the women mill around the tomb's entrance, but they themselves apparently kept their distance due to fear. Did they stay on long enough to

After convening an assembly of the elders, the chief priests handed the guards a handsome sum of money and told them to spread a rumor that Jesus' disciples had stolen the body in the night.

hear the angel speak to the women about the empty tomb and Jesus' resurrection? Matthew never says so, but it seems likely that they did. After convening an assembly of the elders, the chief priests handed the guards a handsome sum of money and told them to spread a rumor that Jesus' disciples had stolen the body in the night (Matt 18:13). This means they knew the tomb was empty and that it needed a non-miraculous explanation if the inevitable Jesus craze was to be minimized. That the priests *paid* the guards to spread this explanation proves beyond doubt that they knew it was false. So intense was their hatred for Jesus and so repulsed where they by his claims and teachings that they would stop at nothing to escape submitting to him as Lord.

Meanwhile, Mary Magdalene reached Peter and the disciples before the other women. She had gotten a head start, you recall. Finding Peter she reported, "They have taken the Lord out of the tomb, and we don't know where they have put Him!" (John 20:2). Obviously Mary believed the body had been stolen away by Jesus' enemies. An isolated reading of John leaves the reader under the impression that Peter was driven straight out the door by Mary's dire report, but pulling Luke's account into the mix reveals that the other women arrived on

Mary's heels and gave an ecstatic report that mixed poorly with Mary's pessimism. As Luke describes it, the emotion-packed scene descended into confusion. The words of Mary Magdalene, Joanna, Mary the mother of James, and all the other women combined to make unbelievable nonsense (Luke 24:11). On one hand Mary Magdalene reported a theft; on the other hand her late-arriving compan-

The Women at the Tomb by Memling.

ions told tales of a living Jesus wandering along the roadway. Believing none of it but compelled to investigate, Peter ran for the tomb. John, once again identified as the disciple whom Jesus loved, joined the sortie but soon outpaced the older Peter (John 20:4).

John reached the tomb first and stooped low at the open entrance. He saw that Jesus' linen cloths were lying empty within. He dared not enter for a closer look. That was the work of a rasher man, Peter. He caught up to John, brushed by him, and entered the tomb in pursuit of truth,

On one hand Mary Magdalene reported a theft; on the other hand her late-arriving companions told tales of a living Jesus wandering along the roadway.

whatever it may be. There he found that the linens told an odd tale, one which we are still puzzling over 2,000 years later. The cloth that had been wrapped around Jesus' head was folded up neatly and placed in a spot separate from the cloth that had wrapped his body (John 20:7). It seems that "folded up" may mean that the head cloths had kept the form which was given them by the contours of Jesus' head. This would seem to imply that Jesus simply passed through his grave clothes. Certainly he could not have unwrapped them himself when he came back to life, for his arms were pinned snugly against his body by the swaddling cloth. Bear in mind also that when the angel opened the tomb Jesus did not come walking out. He had already vacated the chamber and was nowhere in sight. Thus we see that Christ's resurrection did not involve him simply coming to, unwrapping himself, arranging for the sealing stone's removal, and then exiting the chamber in the normal manner. Instead, Jesus' resurrection was altogether supernatural. One moment he was dead and swaddled inside a silent tomb; the next he was alive and transported elsewhere, unhindered by

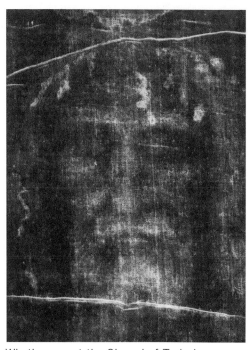

Whether or not the Shroud of Turin is authentic, it does seem to match what John describes as a head cloth. In any event the cloth John saw was a powerful evidence for Christ's resurrection.

obstructing cloth or stone. John seems to have deduced all of this immediately once he mustered the courage to enter the tomb and take a close look at the linens, for he looked on them "and believed" (v. 8). The state of the head cloth was so striking

> *The state of the head cloth was so striking that John's final doubts were overturned.*

that John's final doubts were overturned. Peter was slower on the uptake, for Luke tells us he went home "amazed" at what he had seen (Luke 24:12). Amazement is not belief, and so for Peter much remained unresolved as he pondered the meaning of the empty grave clothes.

Mary Magdalene had returned to the tomb site as well, though she was in a morose state of mind. Inconsolable even by news of the odd cloth, she let Peter and John return home without her. For John the linens confirmed that Jesus had risen; for Peter they were tantalizing evidence that something wonderful might have happened; for Mary the empty cloths only reminded her of her empty heart. As Merrill Tenney has said, "She had hoped for the sad consolation of completing the burial, and even that had been taken from her [with the theft of the body]."[2] Mary's Lord was dead, and some black soul had carted away his body. And so when John and Peter left, she stayed facing the tomb, crying and looking in on the scene of a crime. When

> *For Mary the empty cloths only reminded her of her empty heart.*

she stooped to get a closer look inside, she found that two angels were now sitting there. She did not recognize them as angels, for again they appeared simply as young men arrayed in splendid white clothing. The angels asked her why she was crying. She repeated the same assessment she had been sharing all morning: "Because they've taken away my Lord and I

Don't Cling to Me by Tissot. Mary initially thought the risen Jesus was merely a gardener. Realizing his true identity, she rejoiced and embraced him.

don't know where they've put Him" (John 20:13). She then turned back around to exit the dark tomb, perhaps intending to scour the sunlit ground for sign of the thieves. As she emerged into the brightness, she noticed that yet another man had joined them. It was Jesus, but Mary did not recognize him; either her eyes were still adjusting to the light or else something about the risen Lord fooled her perceptions, as would happen in several later sightings. Like the angels inside the tomb, this third man wanted to know why Mary was crying and whom she was looking for.

Supposing it was only the gardener (recall that the tomb was located in a garden area near Golgotha), she made a plea: "Sir, if you've removed Him, tell me where you've put Him, and I will take Him away" (v. 15). Here, with this heartfelt plea, is where Mary's world took up a bright new Son-bound orbit it would never relinquish, for the "gardener" spoke her name with a familiar gentleness and depth of caring. She spun back to face

Mary's world took up a bright new Son-bound orbit it would never relinquish.

Jesus and cried out, "Teacher!" as she embraced him (v. 16).

To Mary's act of elated devotion, Jesus gave a fascinating and unexpected reply: "Don't cling to Me" (John 20:17). His reasoning was simple: "I have not yet ascended to the Father." In other words, he told her that he was not leaving earth just yet. Mary was clinging to him as if he would lift away any moment, gone forever through the skies above. Jesus went on to assure her that he *would* ascend to the Father before long, and he sent her to report this to the disciples. Now she who had been sorrowful all morning raced away to share in the joy that had already dawned over John and the other women. "I have seen the Lord!" she told them, and she repeated all that Jesus had said to her (v. 18).

Road to Emmaus

Later in the day on Sunday, two of Jesus' disciples, Cleopas and an unnamed companion, struck out from Jerusalem intent on stopping in Emmaus, a village that lay seven miles in the distance. These men were not members of Jesus' inner group, the Twelve which was now reduced to the Eleven with the apostasy of Judas. Rather, these travelers were part of the much larger pack of supporters who gathered periodically around Jesus during his journeys. Many such people had come with Jesus to Jerusalem for Passover, and though these men were not of Jesus' inner circle, they had associated closely enough with that group to have heard

The Road to Emmaus by Führich. Jesus walked to Emmaus with Cleopas and his companion, but both men were prevented from recognizing Jesus (Luke 24:16).

incomplete rumors about remarkable things that were said to have transpired earlier that day at Jesus' tomb. But the news had come chiefly from women. Could they be trusted to give accurate accounts? As with every other society of the time, among Jews the testimonies of women were not valid in legal proceedings, and in general men regarded women as too excitable to be trustworthy in dramatic situations. This attitude seems remarkably ill-founded to us today, but such was the dominant thought of that far-

Travelers on the road from Jerusalem to Bethlehem in 1893. The road to Emmaus was probably near here.

gone time. And so the men discussed these reports and argued over the meaning of it all as they made for Emmaus.

Soon the men were joined by a third traveler. It was Jesus, but the men "were prevented from recognizing Him" (Luke 24:16). This reminds us of Mary's encounter outside the tomb. Whether there was something unusual in Jesus' appearance or in exercise of divine powers he chose to dull their perceptions for some higher purpose is not made clear at this point, but later evidence indicates that their failure to recognize him was due to dulled perceptions. In any event Jesus joined the men as a stranger and asked about the details of their debate. His question troubled them. They both stopped in their tracks and slouched under the weight of discouragement. Finally

Jesus joined the men as a stranger and asked about the details of their debate.

Cleopas responded, "Are You the only visitor in Jerusalem who doesn't know the things that happened there in these days?" (v. 18). The controversial sentencing and execution of Jesus; the earthquake and daytime darkness that attended his crucifixion; the supernatural tearing of the temple veil—how could anyone have missed these things? Together Cleopas and his companion explained to their uninformed guest that Jesus had been regarded as a prophet "powerful in action and speech before God and all the people" and that the chief priests had unjustly arranged for his execution. The death of Jesus dismayed the men deeply because they had hoped that he was Israel's Redeemer (vv. 19–21). But perhaps that hope was not entirely extinguished. Voices rising, they explained to Jesus that "some women from our group astounded us. They arrived early at the tomb [today], and when they didn't find His body, they came and reported that they had seen a vision of angels who said He was alive. Some of those who were with us went to the tomb and found it just as the women had said, but they didn't see Him" (vv. 22–24).

Basically these men explained to Jesus that none of the disciples (inner *or* outer circle) expected Messiah to suffer and die or rise from the dead. After hearing their explanation, Jesus (whom the men still had not recognized) proceeded to chide them for their lack of understanding. "How unwise and slow you are to believe in your hearts all that the prophets have spoken! Didn't the Messiah have to suffer these things and enter into His glory?" (Luke 24:25–26). Jesus then explained that the Old Testament teachings had revealed these things about Messiah. Without doubt the men were fascinated to discover that predictions of Messiah's suffering, death, and resurrection were sprinkled throughout the holy books. We know from studying their ancient commentaries that the Jews simply were not expecting such an outcome for Messiah; not even those who most thoroughly devoted themselves to the study and teaching of the Scriptures—the scribes, priests, and elders—had foreseen it. In contrast to this, Jesus taught about the necessity of Messiah's death and resurrection throughout much of his ministry. In one setting after another, his disciples either failed to understand or refused

> *These men explained to Jesus that none of the disciples (inner or outer circle) expected Messiah to suffer and die or rise from the dead.*

> *Without doubt the men were fascinated to discover that predictions of Messiah's suffering, death, and resurrection were sprinkled throughout the holy books.*

to accept that such things could come true of God's Messiah. Now Scripture after Scripture was opened to Cleopas and his companion, and in light of recent events, they were better prepared to accept that Messiah really was destined to suffer, die, and rise gloriously from death.

When the party reached the outskirts of Emmaus, Cleopas and his companion urged Jesus to spend the night with them in the village since evening was quickly approaching. They were simply showing kindness to an interesting stranger. Jesus agreed to join them. Once they were reclined at the table, Jesus assumed the role of host by breaking bread and blessing it for their meal. At this moment "their eyes were opened, and they recognized Him"

(Luke 24:31). More precisely, *Jesus opened their minds to his identity.* That is the meaning of the text. Unnamed obstacles to true perception fell away, but even as one veil was lifted, another dropped down before them: Jesus disappeared into thin air (v. 31). Once they got over the shock of his disappearance both men said they should

Christ at Emmaus by Rembrandt. Jesus revealed his identity when he broke and blessed the bread.

have known all along that it was Jesus who traveled with them, for their hearts had been "ablaze" when Jesus explained from Scripture the necessity of Messiah's suffering, death, and exaltation. After reminiscing about this for a short while, the men sped back through the darkness to Jerusalem where they found the Eleven gathered together. They came from Emmaus eager to share their incred-

> *As soon as they recognized him, Jesus disappeared into thin air.*

ible report, but before they could make good on this plan, they were told by everyone gathered there that Jesus had put in an appearance to Simon Peter. The women had not been mistaken after all, as Cleopas and his companion had already deduced. Women brave and good, tellers of truth!

We are not given details about Peter's private meeting with Christ on Sunday. We know it occurred sometime before Jesus appeared to the rest of the male disciples in a closed-door meeting (which we detail below) because 1 Corinthians 15:5 says the risen Christ "appeared to Cephas [alternative name for Peter], then to the Twelve." By now no one doubted that the sightings were really happening, but what exactly were they seeing? Some of them (such as Mary) had touched the risen Jesus, but what were they to make of the fact that Jesus disappeared into thin air before the watching eyes of Cleopas and his companion? The disciples were elated to have seen Jesus back from the dead, but deep questions remained about what was happening.

> *The disciples were elated to have seen Jesus back from the dead, but deep questions remained about what was happening.*

Locked Doors and Pierced Hands

While the disciples were still sharing their experiences of the day, Jesus suddenly stood among them. "Peace to you!" he said and sent a jolt through them all (Luke 24:36–37). Terrified, they thought a ghost had dropped into their midst from the spirit world. There's little wonder why they thought such a thing. Human bodies do not come and go in a flash, nor do they pass through doors that are closed and locked (John 20:19). No one doubted that Jesus had sprung up several times and in diverse places throughout this strange day. What began with the women had continued later in the day with Peter, Cleopas, and his unnamed companion. Now, packed together in a room with four walls and shut

Though the doors were closed and locked, Jesus appeared amid the disciples.

doors, everyone had gotten in on the experience. But exactly what *kind* of experience was it? Had the real flesh-and-blood Jesus come back from the dead, or was a come-and-go phantom mimicking bodily life?

Sensing that his disciples were troubled rather than elated, Jesus asked them why doubts remained among them (Luke 24:38). He already knew the answer. No rational person could be unshaken at the sight of a dead man walking, talking, and

bouncing in and out of sight as Jesus had done throughout the day. As Jews these men believed in the power of God, and upon Jesus they had pinned all their hopes of salvation, but what they were seeing was unprecedented. It would take solid evidence for them to conclude that the real Jesus was standing before them. For this reason Jesus

Emmaus (detail) by Caravagio. To convince the confused disciples that he was real, the risen Jesus ate some food as they watched.

said, "Look at My hands and My feet, that it is I Myself! Touch Me and see, because a ghost does not have flesh and bones as you can see I have" (v. 39). This was a good start toward settling matters, but still their joy and amazement were mixed with unbelief (v. 41). To settle the matter once for all, Jesus decided to have a meal with them. He had broken bread with Cleopas and the other disciple in early evening but never got around to eating since he blinked out of sight the instant they recognized him. Now he took the next step. He asked them for food. The disciples handed over some broiled fish. Never

Never in history was an audience more eager to see a man chew up and swallow a bit of food.

in history was an audience more eager to see a man chew up and swallow a bit of food. Jesus did not disappoint them; while everyone looked on, he "ate in their presence" (v. 43). Assured that no ghost could partake of a meal, the disciples could now tear away their last restraints and celebrate the genuine bodily resurrection of Jesus Christ (John 20:20).

Prelude to a New Mission

Having won the confidence of everyone in the room, Jesus began sharing with them the same things he had spoken to Cleopas earlier. He demonstrated that the books of Moses, the Prophets, and the Psalms had foretold that Messiah would suffer death but then be raised again to new life. No one Scripture tells the whole tale, of course; but by piecing many Old Testament witnesses together, you arrive at a picture of a suffering, dying, rising Messiah

Jesus demonstrated that the books of Moses, the Prophets, and the Psalms had foretold that Messiah would suffer death but then be raised again to new life.

that was foretold many hundreds of years before Jesus was nailed to a cross on Golgotha. Jesus taught these things before

No one Scripture tells the whole tale, of course; but by piecing many Old Testament witnesses together, you arrive at a picture of a suffering, dying, rising Messiah that was foretold many hundreds of years before Jesus was nailed to a cross on Golgotha.

his crucifixion, but his words had fallen on deaf ears. Now the audience was in a better position to understand. Jesus ensured that they did so by supernaturally opening their minds to receive the truth of God's revelation (Luke 24:45). He went on to say that in light of his victory over death, repentance for forgiveness of sins should be preached in his name to the entire world, beginning from the very room in which he was standing (v. 47). "You are witnesses of these things," Jesus told them, and he instructed them to wait in Jerusalem until God empowered them permanently by the gift of the Holy Spirit (vv.

48–49). To close out this prelude to the mission he was assigning them, Jesus bestowed the Spirit's presence upon them that they might grow in their comprehension of the new life he was leading them to embrace. All the disciples gladly accepted this gift except for the one member who was absent: Thomas. It is good for us that Thomas stayed away that night, for Jesus' later reception of this doubter offers hope for us all.

Doubting Thomas

The Bible does not tell us why Thomas did not join the rest of the disciples that night, but it is not difficult to guess the cause. Most likely Thomas was easing himself away from the community of faith. At an earlier time in Jesus' life, when he was heading off to the city where his friend Lazarus lay dead in a tomb, Thomas had told the other disciples, "Let's go [also] so that we may die with Him" (John 11:16). Here we see that

Most likely Thomas was easing himself away from the community of faith.

Thomas was a brave and loyal follower of Christ, but we also catch a glimpse of deep-seated pessimism and possibly even doubt about Jesus' identity. No Jew expected Messiah would die in any circumstance, much less that he would die at the hands of a mob grown angry at his healing powers. If at that point Thomas had started to suspect Jesus' ministry would end in his death, it was not because he alone among the disciples had seen this from Scripture or that he had risen above the dominant paradigm that kept everyone else from comprehending Jesus' death-and-resurrection predictions. Rather,

The gears of Thomas's soul were turning fitfully, catching here and there on doubts, troubles, questions.

most likely Thomas expected Jesus might die because he was struggling with doubt about Jesus' true identity as Messiah even at this early date. We see this struggle play out yet again in John 14. After Jesus told the disciples that he was going to prepare a place for them and that he would come back for them so they could all be together, Thomas blurted out his deepest doubts by saying, "We don't know where You're going. How can we know the way?"

(John 14:5). To this Jesus replied, "I am the way, the truth, and the life. No one comes to the Father except through Me" (v. 6). Did Thomas believe this? Possibly not. The gears of his soul were turning fitfully, catching here and there on doubts, troubles, questions.

Though Thomas was not with the disciples for Jesus' Sunday night appearance, he was filled in on all the details by his excited brethren. Again and again they told him, "We have seen the Lord!" but Thomas would have nothing to do with such talk. "If I don't see the mark of the nails in His hands, put my finger into the mark of the nails, and put my hand into His side, I will never believe!" (John 20:25). Can the bar of proof be raised any higher than this? By now Thomas was a hard-shelled skeptic. If he was to be won over to the believing crowd that gushed all around him, it would take nothing less than indisputable evidence.

On the next Sunday after Jesus' abrupt appearance to the disciples, the gang all gathered again behind barred doors. This time Thomas was present. Picture him sitting there spinning the iron wheels of logic as time stretched on without any sign of the risen Jesus. The Lord's no-show was not a cause for celebration on his part; far better to find that Jesus was alive after all, but in the absence of proof, Thomas would not be carried away by false hope. Then a familiar voice called out, "Peace to you!" It was Jesus. Once again he appeared among them though the doors were shut against his entry, but he was not here to wow the crowd with tricks of mobility. He had come to win Doubting Thomas to his cause. Looking at him, Jesus said, "Put your finger here and observe My hands. Reach out your hand and put it into My side. Don't be an unbeliever, but a believer" (John 20:27). Jesus offered Thomas the exact evidence he had named as necessary for overturning his disbelief. We have every expectation that our resurrected bodies will be whole and complete, not crippled or marked by scars. Jesus, however, will forever bear the scars that prove his love for us. Thomas gazed at the marks in Jesus' flesh but found that he did not need to poke around in

Picture Thomas sitting there spinning the iron wheels of logic as time stretched on without any sign of the risen Jesus.

them after all. There could be no doubt about the reality of the flesh-and-bone man standing before him. "My Lord and My God!" he exclaimed (v. 28).

Here we see that Jesus had regard for the doubter. Far from scolding Thomas, Jesus met him at the crossroads of doubt and faith and showed him signs indicating that the path of belief was safe, rational, and true. The signs Thomas beheld are not available to us today, nor should we seek after them. The resurrection of Christ was a one-time event, and Thomas was positioned in a place and epoch that allowed him to see the proofs personally. Though today the body and scars of Christ are not offered for our examination, we do have

The Incredulity of Thomas by Caravaggio. Jesus said to Thomas, "Put your finger here and observe My hands. Reach out your hand and put it into My side. Don't be an unbeliever, but a believer" (John 20:27).

the eye-witness, Spirit-inspired testimonies given through the New Testament authors. Time and again we see in these writings that all the leading disciples doubted at some point or another. Like Thomas, several were even converted from hardcore skepticism regarding Jesus' resurrection and claims to divinity. When we struggle with doubts, we should lay them bare before God, as Thomas did. If our hearts and minds are prepared to be instructed and if we are willing to do the hard work of studying the biblical testimonies, faith will be our reward. We shall know without seeing, feel without touching, and

Jesus met Thomas at the crossroads of doubt and faith and showed him signs indicating that the path of belief was safe, rational, and true.

believe with a firmness of conviction that cannot be overturned by unanswered questions. As Jesus said, "Those who believe without seeing are blessed" (John 20:29).

Catch and Release

Some time after Jesus' second appearance behind closed doors in Jerusalem, he came out to the Sea of Tiberias (aka Sea of Galilee) and watched from the shore as Peter, Thomas, and a number of other disciples were fishing. Jesus had instructed them to return to Galilee after his resurrection, and so in compliance with his wishes they returned to their old haunts. Many of them had been professional fishermen before Jesus

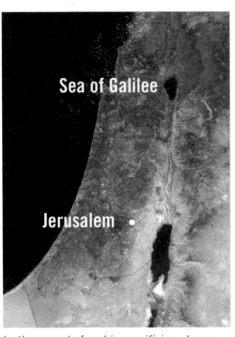

called them to follow him three years earlier, and they naturally began to fall back on their old trade in the days and weeks before Jesus gave them their definitive commission to abandon such things and reach the world. They had seemingly lost their former touch for fishcraft, for they spent the whole night on the waters and caught nothing. Not one fish could be teased into their nets.

In the years before his crucifixion, Jesus based his ministry in Capernaum on the northwest shore of the Sea of Galilee, about 85 miles from Jerusalem. This is where the disciples likely met the risen Jesus.

At daybreak Jesus arrived at the shoreline and called out to the men, "You don't have any fish, do you?" (John 21:5). He knew their lack, just as he knows yours and mine. The fishermen did not recognize that it was Jesus who hailed them. The light was still dim, and the morning fog clung to the shore at this early hour. When the men answered that they indeed had no fish, Jesus called back and said that they would catch plenty if they would just throw the net over the right side of the boat. He offered no explanation for why it should turn out that way, nor did he disclose who he was. Having nothing to lose, the disciples obeyed the stranger's prompting and wound up catching so many fish that they were unable to lift the bulging net into the boat. John immediately realized it was Jesus who had called out to them. Who else could it be? Jesus had done this same service for them years earlier. Peter agreed and put on his outer garment (he had been stripped to the waist while working) and swam a hundred yards to meet Jesus. Hasty Peter kept true to form. Would he not have done better to leave his outer garment aboard the boat, dry and ready for use once he toweled off on the shore? Never mind that. We love Peter for his determined pursuit of God, and we know that his urgency was driven all the harder by remembrance of his failures. His deni-

The Miraculous Catch of Fish by Witz. By following Jesus' command, the disciples caught so many fish that they were unable to lift the bulging net into the boat.

als and curses were still fresh to him, and every rooster crow echoed in ears that burned to hear the Lord's pardon. Would he receive it on the morning shore? Would Jesus release him from his burden? Peter stroked and kicked in the chill water, hoping to salve his conscience on shore.

> *Peter stroked and kicked in the chill water, hoping to salve his conscience on shore.*

The rest of the men piloted the boat to shore and left the cinched net resting in shallow water. To their amazement Jesus had fish and baked bread ready and waiting for them. Nevertheless Jesus was unwilling to waste the miracle catch. He instructed the men to bring some of the fish they had netted. Peter, drenched and still panting from his swim, leaped up and dragged the net to shore all by himself. The men counted out 153 fish as they separated them according to kind. Altogether the fish and soaked net probably weighed 300 pounds—quite a weight for one man to drag up the bank. Peter was working hard to make reparation unto the Lord whom he had betrayed, but he would soon learn that such works were not necessary.

When breakfast was finished, Jesus turned his attention to

Peter. It was time to bind up this man's wound once and for all. Three times in front of the whole group, Jesus asked Peter if he loved him. Much as doctors do, Jesus chose to probe the wound before healing it. Each time the question was put to him, Peter assured Jesus with increased urgency that he did indeed love him, and each time Jesus accepted Peter's answer and said that he should tend the flock of God. The implications are liberating and far-reaching: Jesus was telling Peter that his love for Messiah was enough. Peter did not need to earn back Jesus' acceptance. Acceptance was his forever through love and faith in the Savior no matter what mistakes he had made. Further, not only was Peter still accepted; he was still fit for Christian service. Jesus made this clear by his repeated admonition that Peter should feed and tend God's sheep. Here Peter learned that

Jesus is not just a partial Savior. He saves the whole soul and the whole life of the one who comes to him in faith, affecting a complete redemption that needs no supplementation by human efforts.

Jesus is not just a partial Savior. He saves the whole soul and the whole life of the one who comes to him in faith, affecting a complete redemption that needs no supplementation by human efforts. Peter was going to be okay because his Savior made him so. Praise God for his vast mercies!

Parting Words; Parting Worlds

Two final episodes in the life of the risen Christ demand our attention: First, in what has been called the Great Commission, Jesus more fully explained the new life mission he had initially described to the disciples during his first appearance in the locked room (Luke 24:47). This time Jesus and the Eleven eschewed the indoors and ascended a mountain in Galilee, a destination of Jesus' own choosing (Matt 28:16). Some of the Eleven worshipped Jesus openly in this place while others held back, struggling with doubts not about the Lord's authentic return to life but rather the appropriateness of worshipping Jesus in such an unbounded manner. Can heaven approve of such open adoration? Jesus is God the Son, but should the

Son receive adoration equal to the Father? Absolutely yes. But some of the disciples were unsure. Sensing this reservation and wishing to speak in definitive terms about his status and

Can heaven approve of such open adoration? Jesus is God the Son, but should the Son receive adoration equal to the Father? Absolutely yes.

the requirements of true discipleship, Jesus said, "All authority has been given to Me in heaven and on earth. Go, therefore, and make disciples of all nations, baptizing them in the name of the Father and of the Son and of the Holy Spirit, teaching them to observe everything I have commanded you. And remember, I am with you always, to the end of the age" (vv. 18–20). In this short string of sentences, Jesus summarized his power, stated the disciples' God-given and enduring purpose, and made a promise to be with his disciples down through the ages as they bear witness of him to a lost

and dying world. This is God's ultimate purpose in the dramatic crucifixion and resurrection of Messiah: that to the praise of his love and grace peoples from every nation would be redeemed and made holy children of God, secured for eternity by the Lamb who bore human sins, endured the Father's punishment, and slew death as he rose up amid angels on the third day.

The Savior of the World by El Greco.

Second, sometime after the mountaintop commission, Jesus and his disciples were again gathered outdoors (Acts 1:4–11). It was now 40 days since Jesus had conquered death, and in that span of time, he had "presented Himself alive to them [the apostles] by many convincing proofs" (v. 3). No doubt remained among the disciples. Jesus was obviously alive, and he had made it clear that all peoples of earth should be taught to believe in him and thus count their sins forgiven through his sacrifice on their behalf. Now, in his closing moments with them, Jesus again admonished the disciples to wait in Jerusalem until the Holy Spirit was poured out on them. Once this happened, they would be scattered by the hand of God, destined for various appointments across the known world. Some of the disciples had supposed Jesus would not leave for heaven without first restoring Israel. To this presumption Jesus made a reply that should not dart quickly past our own ears: "It is not for you to know times or periods that the Father has set by His own authority" (v. 7). In other words: the end times will come at the hour appointed by God. As for you—get on with the commission I've given you.

Jesus made it clear that all peoples of earth should be taught to believe in him and count their sins forgiven through his sacrifice on their behalf.

Even as his last words still rang in their ears, the disciples watched as Jesus was caught up by a cloud and lifted from among them. In a moment he was gone. The disciples stared after him in wonderment and holy dread. Then two angels abruptly appeared next to them. Arrayed in brilliant white clothing, they said, "Men of Galilee, why do you stand looking up into heaven? This Jesus, who has been taken from you into heaven, will come in

The Ascension of Christ by Garofalo.

the same way that you have seen Him going into heaven" (Acts 1:11). He will return, they understood, but in such a time as is appointed by God. In the meantime the disciples had a world to reach. Together they undertook the daylong journey back to Jerusalem where they united in continual prayer as they waited for the breath of God to fall on them. So began the church of Jesus Christ.

Notes

1. The reconstruction presented in this book for the resurrection and the appearances that followed does not include the data found in Mark 16:9–20. Based on the absence of this passage in key ancient manuscripts, most scholars (conservative and otherwise) do not believe it was originally a part of Mark's Gospel. This means verses 9–20 were most likely added at some later date by a scribe who believed that Mark had originally included a longer ending. In any event the decision to exclude these verses has a significant impact on how one may reconstruct the events of Easter Sunday. In fact, it makes such reconstructions easier and possibly closer to the true sequence of events that unfolded on that magnificent day. The reconstruction offered in this book should not be taken as anything more than a studied effort to bring the various accounts together in a way that communicates the truth of Christ's resurrection most effectively. If it happens to reflect the true historical sequence, so much the better! If not, we have erred in a matter that the Gospel writers found comparatively insignificant.

2. Merrill Tenney, *John*, Expositor's Bible Commentary, vol. 9 (Grand Rapids: Zondervan, 1981), 190.

Part IV
Jesus' Teachings

Chapter 15
The Son Confesses

I've probably never met you, but if I wanted to get to know you, I could track you down and pose a series of questions. I would start by asking about your origins: the time and place of your birth and details about your family background. Next I might want to know about your present life: who your friends and family are, what you do for a living, and what beliefs and purposes drive you. Finally I would ask for a snapshot of your plans for the future: where you are going and what you want your life to look like in the end. If you gave me all this information I would have a pretty clear understanding of who you are. To eliminate the possibility that you have misrepresented yourself, I

If I wanted to learn about you, I could ask you to step up to the microphone and tell me all about yourself. But what if I wanted to learn about Jesus? Where would I turn?

could do some quick checking among your acquaintances. If their reports agree with yours, I can be confident that I know a great deal about who you are.

What about Jesus? I may wish to learn about him, but I cannot interview him in person. His friends cannot sit for my questions either, for they are long dead. Does this mean I can't do any better than make vague guesses about Jesus' identity? Fortunately not. By reading the four Gospels, anyone can meet Jesus Christ and learn vital biographical facts about his life. Granted, these books were not written by Jesus himself. However, his closest followers wrote them, and we have compelling reasons to trust that they delivered true facts about the most fascinating life ever lived (see chapters 19 and 20). Furthermore, much of the Gospel material preserves Jesus' teachings. We read his confessions about his origin and destination, his family and his beliefs, his purposes and crowning achievements. Thus in a real sense we *can* sit Jesus down for a personal interview, for in the Gospels he tells us everything we need to know about his identity, purposes, and accomplishments. In this chapter we will examine Scripture passages in which Jesus describes himself as or shows himself to be God the Son, the Messiah, the Good Shepherd, and the Great Physician.

By reading the four Gospels, anyone can meet Jesus Christ and learn vital biographical facts about his life.

In the Gospels we read Jesus' confessions about his origin and destination, his family and his beliefs, his purposes and crowning achievements.

Jesus Is God the Son

Modern people commonly doubt or even deny that Jesus claimed to be God. Their image of Jesus is one of a great moral sage who went around teaching people to love one another and get along. Far from drawing attention to himself, they suppose he only meant to spread love for humanity through acts of service and sacrifice. While it is certainly true that Jesus loved humanity and upheld the necessity of serving others, it is absolutely insupportable to say that he made no grand claims about himself. All the earliest biographical books about Jesus

All the earliest biographical books about Jesus affirm that he claimed to be nothing less than God's own divine Son. affirm that he claimed to be nothing less than God's own divine Son. We will examine 14 such teachings in the following pages.

Jesus came from the Father. Jesus was constantly embroiled in controversy because of his distinctive teachings and works of power. People either loved him or hated him (or both), and the crowds often narrowed the whole situation down to the question of origin: Where did Jesus come from? On one occasion he answered them in the following way: "You know Me and you know where I am from. Yet I have not come on My own, but the One who sent Me is true. You don't know Him; I know Him because I am from Him, and He sent Me" (John 7:28–29). This response might seem a touch vague to untrained modern eyes, but Jesus' original audience certainly caught his drift. They understood him to say that in one sense he was from Nazareth, as they well knew, but that in another sense he was also *from God.* Angered by such an audacious claim, the crowd tried to seize Jesus for an impromptu execution (vv. 25, 30).

Jesus was often threatened with death because of his claims to deity.

Jesus returned to the Father. After the crowd failed to kill Jesus for claiming to be from heaven, the chief priests and Pharisees deployed the temple police in a bid to arrest him for blasphemy (John 7:32). Jesus stood down the advancing patrolmen with the following statement: "I am only with you for a short time. Then I'm going to the One who sent Me. You will look for Me, but you will not find Me; and where I am, you cannot come" (vv. 33–34). The arrest party was unsure what to make of this. Some suggested Jesus meant he was planning to flee the opposition he faced in Israel by running off to join the

The Ascension by Tintoretto. Jesus ascended to heaven enveloped in clouds as the disciples gaped at him.

Jews who had dispersed into Greek-flavored cities such as Alexandria in Northern Egypt. Perhaps those Jews, who were a bit more liberal in their thinking, would be more receptive to his radical message and personal claims. In any case the arrest party must have felt his emigration would solve their problems. Let him go pester someone else! But of course this was not Jesus' meaning. In keeping with his teaching from a few verses earlier, Jesus meant he was on a trajectory to reenter his place of origin: heaven. Quite a claim! In the age before rockets and airships, no man could fake such an ascension. How would he pull it off? As it turns out, we have multiple attestations that Jesus did in fact ascend to heaven. In both his Gospel and his book about the church's earliest days, Luke reports that Jesus ascended to heaven enveloped in clouds as the disciples gaped at him (Luke 24:50–53; Acts 1:4–11). Thus God the Son returned home, proving that heaven was his true place of origin.

We have multiple attestations that Jesus did in fact ascend to heaven.

Jesus is coequal to the Father. One of the most breathtaking things Jesus ever said came at a time when threats had grown up all around him. Soon he would be arrested, killed, and friendless. Jesus foretold that even strong-willed, immovable Peter would wilt under pressure and deny knowing him (John 13:36–38). It must have seemed to the disciples that everything they believed in had failed. Sensing their broken spirits, Jesus reassured them with words that demonstrated his equality with God. "Your heart must not be troubled," he told them. "Believe in God; believe also in Me" (14:1). This would be utter blasphemy for anyone except God the Son.

Jesus backed his right to commission the disciples to take the gospel to the world by saying, "All authority has been given to Me in heaven and on earth."

Later, in another demonstration of his coequality with the Father, Jesus backed his right to commission the disciples to take the gospel to the world by saying, "All authority has been given to Me in heaven and on earth" (Matt 28:18). None but God can wield such authority.

Jesus bore the Father's authority. The skeptics who listened to Jesus often questioned the authority of his teachings and miracles. They took him to be a blasphemous conjuror and sought to scare people away from listening to him. In answer to this sort of thing, Jesus once cried out, "The one who believes in Me believes not in Me, but in Him who sent Me. And the one who sees Me sees Him who sent Me" (John 12:44–45). Similarly, "If you know Me, you will also know My Father. From now on you do know Him and have seen Him" (14:7). By such statements Jesus did not mean to conflate his personal identity into the Father's such that no distinction could be drawn between Father and Son, nor did he mean to say God sometimes appears as Father and at other

The Triqueta has traditionally been used to represent the Trinity. God the Father, God the Son, and God the Holy Spirit are three persons united in one divine essence. Image © 2007 Petr Sládek.

times as Son. The Father and Son are two persons unified in one divine nature. Their identities are unmixed and both exist simultaneously forever. What Jesus *did* mean is that he is from the Father, that he carries out the Father's will, and that he shares divinity equally with the Father.

Jesus is eternal. On one of the many occasions when detractors were questioning Jesus' identity, someone called out, "Aren't we right in saying that You're a Samaritan and have a demon?" (John 8:48). Samaritans were despised by Jews because they had mixed several different religions, forsaking the one true God. To be Samaritan was to be a compromiser, an unbeliever. In reply to these charges, Jesus said he had no demon and that anyone who kept his word would never die. This sparked off an incredulous response. Even the best teachers in Jewish history had not produced immortal pupils! "Are You greater than our father Abraham who died? Even the prophets died. Who do You pretend to be?" (v. 53).

Samaritans at Jacob's Well. Mount Gerizim, in the background, served then and now as the Samaritan center of worship rather than the temple at Jerusalem. The Samaritans were viewed as compromisers by the Jews because they mixed several different religious streams.

This was a nicely laid trap. As father of all Jews and the man with whom God established his covenant, Abraham was the most venerated figure in Jewish history. He walked with God, made treaties with him, enjoyed unparalleled blessings, and yet he died, same as everyone else. If a man as great as Abraham could not evade death or teach his descendants such an art, how could Jesus claim this ability? For this reason Jesus' enemies sought to highlight his claim of superiority over Abraham, for it would ruin his credibility among devout Jews. But Jesus was cleverer than they supposed. His carefully crafted answer paid respect to Abraham

If a man as great as Abraham could not evade death or teach his descendants such an art, how can Jesus claim this ability?

and yet left no doubt as to his superiority over the ancient patriarch. Here is what Jesus said in John 8:54–56:

> If I glorify Myself, My glory is nothing. My Father—you say about Him, "He is our God"—He is the One who glorifies Me. You've never known Him, but I know Him. If I were to say I don't know Him, I would be a liar like you. But I do know Him, and I keep His word. Your father Abraham was overjoyed that he would see My day; he saw it and rejoiced.

By this answer Jesus claimed to know God the Father, receive glory from him, and obey his word; but he also said that Abraham, to whom God revealed many secrets, saw Messiah's day coming (meaning his ministry and purpose) and rejoiced

Abraham by Molnar. Abraham, to whom God revealed many secrets, saw Messiah's day coming and rejoiced over it.

over it. Keep in mind that Abraham lived in the third millennium BC, something like 2,500 years prior to the date on which Jesus addressed this crowd of skeptics. This presented an obvious problem. How could Jesus know what ancient Abraham had or had not seen? Certainly the Bible never reports Abraham as saying anything about Messiah. And so the crowd said to Jesus, "You aren't 50 years old yet, and You've seen Abraham?" (v. 57). A very sensible retort! Jesus, who was roughly 30 years old, could not have walked with Abraham two dozen centuries ago. How would Jesus talk his way out of this one? By telling a most unusual truth, of course. "I assure you: Before Abraham was, I am" (v. 58). This response sent his opponents to their knees—not to worship but to gather stones. It's an obscure statement to modern readers, but the Jews recognized that Jesus had mimicked the words God used when he told Moses to return to Egypt, seek out the Hebrews, and tell them, "I AM has sent me to you" (Exod 3:14). Jesus' answer also recalled passages from Isaiah in which God disclosed ageless facts of his

Jesus said, "I assure you: Before Abraham was, I am."

identity. "I am He. No god was formed before Me, and there will be none after Me. . . . I am He alone, and no one can take anything from My hand. I act, and who can reverse it? . . . I am He; I am the first, I am also the last" (Isa 43:10,13; 48:12). Jesus intentionally mimicked this kind of language so his claims to divinity would be clear and embedded in the biblical tradition. The point was not lost on the crowd. They attempted to stone him for heresy but were thwarted because Jesus "was hidden and went out of the temple complex" (John 8:59). According to the divine plan it was not yet time for the eternal "I am" to die for the people.

Jesus has supernatural knowledge. God knows all things past, present, and future. This fact runs throughout the Bible. For instance, King David said, "Before a word is on my tongue, You know all about it, LORD" (Ps 139:4). Through Isaiah the Lord proclaimed, "I declare the end from the beginning, and from long ago what is not yet done, saying: My plan will take place, and I will do all My will" (Isa 46:10). Theologians call this divine ability *omniscience*, a word that literally means "all knowledge." God simultaneously comprehends every fact in every place in every age past, present, and future.

God simultaneously comprehends every fact in every place in every age past, present, and future.

As the Son of God who took on genuine human existence and submitted to the Father who sent him, we ought not to expect that Jesus went around dropping supernatural knowledge on everyone. It seems that in some matters the incarnate Son of God chose to yield his divine right to know, such that the Father alone exercised or made use of the unqualified omniscience that each member of the Trinity has shared equally from all eternity (see Matt 24:36). Nonetheless Jesus on several occasions demonstrated the possession of supernatural knowledge. A good example is when he called Nathanael to be his disciple. When Nathanael met Jesus for the first time, Jesus already knew about him—not just his name, profession, or place of residence but details about the hidden things of the heart. "Here is a true Israelite; no deceit is in him," Jesus said as Nathanael approached (John 1:47). Nathanael was perplexed at this announcement, just as you would be if a stranger called out secret details of your life as you strode down the sidewalk. When Nathanael asked Jesus how he knew these things, Jesus answered, "Before Philip called you, when you were under the fig tree, I saw you" (v. 48). Here "saw" does not mean Jesus looked with his eyes. Even if Nathanael had been camped out under a nearby

Jesus by Martini.

tree, allowing Jesus to take a good long look before meeting him, such benefit would not have given Jesus information about Nathanael's spiritual life. Thus "saw" means something more like "knew and comprehended in a supernatural way."

> *Nathanael replied to Jesus, "Rabbi, You are the Son of God! You are the King of Israel!"*

Nathanael realized this immediately. For this reason he replied to Jesus, "Rabbi, You are the Son of God! You are the King of Israel!" (v. 49).

Jesus never sinned. God alone is without sin. Due to the corruption of humanity in Adam and Eve's fatal choice, all humans are born in sin and bear that reality out by making choices that contradict God's moral will. God the Son is the lone exception. He took on our flesh but not our sin nature. Since our sin nature is a *fact* of the human condition but not a *necessity* for being genuinely human, Jesus can be truly human and yet not share in our native spiritual corruption. He staked this claim indirectly by asking in John 8:46, "Who among you can convict Me of sin?" No one stepped forward to do so, and Jesus knew they could not. He was not a sinner. Everything we know

All humans are born in sin and bear that reality out by making choices that contradict God's moral will.

about Jesus from the Gospels and the rest of the New Testament writings agrees with this conclusion. Jesus could not be an acceptable sacrifice to the Father on our behalf if he had sinned at any point in his life. Convinced of this, Peter affirmed of Jesus, "He did not commit sin, and no deceit was found in His mouth" (1 Pet 2:22).

Jesus is Lord of the Sabbath. By God's command the Sabbath, which the Jews celebrated on Saturday, is a day on which humans are to rest and reflect on the works of God in creation. To ensure that people really did rest, in Jesus' day all sorts of rules defined what actions were and were not permissible during Sabbath. Some of these rules genuinely came from God; others were the creations of men. As Jesus explained it, the rules that were from God were couched in a spirit of grace, but the Pharisees misunderstood these matters and made Sabbath law into a rigid system that suppressed rather than refreshed God's followers. Thus when Jesus and his disciples walked through a

Jesus in the Fields by Olivier. When Jesus and his disciples walked through a grain field on the Sabbath, the Pharisees threw themselves into an uproar when they saw them picking heads of grain as they passed along. To pharisaical eyes this looked like work, not Sabbath rest.

grain field on the Sabbath, the Pharisees threw themselves into an uproar when they saw them picking heads of grain as they passed along. To pharisaical eyes this looked like *work*, not Sabbath rest. In response to their charges, Jesus gave several Old Testament examples of Sabbath-law lenience. These demonstrate that "the Sabbath was made for man and not man for the Sabbath" (Mark 2:27). Jesus went on to say, "If you had known what this means: 'I desire mercy and not sacrifice,' you would not have condemned the innocent [for casually picking the heads of grain during a Sabbath stroll]. For the Son of Man is Lord of the Sabbath" (Matt 12:7–8). Since the Sabbath was an ordinance of God (Exod 20:8–11), Jesus' claim to be Lord of the Sabbath counts as an unveiled claim to being God.

Jesus has life in himself. Jesus promised his disciples they would live forever. "Anyone who hears My word and believes Him who sent Me has eternal life and will not come under judgment but has passed from death to life" (John 5:24). The question naturally arises, Can Jesus deliver on this promise? His next sentences provide the answer. "I assure you: An hour is coming, and is now here, when the dead will hear the voice of the Son of God, and those who hear will live. For just as the Father has life in Himself, so also He

> *Jesus said, "I assure you: An hour is coming, and is now here, when the dead will hear the voice of the Son of God, and those who hear will live.*

has granted to the Son to have life in Himself" (vv. 25–27). The power of life and death is God's alone. Jesus, who as the eternal Son of God is fully equal to the Father but willingly subordinate to him in his assignments, says the Father has granted him the right to have life in himself. This offers us a remarkable glimpse at the inner life of the Trinity. The divine Son chooses to submit to the Father, and the Father freely bestows on his humble Son the right to wield and exercise the choicest prerogative of divinity: the gift of life itself.

Jesus testifies about himself. When we speak about important topics, we often appeal to expert opinion to back our claims. In this way our words are seen as having higher authority because we have cited someone above us. Jesus did not speak this way. Instead, he always spoke as if he himself were the authority. When he taught about himself in this way, his enemies saw an opportunity to undermine him. "You are testifying about Yourself. Your testimony is not valid," said the Pharisees (John 8:13). This was a reasonable objection on the face of it. After all, Jesus was a human claiming also to be God and to bear divine authority. As Jesus explained in his response, the validity of his self-attestations rested on the issue of origins: where did he come from? Here is how he explained it: "Even if I testify about Myself, My testimony is valid, because I know where I came from and where I'm going. But you

Jesus in the Synagogue by Doré.

don't know where I come from or where I'm going. . . . Even in your law it is written that the witness of two men is valid. I am the One who testifies about Myself, and the Father who sent Me testifies about Me" (vv. 14,17–18).

Then and now Jesus knows who he is, and the Father joins him in testifying to the Son's divinity.

Jesus forgives sins. God alone can forgive sins. You and I may forgive one another, erasing offenses and healing hurts, but ultimately it is not our right to pardon sin or sinners because it is not *our nature* that sin has offended. Rather, sin

God personally must be appeased even if no human holds your sins against you.

is an attack on God's holy nature. For this reason you and I may announce to someone, "I forgive you for your sin against me," but we can never take it upon ourselves to say, "Your sins are forgiven," since this would imply that the sinner has been granted good standing with God. God personally must be appeased even if no human holds your sins against you. With these facts in mind, please notice that Jesus openly spoke of forgiving sins. When a paralyzed man was brought to him on a stretcher by thoughtful friends, the Lord said, "Have courage, son, your sins are forgiven" (Matt 9:2). Some scribes were standing nearby. When they heard Jesus announcing pardon for sins, they said, "He's blaspheming!" (v. 3). They were dead right . . . unless Jesus happens to be God. In response Jesus noted that it is far easier to say, "Your sins are forgiven," than to say, "Get up and walk," to a paralyzed man. Why? Because anyone can *say*, "Your sins are forgiven," but actually having the power to make it so is another matter entirely. To demonstrate that he did indeed have the divine right to forgive sins, Jesus next told the

The Paralyzed Man Let Down Through the Roof by Tissot. To demonstrate that he had the right to forgive sins, Jesus told the paralytic to pick up his stretcher and go home (Matt 9:6).

paralytic, "Get up, pick up your stretcher, and go home" (v. 6). When the man obeyed, everyone recognized it as a divine work. To eyes of faith, this episode proved that Jesus truly had the right as God's Son to forgive sins.

Jesus accepts and even requires worship. We all like to be appreciated. Hail me as a hero or a rare genius, and I'll love you forever. But if you bow at my feet and make offerings, I'll run from you or beat you back with a hardwood stick. In the Gospels we find many situations in which the disciples or others worshipped Jesus or ascribed to him titles of deity. Never

Jesus received worship and the ascription of diety. In fact he found such things fitting and even necessary.

once did Jesus correct them. He instead found such things fitting and even necessary. For instance, as he entered Jerusalem for his final Passover, the crowds praised him. The Pharisees looked on and said,

"Teacher, rebuke Your disciples," but Jesus replied, "I tell you, if they were to keep silent, the stones would cry out!" (Luke 19:39–40). Call it a law of the universe: God the Son *must* be praised. If people should fail to meet this requirement, the creation itself will call out praises to its Maker. Fortunately not all humans failed to recognize Jesus' right to receive worship. The wise men worshipped him as a young child (Matt 2:2), Nathanael called Jesus "the Son of God" after seeing proof of his supernatural knowledge (John 1:49), a boatload of terrified disciples worshipped Jesus during a storm (Matt 14:33), and Thomas said, "My Lord and My God!"

Herod's Gate in Jerusalem, 1910. Jesus said stones would cry out praises to him if the people didn't openly worship him.

once his final doubts were overturned by the risen Lord (John 20:28).

Jesus says our fate rests in his hands. If you came to dislike me, I might try to talk you out of it or offer evidences against your assessment; but at the end of the day, not much hangs on your opinion of me. Your life will get on just fine even if you are completely mistaken about what sort of person I am. Not so with Jesus. Everything of lasting importance hangs on the balance of what we think of Jesus and how we respond to his teachings. In this vein Jesus once said:

> *Everything of lasting importance hangs on the balance of what we think of Jesus and how we respond to his teachings.*

"Everyone who will acknowledge Me before men, I will also acknowledge him before My Father in heaven. But whoever denies Me before men, I will also deny him before My Father in heaven" (Matt 10:32–33). In other words, your decision about God the Son has direct bearing on what sort of reception you receive from God the Father. Why? Because it is the Son who mediates between you and the Father. We sinners cannot approach the Father except through the Son who became human so he could represent us before holy God. In this light our allegiance to Jesus must outpace everything else. "The person who loves father or mother

Your fate rests in Christ's hands. Have you received him by faith?

more than Me is not worthy of Me; the person who loves son or daughter more than Me is not worthy of Me" (v. 37). Finally, Jesus also said, "If you do not believe that I am He, you will die in your sins" (John 8:24). Your fate rests in Christ's hands. Have you received him by faith?

Jesus' prayer for himself reveals his deity. John 17:1–5 records the first segment of one of the last prayers Jesus uttered while on earth. It is nothing less than a confessional anthem to the deity of God's Son.

Father, the hour has come. Glorify Your Son so that the Son may glorify You, for You gave Him authority over all flesh; so He may give eternal life to all You have given Him. This is eternal life: that they may know You, the only true God, and the One You have sent—Jesus Christ. I have glorified You on the earth by completing the work You gave Me to do. Now, Father, glorify Me in Your presence with that glory I had with You before the world existed.

We could justifiably spend the rest of this book unpacking these five verses. Impoverished for space, we take a narrower focus and highlight only the final statement: "Now, Father, glorify Me in Your presence with that glory I had with You before the world existed." If we could trace a history of the Son's life based on this testimony, we would say that he had eternally shared glory with the Father in heaven, that he chose to veil (not shed) this glory and descend to earth, taking on the form of a lowly human servant, and that at the end of his

Near the end of his life, Jesus requested a return to the Father where he would again enjoy undimmed manifestation of deity's full-orbed glory.

duties he requested a return to the Father where he would again enjoy undimmed manifestation of deity's full-orbed glory.

Conclusion

We have examined 14 of Jesus' teachings that demonstrate he claimed to be God. In response to his teachings, many people took him at his word and thus followed him by faith, but many others rejected his claims and took him to be a blasphemer. Neither result—that some worshipped him while others branded him a blasphemer worthy of death—makes sense unless Jesus did in fact claim to be God the Son, as the New Testament reveals time and time again.

Christ and the Tribute by Massaccio. The New Testament leaves no room for doubt: Jesus claimed to be God.

Jesus Is Messiah

On what basis do Christians say Jesus was (and is) Messiah? If this identification became obvious to Jesus' earliest followers, why didn't the rest of the Jews agree and follow Christ as Lord and Savior? In this section we review three key evidences that demonstrate that Jesus is God's Messiah.

Jesus accepted identification as God the Messiah. Pious Jews of the first century anxiously awaited the Messiah promised by God. Opinions were mixed as to what Messiah would be like and what exactly he would accomplish, but few if any Jews imagined he would be God incarnate and that he would suffer rejection and death on behalf of sinners. Jesus' disciples, piece by piece, came to learn otherwise about Messiah. They

Peter by Nogari. Peter burned away the fog by saying, "You are the Messiah, the Son of the living God!" (Matt 16:16).

walked and talked with him daily for several years. They were slow learners because they were sinners with minds dulled to spiritual truth but also because they inherited a religious paradigm that needed a little rearranging. When the light finally started to break through on them, Peter made the grandest confession in all of Scripture. Jesus wanted to know who people thought he was. After the disciples reviewed some popular misidentifications,

Peter burned away the fog by saying, "You are the Messiah, the Son of the living God!" (Matt 16:16). This was a bold move since it went against the grain of so many expectations about Messiah, but it was a dare worth taking. Jesus rewarded Peter's confession by saying, "Simon son of Jonah, you are blessed because flesh and blood did not reveal this to you, but My Father in heaven" (v. 17). In other words: Peter's knowledge was too high to be of human origin. He

Peter's knowledge was too high to be of human origin. He knew Jesus as divine Messiah and Son of God because God the Father had implanted that conviction in his heart.

knew Jesus as divine Messiah and Son of God because God the Father had implanted that conviction in his heart.

Jesus fulfilled the Father's will. Jesus did not come to start a new religion. As Messiah, he came to *fulfill* that which was revealed in the Old Testament, not overturn it (Matt 5:17–20). For this reason Christianity is not a departure from the historic Jewish faith but is instead its proper extension, accomplished by God himself. As Jesus once explained to the disciples, "My food is to do the will of Him who sent Me and to finish His work" (John 4:34). This last phrase is particularly interesting, for Jesus himself is the completion of God's work. All of God's promises for redemption are completed only in Christ. The animal and grain offerings, the priesthood and their sacred rituals, the idealization of David's kingship, the renowned wisdom of Solomon, the piercing words of condemnation and hope uttered by God's prophets—all of these shadows were fulfilled in the substance: Christ himself. When Jesus came to accomplish this, he did so in glad submission to the Father's will. "I assure you: The Son is not able to do anything on His own, but only what He sees the Father doing. For whatever the Father does, the Son also does these things in the same way" (John 5:19). This union of will and purpose between Father and Son is one reason Jesus can say, "Anyone who does not honor the Son does not honor the Father who sent Him" (v. 23).

> *Jesus did not come to start a new religion. As Messiah, he came to fulfill that which was revealed in the Old Testament, not overturn it.*

> *Christianity is not a departure from the historic Jewish faith but is instead its proper extension, accomplished by God himself.*

Jesus not only followed the example he had seen in his Father; he also taught in alliance with the Father's teaching. "My teaching isn't Mine but is from the One who sent Me" (John 7:16). Ironically, fidelity to the Father's teaching thrust Jesus into harm's way. Just as the prophets were despised and persecuted in olden days because of the unpopular truths they taught, Jesus' rough reception among the hard-hearted was a direct reflection of God's authentic voice speaking into darkness. But in some hearts the darkness parted. As Jesus claimed,

"Everyone who has listened to and learned from the Father comes to Me" (John 6:45).

Jesus is our Substitute. As Messiah, Jesus came to lay his life down on behalf of sinners (John 10:11). This was a purposeful but merely temporary surrender to the court of human injustice. "This is why the Father loves Me, because I am laying down My life so I may take it up again. No one takes it from Me, but I lay it down on my own . . . and I have the right to take it up again. I have received this command from My Father" (John 10:17–18). Jesus was steadfastly committed to his death mission, but his followers would have kept him from completing it if they could have had their way. For instance, when Jesus began explaining to the disciples that he would die for the people, Peter seized his arm and led him aside for a private rebuke. "Oh no, Lord! This will never happen to You!" (Matt 16:22). Though it was understandable that Peter would instinctively object to a dying Messiah, Jesus had no tolerance for such interference. "Get behind Me, Satan!" he said. "You are an offence to Me because you're not thinking about God's concerns, but man's" (v. 23). The gravity

Christ Before Pilate from the Rossano Gospels. Jesus temporarily surrendered to the court of human injustice.

of Jesus' response does not make sense unless you first understand the gravity of his appointment with death. It is well for us that Jesus took his death duty so seriously, for as he says, "Unless a grain of wheat falls into the ground and dies, it remains by itself. But if it dies, it produces a large crop" (John 12:24). And again, "As for Me, if I am lifted up from the earth [on a cross] I will draw all people to Myself" (v. 32). Salvation would be impossible if the Son had not chosen to fall to earth and die as the seed from which grows our redemption, nor could the cross save us if it had never supported the frame of God's own Son—a willing sacrificial victim who let nothing get between himself and the death he came to accomplish.

Jesus Is the Great Physician

Jesus came to heal the spiritually ill. Early in his ministry Jesus created a stir among the religious set by hanging around sinners and ill reputes, even dining with them in the intimacy of their homes. Seeing this, the Pharisees asked Jesus' disciples, "Why does your Teacher eat with tax collectors and sinners?" (Matt 9:11). As with many of their questions, there was a certain reasonableness to this query. After all, Jewish Scripture warned, "Don't set foot on the path of the wicked; don't proceed in the way of evil ones" (Prov 4:14). Did Jesus share the low morals of his dining club? The Pharisees suspected so, but in reality Jesus came among the spiritually ill as a Great Physician to whom the disease of sin could not cling, and he came intent on practicing the art of mercy among those whom the self-righteous had forsaken as lost causes. As Jesus explained to the Pharisees, "Those who are well don't need a doctor,

Jesus created a stir among the religious set by hanging around sinners and ill reputes.

but the sick do. Go and learn what this means: I desire mercy and not sacrifice. For I didn't come to call the righteous, but sinners" (Matt 9:12–13). This is a remarkable fact. Think of the times you have been ill and have gone to the doctor. Doctors must possess special fortitude and compassion, for each day they touch, examine, and speak with people who have communicable illnesses. They are in harm's way each day they go to work. Additionally, they must clean and patch grotesque wounds. Now consider Jesus. As God's own Son in human

Jesus came among the spiritually ill as a Great Physician to whom the disease of sin could not cling.

flesh, Jesus was not only sinless; he was the total *antithesis* to sin. Rebellion against God's will was unthinkable and repulsive to him, and yet he waded into the sea of stricken sinners and did not flinch as he touched them, probed their spiritual and physical diseases, spoke with them, ate with them, and invited them to forsake lifestyles of death and follow him to godliness and life.

Jesus healed many physically ill people. God the Son did not come to earth primarily to set broken bones, align warped spines, revive deadened nerves, or gift the blind with sight. He came instead to mend the permanent and universally ailing part of human beings: the soul. However, as our Maker and brother, Jesus had great compassion for those who suffered physical afflictions. We learn a lot about God by this, and Jesus himself said his works offered windows into his divine nature (John 10:25). For this reason we can say that every

healing miracle in the Gospels gives us a look into God's heart. Consider his heart for the widow who, in addition to the sorrows of losing her husband, suffered the death of her only son, an adult who was likely her sole hope for provision. The widow and the locals were in a procession heading for the burial grounds when Jesus came along. She

Jesus Raising the Son of the Widow at Nain by Tissot. Jesus raised a widow's son from the dead (Luke 7:11–17).

was a stranger to him, as was everyone there, and yet Jesus was moved with compassion. "Don't cry," he gently told her, and then he ordered the dead man to live again (Luke 7:13–14). The corpse had no will to obey, of course, and dead men do not hear even the sternest commands. Even so, this widow's son obeyed, and great fear fell on everyone as he sat up in his coffin. They also glorified God for his mercies to a woman whose prospects had been so bleak. Here is the heart of God. Bitter winds blow against every life, but in Christ God showed that the destitute are not forgotten. Christians have a high and serious charge to follow Christ's example by serving the weak and weary.

Every healing miracle in the Gospels gives us a look into God's heart.

There is another aspect to God's heart for the ill and lame that should give us great pause. The Bible assures us that God exercises sovereign governance over the universe, and yet we often fall into thinking of illnesses and disabilities as chance

Bitter winds blow against every life, but in Christ God showed that the destitute are not forgotten.

happenings that God has let slip through his net. Alternatively, one sometimes hears that all such afflictions are sent by the devil and they would clear away if only we prayed enough or believed enough. Finally, a great many people suspect that illnesses (except their own?) are evidence that God is dealing out punishment. None of these theories adequately reflect reality; the truth is more complicated than they allow and also a good deal more comforting if we are willing to humble ourselves before God and trust his wisdom.

A powerful illustration of this subject is found in John 9, where Jesus and his disciples passed by a roadside beggar who was born blind. The disciples wanted to know who had sinned to make the man suffer blindness. His parents? The man himself before he was born? It seems the disciples went in for the second theory above: affliction is divine punishment. After assuring them that sin was not the cause of the man's blindness, Jesus said something remarkable: "This came about so that God's works might be displayed in him" (John 9:3).

Jesus Healing the Blind by Duccio. Jesus said the beggar's blindness allowed the works of God to be displayed.

What did Jesus mean by "God's works" being on display? Primarily he meant the man's blindness became a platform for showing forth God's works of power when Jesus healed him by the roadside (vv. 6–12). A lifetime of blindness (and the suffering that attended it) as preparation for a flash-bang show of God's power? Can such a thing be fair and good? In

God's economy, yes. Consider two points: First, few people in history have ever been touched by God in so special a way as this sightless man. After he met Jesus, do you suppose he would have traded the long darkness he had lived through for sight from birth? Absolutely not. It was his blindness and long suffering that primed him to be the object of Jesus' special care and taught him how deeply he should appreciate that care. Extending the argument to include all believers who suffer from debilitations, we may suggest that at the resurrection all Christians who have suffered disability and debilitating illness will realize that their sufferings have been worthwhile when the Son heals them in a way the able-bodied shall not experience.

Few people in history have ever been touched by God in so special a way as this sightless man.

They will experience an "uplift" that is unparalleled among the children of God who never suffered these conditions. In my experience, believers who suffer from bad health find this argument persuasive and encouraging. Second, God's values are the highest possible values. This is because he is the highest good in the universe and serves as the only standard for measuring morality. We are tempted to find it dissatisfactory, but the simple truth is that God does what he wants and he is always pure, holy, and right in doing so.

We are tempted to find it dissatisfactory, but the simple truth is that God does what he wants and he is always pure, holy, and right in doing so.

Thus God's choice to bestow disability on this (or any) person for the purpose of displaying his good works is justified even if humans struggle to understand or accept it.

None of this should be taken to mean that God delights in human illness or disability. Far from it. Ours is a fallen world, and we are a sinful race set against our Maker. As a result we are under God's curse. In such a context God ordains and permits things that do not reflect his best hopes for earthly life, but *we* have cut ourselves off from those best hopes by our sins. And so people of faith look to God for the mercies he grants in his Son, Jesus Christ. Some sufferings God will choose to alleviate in this lifetime; others will not be overthrown until all things are made new in the eternal kingdom. Either way, it is the heart of God to heal his children, as Messiah powerfully displayed at a son's funeral and a dusty roadside in the holy land.

Some sufferings God will chose to alleviate in this lifetime; others will not be overthrown until all things are made new in the eternal kingdom.

Jesus Is the Good Shepherd

Jesus is protective of his sheep. Sheep are not very bright animals. Untended, they will wander into dangers or become lost. We like to think we differ from sheep. Certainly we are smarter, but we stray into wolf packs and hostile lands just as easily. The prophet Isaiah, a man who beheld the glory and presence of God as no other man in history, described our stray spirituality in this way: "We all went astray like sheep; we all have turned to our own way" (Isa 53:6). Jesus came among us as the Good Shepherd, God in human flesh sent to guard and

guide us through life's journey. As for sheep that persist in going astray, what view does Jesus take of them? If he were much like you and me, I imagine he might say, "Fine, have it your way. But don't call for me when the wolves

The prophet Isaiah said, "We all went astray like sheep; we all have turned to our own way" (Isa 53:6).

nip at you." Fortunately Jesus is more compassionate and protective than this. He once told a parable that reveals his heart for lost sheep. Here is how Luke reports it (15:4–7):

What man among you, who has 100 sheep and loses one of them, does not leave the 99 in the open field and go after the lost one until he finds it? When he has found it, he joyfully puts it on his shoulders, and coming home, he calls his friends and neighbors together, saying to them, "Rejoice with me, because I have found my lost sheep!" I tell you, in the same way, there will be more joy in heaven over one sinner who repents than over 99 righteous people who don't need repentance.

Matthew indicates (18:1–14) that Jesus told this parable moments after the disciples asked who was the greatest in the kingdom of heaven. They were expecting to notch their own names high up on the board. In response to this, Jesus summoned a child and had him stand in their midst. He then explained that true greatness in God's kingdom comes to the one who adopts childlike humility. He also said that whoever leads such a humble follower of Christ astray is marked out for severe condemnation. In fact, "it would be better for him if a heavy millstone were hung around his neck and he were drowned in the depths of the sea!" (v. 6). Better to drown in uncharted depths than to teach false beliefs and crooked paths to a follower of Christ? Yes. It is not merely for show that shepherds carry a staff. When wolves come against the sheep, a sharp whack on the aggressor's nose pre-

Palestinian women milling flour, 1895.

serves the flock unharmed. Jesus wields his staff for the same purpose. As our Good Shepherd, Jesus is committed to guiding us safely to pastures that lie beyond this world's horizon. Anyone who comes against us on the journey shall suffer for it, for Jesus is the Shepherd who seeks out his lost sheep and lays his life on the line for their protection (John 10:11).

Jesus is the only true Shepherd. The world has no lack of self-appointed spiritual guides. They arise in every age and every land. In our day they span the entire globe via television, Internet, and podcasts. They write best-selling books and go on talk shows to receive praise for their insights on divinity. Which of them should you follow? Whom can you trust? Jesus taught that there is great danger in following such people. "I assure you: Anyone who doesn't enter the sheep pen by the door

As our Good Shepherd, Jesus is committed to guiding us safely to pastures that lie beyond this world's horizon.

but climbs in some other way, is a thief and a robber" (John 10:1). As followers of Christ, we must train our ears (by Scripture reading and cultivation of the Christlike life) so that only the voice of the true Shepherd prompts our obedience. Other voices will only mislead us. The one true Shepherd says, "I am the way, the truth, and the life. No one comes to the Father except through Me" (14:6).

Art from the catacomb of Domatilla showing Jesus as the Good Shepherd, c. AD 200. Jesus said, "I am the way, the truth, and the life. No one comes to the Father except through Me."

Jesus provides for his sheep. Finally, Jesus said that as our Good Shepherd he came among us to fill our lives with goodness. "I have come that they may have life and have it in abundance" (John 10:10). The Christian life is not meant to be austere and joyless, nor does God abandon us to the scrummage and tell us to tough it out on our own strength. He is with us as a God who provides. Jesus twice demonstrated this by filling a throng of empty bellies with fish and bread (Matt 14:13–21; 15:32–39). On the occasion of the first feeding, Jesus had taken a boat out onto the waters in search of solitude. He had just learned that John the Baptist had been beheaded by Herod, a descendant of the man who had sought to kill him as a toddler in Bethlehem 30 years earlier. A great mass of people, totaling 5,000 men and an undetermined number of women and children, ventured out past the villages and gathered on the remote shore in anticipation of Jesus' return. They too felt the sting of John's murder. He had been a beloved prophet and a sign of God's renewed involvement with Israel. Grieving as a community of God's faithful, they searched for Jesus in hopes that he could offer words of comfort. As for Jesus, he had known of John and his special calling from childhood since John was the son of Mary's relative, Elizabeth, and of course it was John who had baptized Jesus and served as herald to introduce his ministry. A great one had fallen among the Jews. None felt it more keenly than Messiah.

> *The Christian life is not meant to be austere and joyless, nor does God abandon us to the scrummage and tell us to tough it out on our own strength.*

When Jesus returned to shore, he felt compassion for the crowds. Some of the people were sick. When they were put forward for Jesus' consideration, he healed them as lake waters rhythmically lapped the shore behind him. The sun fell westward. Jesus' focus was on the people, and so his disciples pointed out that it was getting late and they were deep in the backcountry. "Send the crowds away so they can go into the village and buy food for themselves," they suggested, for no one had come prepared to tarry so long (Matt 14:15). Jesus answered that there was no need of this. "You give them something to eat," he said (v. 16). The disciples replied that only two fish and five

A mosaic from the Church of the Multiplication of the Loaves and Fishes in Taghba near where the miracle took place. Jesus took two fish and five loaves and multiplied them enough to feed 5,000 men and an undetermined number of women and children.

loaves of bread were on hand! After listening patiently to the inventory report, Jesus told the men to bring the food to him. In an event that has come to be called the "miracle of multiplication," Jesus said a prayer over the food and then began distributing it to his disciples, who in turn passed it into the crowds loaf by loaf, fish by fish in a delivery train that never halted until every man, woman, and child had been filled to satisfaction. Two fish had become thousands and the loaves more plentiful than a bakery could produce in several days. As if this were not remarkable enough, those who set out to gather the leftovers collected the equivalent of 12 basketfuls, which means the remainder was many times larger than the original supply had been. Jesus is the giver of abundance!

Conclusion

Jesus taught without reservation or ambiguity that he was God the Son, the Messiah promised long ago through the prophets. By his life and teachings, he proved that he had come among humans as a genuine man and a selfless divine Servant for the purpose of restoring us to God's good standing. He is willing. He is able. He is the one and only *As God the Father once proclaimed, "This is My Son, the Chosen One; listen to Him!"* Shepherd who can provide for our every need. As God the Father once proclaimed, "This is My Son, the Chosen One; listen to Him!" (Luke 9:35).

Chapter 16
The Kingdom Way

Early Christians called themselves followers of "the Way" (Acts 24:14) because Jesus proclaimed himself to be "the way, the truth, and the life" (John 14:6) and because his lifestyle and teachings showed what kind of life pleases God. In this chapter we use Matthew's Gospel as the primary guide to some of Jesus' key instructions for living life the Kingdom Way.

The Life God Blesses

How should we approach God? What kind of lifestyle invites his blessings? In this section we will examine what Jesus taught about successfully relating to God in our daily lives.

Fear and love. No matter how vigorously you stir them together, water and oil will not unite into a uniform liquid. This is because they are fundamentally different on the molecular level, which means they lack the appropriate gear for forming mutual

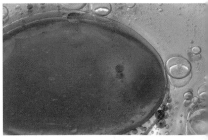

Water and oil do not mix. What about fear and love?

bonds. Put both in a mixer and set it to run full out until world's end, and still they will remain in disharmony.

We think of love and fear in the same way. Pour a draught of genuine fear into a relationship filled with love, and the harmony is wrecked, possibly forever. After all, love is a warm and peaceful feeling that draws us in whereas fear is cold, black, and repulsive. Love and fear mix like water and oil. Paradoxically, in our relationship with God, love and fear *belong* together. In fact, following Jesus' lead you could say they are inseparable.

Paradoxically, in our relationship with God, love and fear belong together.

Jesus once sent his disciples out on a tour to preach and heal, a sort of trial run for the lifelong mission he would give them after his resurrection. Before they left, he gave them instructions to guide their efforts. Knowing that they would face stiff opposition, one of the chief points Jesus made was that they should not be afraid of men. "Don't fear those who kill the body but are not able to kill the soul; rather, fear Him who is able to destroy both soul and body in hell" (Matt 10:28). By "fear" Jesus did not mean the Father is a dangerous, dark-orbed Being who plots our destruction; rather, he was referring to the need to hold God in reverential fear because God is holy, just, and infinitely powerful. To think of God as a doting old man so full of love and mercies that sins are only winked at is not only wrong but dangerous. Similarly, to live the Christian life timidly because you fear what unbelieving men and women might say is dangerous because it shows that you fear humankind more than humankind's Maker. Followers of Christ must not live this way. As the prophet Isaiah said, "It is the Lord of hosts whom you should regard as holy. And He shall be your fear, and He shall be your dread" (Isa 8:13 NASB). The man or woman who does not genuinely fear God cannot relate to him successfully.

To think of God as a doting old man so full of love and mercies that sins are only winked at is not only wrong but dangerous.

But fear is not the whole story, for fear without love fosters servitude, not heartfelt devotion. In what he dubbed "the greatest and most important commandment," Jesus taught that we should love God with all our being: "Love the Lord your God with all your heart, with all your soul, and with all your mind" (Matt 22:37–38). If other things reside in the deepest holds of your heart, your love for God needs expanding. What about the habits of your mind? Are your most favored and frequent contemplations Godward or merely earthward, centering on self or created things without reference to God? Jesus said the emotions of our hearts, the dispositions of our souls, and the trends of our minds should conform to the will of God, whom we must love above all.

> *If other things reside in the deepest holds of your heart, your love for God needs expanding.*

Practice secret righteousness. People who are very religious in an outwardly visible manner may be farther from God than you think. Loud public prayers that wind down florid lanes, showy offerings of money to church causes, sacrificial

The Pharisee and the Publican by Doré.

acts for the kingdom that become public knowledge with suspicious ease—all of these are signs that someone may be blowing trumpets. If you walk with Jesus through the Gospels, you will notice that this was a significant problem among his countrymen. Many of them had fallen into the trap of practicing public piety, which is a form of false religion. Not only does it fall short of true righteousness; it does not invite God's blessings (Matt 6:2). The same temptation haunts Christ's followers in every land and every age. For this reason Jesus taught that truly righteous persons are harder to identify because they make no show of their devotions. Therefore, if you wish to practice a righteousness blessed by God, learn the model Jesus endorsed: "When you give to the poor, don't let your left hand know what your right hand is doing, so that your giving may be in secret. And your Father who sees in secret will reward you" (vv. 3–4). Such is the power of secret righteousness.

Pray privately and persistently. The power of secrecy applies to prayer as well. Rather than ascending high platforms or cordoning off busy street corners for your prayer venues, Jesus asks that you put in a private appearance before God's throne. "When you pray, go into your private room, shut your door, and pray to your Father who sees in secret. And your Father who sees in secret will reward you" (Matt 6:6). Further, don't feel pressed to pray in endless repetition or exaggerated emotive streams because you believe God's atten-

"When you pray, go into your private room, shut your door, and pray to your Father who is in secret. And your Father who sees in secret will reward you" (Matt 6:6).

tion depends on your angst, your piety, or your word count. "When you pray, don't babble like the idolaters, since they imagine they'll be heard for their many words. Don't be like them, because your Father knows the things you need before you ask Him" (vv. 7–8). God is not like the make-believe pagan deities who were thought to suffer from short attention spans and chronic self-absorption. Rather, he is the caring Lord of your circumstances, and he has plumbed every depth of your heart before you even open it to him. Come to him by simple, earnest faith and make your requests known.

God is the caring Lord of your circumstances, and he has plumbed every depth of your heart before you even open it to him.

But note: this is no prohibition against long prayers or persistence. In fact, Jesus taught that dogged determination before God's throne is not only acceptable but effective. "Keep asking, and it will be given to you. Keep searching, and you will find. Keep knocking, and the door will be opened to you. For everyone who asks receives, and the one who searches finds, and to the one who knocks, the door will be opened" (7:7–8). Often it will open to answers you neither expected nor desired, but God knows best and your requests to him are never ignored.

Do not be anxious—Part I. If your health and safety are entrusted to me, your confidence in me (or lack of it) will determine your state of mind. If you think I am competent and resourceful, you will rest in the belief that your future is secured. On the other hand, if you doubt my abilities, you will most likely feel anxious about tomorrow and its many unknowns. Frankly, anxiety *should* be your *God is the author of the future; wisdom's path starts at his throne; and by the span of his hand the whole universe is measured.* outlook if I am responsible for your care. After all, I know very little of the future, I cannot always see wisdom's path, and the span of my hand measures mere inches—a limitation that renders me powerless to move heaven and earth on your behalf.

If instead of me it is *God* to whom your life is entrusted, your mind should shift onto a different track altogether. After all, God is the author of the future; wisdom's path starts at his throne; and by the span of his hand the whole universe is measured. For these reasons Jesus taught that God is fully reliable. If we make his will our highest priority and entrust all our needs to him, he will take care of us. "Seek first the kingdom of God and His righteousness, and all these things will be provided for you" (Matt 6:33).

Do not be anxious—Part II. There is a second common cause of anxiety: mislaid priorities. If someone mistook up for down and right for left his life would be an aimless mess, not to mention dangerous. In much the same way, mistaken priorities will send a person off in a thousand wrong and hurtful directions. Jesus understood this, and he knew that in our sinful self-absorption we often fall into thinking that care for our body is life's first priority. To this Jesus said:

In our sinful self-absorption we often fall into thinking that care for our body is life's first priority.

> Don't worry about your life, what you will eat or what you will drink; or about your body, what you will wear. Isn't life more than food and the body more than clothing? Look at the birds of the sky: they don't sow or reap or gather into barns, yet your heavenly Father feeds them. Aren't you worth more than they? (Matt 6:25–26).

This is not a prescription for laziness or a haphazard lack of planning. As stewards of the talents and responsibilities God has given us, we must work hard to provide for ourselves and our families. But life is more than these things. Seek God and his priorities above all else, and the causes of your anxiety will fall away.

Hold loosely the things of earth. All treasures bear a testimony about ownership. I don't mean they tell us who owns them, of course. I could own the *Mona Lisa* half a century and nothing about the portrait's elusive smile would identify me as its owner. Rather, treasures tell us something about who owns their *owner.* For instance, a woman whose

I could own the *Mona Lisa* half a century and nothing about the portrait's elusive smile would identify me as its owner. Nevertheless, treasures tell us something about who owns their owner.

expansive wardrobe is stuffed with designer clothes and whose jewelry box is measured in square feet has most likely stored up her treasures in this world, not the next. She is owned by this age rather than the everlasting tomorrow. Jesus wants better things for us, things that are not tethered to this brief life. "Collect for yourselves treasures in heaven, where neither moth nor rust destroys, and where

"Collect for yourselves treasures in heaven, where neither moth nor rust destroys, and where thieves don't break in and steal. For where your treasure is, there your heart will be also."

thieves don't break in and steal. For where your treasure is, there your heart will be also" (Matt 6:20–21). Forsake the pursuit of wealth, which passes into nothingness. Help orphans and widows, haul a hurting person up from despair, spread the gospel personally, and give financial gifts to your church and its selected missions agencies. Do this, and all the treasures you forsook on earth will be heaped tall and broad upon you in heaven.

Value God's kingdom above all. Admission to God's kingdom is reserved for the swift footed, spiritually speaking. Those who stall or drag their feet because they have other business or pleasures to pursue first may find that life's path never again crosses the sacred entryway. Worries and worldly pursuits grow up like woody vines, obscuring the view and choking out the light. Jesus warned two would-be followers about this when they came saying they would follow him only *after* they first took care of their household priorities. Jesus' stern reply should shake us all: "No one who puts his hand to

Samarian farmer ploughing, 1893. Jesus said, "No one who puts his hand to the plow and looks back is fit for the kingdom of God" (Luke 9:62).

the plow and looks back is fit for the kingdom of God" (Luke 9:62). This means no one who sets out to commit to the kingdom and its mission can then glance back longingly at the life he's left behind. Elsewhere Jesus said the kingdom is like a treasure that a man found buried in a field (Matt 13:44). Upon finding it, he quickly reburied it and ran to sell all his possessions. Money in hand, he purchased the field and made the treasure his own. The kingdom of God is this urgent! Take possession while you can, even if it requires forsaking everything you value. Entrance into God's kingdom is worth any sacrifice, even if your own family disowns you. "I assure you, there is no one who has left house, brothers or sisters, mother or father, children, or fields because of Me and the gospel, who will not receive 100 times more, now at this time . . . and eternal life in the age to come" (Mark 10:29–30).

Simply tell the truth. Few things are more powerful than lies. Lob just one of them into your life, and it can set off a series of rapid-fire reactions that escalate out of control. Before long someone is hurt or something beautiful (a relationship, a virtue, a dream) is ruined. Never underestimate a lie's power. The first one seared the earth from age to age: "No! You will not die," the serpent said to Eve (Gen 3:4). The rest is history, *fallen* history.

In ancient lore it was believed that the gods used lies and manipulation to get their way, but the God of the Hebrews revealed himself as a

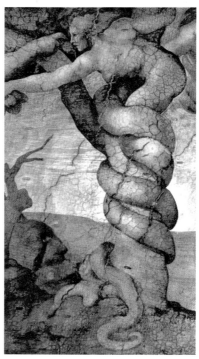
The serpent of Genesis as painted by Michelangelo.

God of truth. "The Rock—His work is perfect; all His ways are entirely just. A faithful God, without prejudice, He is righteous and true" (Deut 32:4). Knowing this, the Hebrews adopted the practice of oath-making, whereby a man or woman attempted to ensure the truthfulness of their claims by placing themselves under God's threat if they should be proven false. Hence they were saying something to the effect of, "I swear to God . . ." Jesus taught that we should make no oaths because oaths are banked against things that are greater than we are or beyond our control. Don't make an oath "by heaven, because it is God's throne, or by the earth, because it

In ancient lore it was believed that the gods used lies and manipulation to get their way, but the God of the Hebrews revealed himself as a God of truth.

is His footstool. . . . Neither should you swear by your head, because you cannot make a single hair white or black" (Matt 5:34–36). Be ever truthful so that your word needs no backing other than your own untarnished reputation for truth telling. "Let your word 'yes' be 'yes,' and your 'no' be 'no.' Anything more than this is from the evil one" (v. 37).

Make peace with God's rights. Possibly the greatest key to relating to God successfully is recognizing his absolute rights over all creation, including you and the details of your life.

Jewish workers at a Jerusalem vineyard, 1860. To illustrate the importance of honoring God's sovereignty, Jesus told a parable about a landowner who paid all his laborers the same wage (Matt 20:1–16).

Permission slips and committee votes have no place in God's government of his world. To illustrate this point Jesus told a parable about a group of laborers who had gathered outside a vineyard. To their delight the owner came out around dawn and agreed to pay each of them a denarius for a day's labor. Fair enough. They spilled into the vineyard and set about their work. At midmorning the owner hired another group of laborers and sent them into the vineyard with a promise to pay them "whatever is right" (Matt 20:4). He did the same thing at noon and then again at three in the afternoon. Finally, the owner hired a fifth group of laborers at five o'clock. Very little of the working day remained, but the owner sent them in to work till the skirts of evening dropped over the vineyard. At that time the landowner arranged to pay the workers their wages, beginning with the last group and proceeding down the line to those who were hired at dawn. Remarkably, the men who had only worked an hour were paid a whole denarius! When the group that had been in the vineyard since dawn saw this, their hopes got up quickly. *What might we receive?* they wondered. *Three or four times the promised wage?* But when the owner passed out their wages, it was a lone denarius for each man! Not surprisingly these work-weary men had something to say. "These last men put in one hour, and you made them equal to us who bore the burden of the day and the burning heat!" (v. 12). You might have said the same thing. I'm sure I would have. This is the genius of Jesus' parable: *no one* who hears it finds it fair that all the laborers received equal pay. To all our protests Jesus replies through the landowner: "Don't I have the right to do what I want with my business? Are you jealous because I'm generous?" (v. 15). Jesus then closed the parable with the oft-quoted line, "So the last will be first, and the first last" (v. 16). God will do as he pleases on earth. It will often seem to us that his favors are handed out unevenly. At times like that, run to receive your denarius with a thankful heart and be glad for your neighbor who, though less deserving in your opinion, receives the same or better from the Landowner's hand.

God will do as he pleases on earth. It will often seem to us that his favors are handed out unevenly. At times like that, run to receive your denarius with a thankful heart.

Put on humility—Part I. There are no big shots in God's kingdom. Whatever talents or positions of influence you have are granted to you by God for his glory and the good of his people. Jesus' disciples had a difficult time understanding this. Seeing that they often made comparisons and jockeyed for position, Jesus brought a child

There are no big shots in God's kingdom.

among them and said: "I assure you, unless you are converted and become like children, you will never enter the kingdom of heaven. Therefore, whoever humbles himself like this child—this one is the greatest in the kingdom of heaven" (Matt 18:3–4). Elsewhere Jesus held a child and said God's kingdom "is made up of people like this" (19:14). The disciples must have been stunned by this revelation. After all, children were essentially invisible to the radar of the

Galilean family, 1894. Children were essentially invisible to the radar of the ancient world.

ancient world. Of course they were treasured by their parents, but they had few rights, little access to education, few capabilities in hard labor, and no place in the debates on politics and religion that dominated the first century. Childhood was a phase to be hurried through on the way to greater, more useful things. Adults never envied children, and yet Jesus said they are favored by God. Jesus' challenge to his followers then and now is this: make yourselves small. Demand no respect. Do not clamor for the top. Love and obey God as young children do their earthly parents.

> *Jesus' challenge to his followers then and now is this: make yourselves small. Demand no respect. Do not clamor for the top. Love and obey God as young children do their earthly parents.*

Put on humility—Part II. One day the mother of two of Jesus' disciples approached the Lord and lobbied that her sons be given the privilege to sit to his right and left in the coming kingdom. "They've served you well," we imagine her saying, "so why not reward them with seats of honor?" Jesus recognized this as another opportunity to teach the importance of humility. He pointed out that though the rulers of the Gentiles lord their rule over the people this is not permitted among

God's people. "On the contrary, whoever wants to become great among you must be your servant, and whoever wants to be first among you must be your slave" (Matt 20:26–27). Jesus then named himself as the exemplar of this attitude: "Whoever wants to be first among you must be your slave; just as the Son of Man did not come to be served, but to serve, and to give His life—a ransom for many" (vv. 27–28). If God the Son came among us to serve, surely we are not above following his example of humility and service to others.

Put on love. Jesus taught that God's greatest commandment is that we love him with all our being. He also went on to name the *second* most important commandment: "Love your neighbor as yourself" (Matt 22:39).

We all have a mental list of exemptions, people whom we suppose Jesus would not expect us to love.

The question naturally arises: Who is my neighbor? Surely not the Muslims, drunks, or homosexuals? We all have a mental list of exemptions, people whom we suppose Jesus would not expect us to love. An expert in the Jewish religion tried this tactic when he heard Jesus' teachings about loving our neighbors, but Jesus headed him off at the pass by telling a story in which a Samaritan (a people group despised by Jews) traveling the road to Jericho came to the aid of a citizen of Jerusalem, presumably an upstanding Jew, who had been waylaid by robbers and left to die (Luke 10:30–35). A Jewish priest and a Levite (a member of one of Israel's most venerable Jewish tribes) had previously passed by the

Good Samaritan by van Gogh. To illustrate the need to put on love, Jesus told a tale about a Samaritan aiding a Jew who despised him.

trampled man and hurried on, not wanting to get involved in roadside complications. How ironic that the injured man was ignored by his countrymen but saved by a hated neighbor. This would be something like a hard-line communist coming to the aid of a fallen Reagan Republican in the 1980s. More fitting to our own day, the Samaritan's service to the Jew is much like a fundamentalist Muslim binding the wounds of an evangelical Christian when other Christians had refused to help. Needless to

> *The Samaritan's service to the Jew is much like a fundamentalist Muslim binding the wounds of an evangelical Christian when other Christians had refused to help.*

say this is a shocking and humbling scenario, and that is exactly what Jesus wanted. When he finished the tale, he asked the Jewish religion expert which of the men had been a neighbor to the wounded Jew. Reluctantly the man admitted it was the Samaritan. To this Jesus replied, "Go and do the same" (v. 37). The mandate for all followers of Christ is this: love one; love all. Make no distinction between worthies and unworthies. You were unlovable because of your sins, and yet in mercy God redeemed you and called you by his name. Now go out in Christ's name and love your neighbors without discrimination.

Family Ties

Every Christian is a member of two intimate groups: a domestic family and Christ's family. Strum through the respective photo albums, and you will find folks you really like and others you can barely tolerate, but even your favorites can get under your skin. After all, every relationship comes across rough patches. When sin pocks the lane, we are tempted to give up the jour-

ney and part ways. In other cases we drive on with the relationship, but we hit every pock at high speed in hopes that we'll jar some sense into the lout beside us. Neither approach pleases God. Therefore, Jesus offered tips for succeeding in our church and domestic relationships.

The Golden Rule. If you could throw a switch and make the whole world conform to a single ethic, you would do well to choose Luke 6:31. Speaking about the need to love our enemies and endure offenses, Jesus said, "Just as you want others to do for you, do the same for them." This means you should never do to another person something you would not want them to do to you in return. Amazingly, Jesus means for us to apply this ethic even to our enemies. "If anyone hits you on the cheek, offer the other also. And if anyone takes away your coat, don't hold back your shirt either" (v. 29). When was the last time you were struck on the face? Maybe it was with words rather than a palm, a betrayal rather than a fist. It hurt, didn't it? You were shocked and offended. How did you respond? Chances are good that you didn't turn the other cheek. Most likely you followed not the Golden Rule but the Goading

> *Jesus said, "Just as you want others to do for you, do the same for them."*

Jesus said, "If anyone hits you on the cheek, offer the other also" (Luke 6:29).

Rule, which says if someone sins against you, you sin right back at 'em! While it is true that our sinful dispositions make the Golden Rule an ideal whose perfect fulfillment must await our final redemption in heaven, the man or woman who walks in the power of God's Spirit can strike near to Jesus' mark. May it be true of us all!

Marriage and divorce. No relationship is more fundamental to God's plan for human community than the lifelong marriage between a man and a woman. By this union we are to discover and enjoy sexual intimacy, produce children, enfold them in love, instruct them in the ways of God, release them to be salt and light to the world, and remain faithful to our partners till death. You don't need me to tell

> *No relationship is more fundamental to God's plan for human community than the lifelong marriage between a man and a woman.*

you that this calling is full of challenges. Intact marriages are rarer now than ever before, but the problem is not new. It is as old as sin, in fact. Jesus addressed the importance of marriage several times during his ministry. The true cost of Christian discipleship comes into focus when we read these teachings, for they ram headlong against the loose marriage ethics that dominate modern society. Consider this: "Everyone who di-

vorces his wife, except in a case of sexual immorality, causes her to commit adultery. And whoever marries a divorced woman commits adultery" (Matt 5:32). When Jesus repeated this teaching at a later date, some listeners objected that Moses had allowed divorce. Jesus replied that this had only been due to the hardness of human hearts (19:8). If we would memorize one statement from Jesus on God's plan for marriage, may it be this one: "What God has joined together, man must not separate" (Mark 10:9).

Forgiveness. Forgiveness has its limits, right? Simon Peter assumed so, but he was unsure just where the boundary lay. He was thinking of a pretty low number when he walked up to Jesus one day and posed the question: "Lord, how many times could my brother sin against me and I forgive him? As many as seven times?" (Matt 18:21). I know what you're thinking. Take care that you don't offend Peter! He keeps a log, and it fills up fast. But in all reality most of us are stingy with forgiveness. In answer to Peter (and us), Jesus said not seven but "70 times seven" (v. 22). This is a figurative way of saying there is no limit. To illustrate this Jesus went on to tell a parable about a slave who owed his king 10,000 talents (vv. 23-34). A single talent was equivalent to

Forgiveness has its limits, right?

6,000 denarii. Recall that in the vineyard parable the laborers worked an entire day to earn a single denarius. In Jesus' made-up example, therefore, he pictures the slave owing a fortune that could never be repaid even in many lifetimes. Realizing the impossibility of full repayment the king elected to sell the slave's family and possessions so that a fraction of the debt could be recovered. "At this, the slave fell facedown before him and said, 'Be patient with me, and I will pay you everything!'" (v. 26). This promise to repay the massive debt was mere bluster, of course, driven by panic and desperation, but the king was moved with compassion. He decided right there on the spot to forgive the slave his entire debt.

Thus freed from doom, the slave went out and seized a fellow drudge who happened to owe him 100 denarii, a whole season's wages. "Pay what you owe!" he screamed as he choked the man (v. 28). Naturally the drudge was unable to pay his debt. Realizing this the slave, though fresh off his own unmerited pardon, had the man jailed. The gall of this action is difficult to describe, but whatever words of scorn we choose will rebound onto our own heads because we emulate this slave's double standard each time we threaten to nurture a grievance or deny mercy to one who has sinned against us. God in Christ has forgiven us an infinite offence. Like the slave we could not have paid the debt

Two Debtors by Fetti. Thus freed from doom, the slave went out and seized a fellow drudge who happened to owe him 100 denarii, a whole season's wages. "Pay what you owe!" he screamed as he choked the man.

in a lifetime of effort. In this light what does God think of us when we withhold forgiveness from others? Jesus answers this by describing what the king did when he learned of the wicked slave's behavior. After dressing him down for his unforgiving heart, the king threw him into prison "until he could pay everything that was owed" (v. 34). We already know that 10,000 talents lay infinitely far beyond his ability to repay. The conclusion is sobering: the unforgiving slave would never live to see the relief of his debts to the king. He would die in chains, condemned by a ledger filled with unpaid dues. For us the implication is clear: If we do not practice forgiveness, it is a sure sign that we have not enjoyed authentic rebirth in Christ. We have played our hand at religion, but our hearts have held out. In such a case our ledger remains unbalanced, and a hopeless debt of retribution remains.

> *If we do not practice forgiveness, it is a sure sign that we have not enjoyed authentic rebirth in Christ. We have played our hand at religion but our hearts have held out.*

Rally 'round the family. Imagine yourself at a family reunion. You see aunts, uncles, and distant cousins for the first time in years. You embrace, swap stories, and laugh till you cry. Then you come across someone you don't recognize. He hugs you, smiles, and chats a bit. You rack your brain trying to dredge up a name, but no luck. Soon you slip away and ask everyone who the guy is, but they have no idea either. After a while it dawns on you: there is a stranger in your midst, an imposter who has no place in your family. You wonder why he has come and what he is planning.

Jesus warned that the family of God is often visited by such drop-ins, and they don't just come for food and fellowship. "Beware of false prophets who come to you in sheep's clothing but inwardly are ravaging wolves" (Matt 7:15). Such men and women come to coax the children of God onto paths that lead away from truth and life. Most often they make the journey seem easier. They tickle our ears with choice words and commendations. Once they earn our trust, they lead us (by teaching, life example, or both) to bypass the narrow gate and its lane of self-denial. They choose instead the broad entries and wide pavements down which seemingly the whole world travels. Be wary of the broad road, Jesus said, for it "leads to destruction, and there are many who go through it" (v. 13). In contrast, "narrow is the gate and difficult the road that leads to life, and few find it" (v. 14).

Be wary of the broad road, Jesus said, for it "leads to destruction, and there are many who go through it."

How do we rally around the family and protect our own in the face of such threats? We begin by learning to distinguish a wolf from a sheep. Speaking of the wolves (false teachers), Jesus said, "You'll recognize them by their fruit. . . . A good tree can't produce bad fruit; neither can a bad tree produce good fruit." (Matt 7:16,18). This means wolves will not live or teach in conformity to the standard for Christian practice and belief: the Bible. They will diverge from paths clearly laid out in Scripture. The Lord's name may be on their lips, but recall Jesus' words of warning about name dropping: "Not everyone who says to Me, 'Lord, Lord!' will enter the kingdom of heaven, but only the one who does the will of My Father in heaven" (v. 21).

Wolves will not live or teach in conformity to the standard for Christian practice and belief: the Bible.

The threat imposters pose to the church is real, and too often we sheep are unwilling to confront wolves, but also beware the danger of setting out on wolf hunts at the slightest provocation, for in our zeal we might end up persecuting genuine sheep instead. When people who profess to be Christians stray into false doctrines or sinful practices, it is not necessarily a sign that they are wolves. Often it just means they need a little correction and guidance from the rest of the sheep, as we will see directly below.

Faithful to correct and restore. Most people today know little about the Bible, but even if they never crack one open, you can bet they know Jesus' words in Matthew 7:1, "Do not judge, so that you won't be judged." It is the most beloved verse of our time. Against all reason it is said that Jesus has given us an exemption card here, meaning no one but God can judge us. A careful reading of the context shows that Je-

"Do not judge, so that you won't be judged" (Matt 7:1). It is the most beloved verse of our time.

sus only meant to warn us away from hypocrisy or nitpicking in our judgments. "With the judgment you use, you will be judged, and with the measure you use, it will be measured to you" (v. 2). This means if you judge harshly or falsely the same oppressive standards will be used against you. Jesus went on to give us a prescription for making balanced judgments that promote health among Christians. "How can you say to your brother, 'Let me take the speck out of your eye,' and look, there's a log in your eye? Hypocrite! First take the log out of your eye, and then you will see clearly to take the speck out of your brother's eye" (vv. 4–5). In this way we can be mutually helpful to one another as we pursue the call to be like Christ. The recognition of sin in someone else's life should

The recognition of sin in someone else's life should first call us to a round of self-examination and repentance.

first call us to a round of self-examination and repentance. Having completed this first priority, we can then approach our Christian brother or sister and invite them to see their troubles and the need to turn back onto the homeward path. Our faithfulness to engage in awkward tasks such as this is evidence of our deep commitments to one another and to Christ. If on the other hand we refuse these duties, it suggests that we love our peace and possibly our own sins more than we love God's kingdom and the health of its citizens. But even willing hearts find the task challenging. Sin, emotions, inadequacies, and relational

If you find yourself tracking down an errant Christian and your foremost hope is not their restoration, stop in your tracks. You've got the log in your eye again.

dynamics come into play when we speak to someone about their sins. Thankfully we are not left to fly blindly. Jesus gave instructions about how to seek repentance and restoration for an erring member of God's family. Speaking specifically of times when someone has sinned against you personally, Jesus said, "Go and rebuke him in private. If he listens to you, you have won your brother" (Matt 18:15). This is of course the aim of the whole enterprise. If you find yourself tracking down an errant Christian and your foremost hope is not their restoration, stop in your tracks. You've got the log in your eye again.

In the event that the errant brother or sister goes on sinning after we speak with them, Jesus instructs us to take along two or more companions for the second attempt at restoration. This allows multiple witnesses to establish the facts at hand, ensuring that no one is executing an agenda. If at this point the sinner remains unrepentant, the entire church (the one he or she attends) should be informed about the situation. Here is where things *really* start getting uncomfortable for the stray lamb. Now the whole church is in the know. If they are faithful to Christ's calling, many members will join the effort to win the sinner back to right living. "But if he doesn't pay attention even to the church, let him be like an unbeliever and a tax collector to you" (Matt 18:17). This means the errant person is removed from the fellowship and is presumed to be lost, separate from Christ and without eternal redemption. The hope is that the expelled person will sober up and realize that their life choices match those of a non-Christian. Church members should contact them periodically to encourage this outcome.

Jesus' teachings on repentance and restoration remind us how important it is to be regularly involved in a local church that faithfully preaches the Gospel and seeks to conform its beliefs and practices to the biblical witness. We need one another so we can be held accountable to the Kingdom Way. Every life will stray off course without regular encouragement and correction from the community of faith. To pull back from church involvement puts us in harm's way and can contribute to the downfall of others because our example tempts fellow Christians to follow suit.

> *The hope is that the expelled person will sober up and realize that their life choices match those of a non-Christian.*

Lamps in Darkness

In this final section we will review three of Jesus' teachings about how Christians should interact with the non-Christian world. As you read, ask yourself two questions: How can you fulfill these teachings, and what would the world look like if all Christians took these callings seriously?

Salt and light. How do you save a doomed world? Jesus says you salt it. In the earliest days of human civilization, when refrigeration and preservative canning were unknown or impracticable sciences, salt was the major means of preserving meat. Workers would mine it from the ground or harvest it from seawater, and then some patient soul would rub it into a freshly

> *How do you save a doomed world? Jesus says you salt it.*

cut slab of meat, pressing down firmly as they worked the heel of their hand back and forth over the slab to ensure that the minerals sunk into the meaty depths. Jesus expects Christians to have the same preservative effect among the lost. We are to infiltrate all segments of society, leaving no portion untouched by Christ's influence. This is the world's lone hope, but it comes at great risk to Christians. Note Jesus' warning: "If the salt should lose its taste, how can it be made salty? It's no longer good for anything but to be thrown out and trampled on by men" (Matt 5:13). Casualties

Jesus expects Christians to have a preservative effect among the lost, as salt does in meat.

are a very real possibility for Christians who bear the gospel into dark places. Much that the world offers is appealing if we take our eyes off Christ. Divert your eyes long enough, and you'll find that the world has transformed you. You are no longer salt but a spent, tasteless mineral that worked its way into the depths of the world only to rot along with everything else. The world wooed you, and you are part of it now. Or are you? As Jesus said, the world accepts shelled-out Christians not as kindred spirits but as laughingstocks: they are useless now except "to be thrown out and trampled on by men." And as they tramp by the fallen Christian, each passerby takes one step farther away from the Christ whom they believe failed another one of his followers.

Jesus also compared his followers to lights burning in perpetual night. Just as no one lights a lamp and then stows it under a basket, Christians should not build enclaves and safe havens that

Christians should not build enclaves and safe havens that horde light and block off the encroaching blackness.

horde light and block off the encroaching blackness. God has made us to be light for a reason. "Let your light shine before men, so that they may see your good works and give glory to your Father in heaven" (v. 16). If you are a follower of God, is your light reaching the darkness or are you only flashing your high beams at Christ's church?

Assist the downtrodden. Jesus spent a great deal of his time in the parts of town we won't even drive through in daylight. Prostitutes, beggars, ill reputes—Jesus palled around with these kinds of people and enjoyed their company more than he did that of the carping religious leaders who trailed after him wanting to talk theology.

> *Jesus spent a great deal of his time in the parts of town we won't even drive through in daylight.*

Granted, Jesus did not come among sinners or bums to approve of what they had done with their lives, but neither did he judge them hopeless or worthless, and he certainly didn't picket or protest outside their doors. Instead, he met them on the heart level and loved them for who they were. Rather than chide them, he spoke plainly and directly, offering pardon for sins and a way out of sinful lifestyles. Jesus also reached out to women, children, the lame, the blind, and indirectly to slaves, demonstrating that God does not regard such people as second class or forgotten. All men, women, and children are equal in the eyes of their Maker.

Your role in national affairs. If you are a follower of Christ, this world is not your home; nevertheless you are here for a lengthy stopover. Like any resident alien you are responsible to the government that rules over you. Jesus made this clear when a group of Pharisees tried to goad him into opposing Rome by speaking out against taxes. "Is it lawful to pay taxes to Caesar or not?" they asked (Matt 22:17). Popular sentiment would have had him say no.

> *Like any resident alien you are responsible to the government that rules over you.*

After all, the Romans were godless pagans, and any monies given to them only helped sustain their oppressive empire. But Jesus would not take the bait. He asked them for a coin. Taking a denarius in hand, Jesus asked,

Render unto Caesar by Titian. A group of Pharisees tried to goad Jesus into opposing Rome by speaking out against taxes. "Is it lawful to pay taxes to Caesar or not?" they asked (Matt 22:17).

"Whose image and inscription is this?" Caesar's, they answered. Now the stage was set for Jesus' clever but deeply meaningful answer: "Therefore, give back to Caesar the things that are Caesar's, and to God the things that are God's" (v. 21).

While we sojourn in this world, we must not be disruptive to governing authorities unless it is demanded by our obligations to God. Following this line of thought, the apostle Paul wrote in his epistle to the Roman church: "Everyone must submit to the governing authorities, for there is no authority except from God, and those that exist are instituted by God. So then, the one who resists the authority is opposing God's command, and those who oppose it will bring judgment on themselves" (Rom 13:1–2). In this light he or she who contemplates using civil disobedience as a tool for social change must be doubly sure that both their cause and their methodology are righteous in God's eyes.

The larger reason Christians should maintain good standing in society is so that the gospel might be spread without organized, government-sanctioned opposition. Just as Jesus carefully avoided giving the impression that he would seek to establish a new government in place of the Roman occupiers, we too must not send signals that convince our unbelieving fellow citizens that we intend to establish a Christian theocracy in place of democratic government. I suspect we have often missed this point. Jesus would have us live with a singular purpose: spread hope in his name, calling people everywhere to place their faith in him for forgiveness of sins and eternal life in heaven.

Chapter 17
Life in Light

In the popular movie *The Matrix,* a young man named Neo stumbles onto the troubling realization that life is not as it seems. Everything Neo had believed about himself and society turned out to be a masterfully orchestrated lie. True human existence was hidden behind an electronic veil that could only be lifted by enlightened prophets such as Morpheus and Trinity, savior agents from a realm where the lie held no power.

The Matrix makes for great fiction, but it also strikes near to deep truths about human existence and life beyond the veil. In this chapter we will examine Jesus' teachings about vital hidden realities of our spiritual condition. We will also explore his message of hope—hope for enlightenment and redemption from the sham that misleads and enslaves the world.

Reality Check

Every time you choose to commit a sin you do so freely. No one forces your hand. Neither the stars above nor social forces here below force you onto a destructive path. Better options are

We humans are free moral agents whose destiny hangs on the choices we make.

always available, so why do you choose sin? The surprising answer is that though you are free in your choices you are also bound by a sort of secret slavery. Can a person really be free and enslaved at the same time? According to the Bible,

It takes a God's-eye view to diagnose our sins, for it is only in relation to divine perfections that sin can be defined.

yes. We humans are free moral agents whose destiny hangs on the choices we make, and yet we make our choices based on the persuasive counsels of an inner nature (heart, mind, soul) that has become corrupted by sin. This is our inheritance from Adam. We freely and gladly choose sin because we are by nature sinners. For this reason Jesus said we are *slaves* to sin (John 8:34). This is the hidden spiritual condition that all humans must identify. The doctors didn't announce this condition at your birth. The bank never sent a notice about your inheritance of Adam's corruption. In fact, though evidence for human sinfulness is far too massive to

escape notice (we all know about murder, genocide, theft, slavery, racism, sexism, slander, envy, greed, elitism, unconcern for the poor and oppressed, etc.), it remains the one reality most people insist on denying. It is the elephant looming large and gray in the room, but few admit its presence even as they slink around it. Ultimately it takes a God's-eye view to diagnose our sins, for it is only in relation to divine perfections that sin can be defined. God has performed this diagnosis vividly in the Bible and also by the ministry of the Holy Spirit who convicts us of sin. So profound is our sin problem that Jesus describes humans as children of the devil (John 8:44). This does not mean Satan is our creator, of course. Rather, it means we are

The Expulsion of Adam and Eve by Masaccio. Sin is our inheritance from Adam.

aligned with Satan in rebellion against God. We love darkness rather than light (3:19).

Can you fix your sin problem via moral reform? Many have thought so, but this is a hopeless tactic. Reformation based on merely human efforts can actually leave you prepared for a greater fall because you suppose that by your own power you have beaten back a darkness that is far greater than you (Matt 12:43–45). Our sin problem is lodged so deeply within us that it is beyond the reach of every medicine, machine, or machination we would set against it. Metaphorically speaking it comprises the very fiber of our hearts and stains our world as we draw hurt and ruin up from within our being (15:10–20). This has not been a popular message in any earth age, but throughout his ministry Jesus persisted in speaking about human sinfulness and God's future separation of the redeemed from the unredeemed.

> *Our sin problem is lodged so deeply within us that it is beyond the reach of every medicine, machine, or machination we would set against it.*

Separations

As the source and standard for all moral good, God cannot allow his holiness to be forever trampled by his riotous creation. Otherwise the pots have risen up against the Potter and overthrown him—an absurdity that should not, cannot, and will not happen. For us the implications are stark: either we will be made holy and acceptable to God, fit for his eternal fellowship, or else we remain against him and apart from him forever. Jesus believed this. He taught it often and unflinchingly. For

The Last Judgment (center panel) by Memling. Jesus said that at the end of the age he will return to earth in glory, attended by innumerable angels, to sit upon a throne of judgment (Matt 24:29–31).

The Last Judgment (right panel) by Memling. Those whose names are found recorded in the book of life will enter everlasting joy with the rest of the sheep, but all others will be "thrown into the lake of fire" for everlasting punishment (Rev 20:15).

instance, he said that at the end of the age he will return to earth in glory, attended by innumerable angels, to sit upon a throne of judgment (Matt 24:29–31). All humans who are alive on that climactic day will be brought before him so they can be separated according to kind. Using imagery that suited the agrarian context of ancient Israel, Jesus said the sheep will be shunted to the right, goats to the left. For sheep the final stop is blessed life in God's eternal kingdom. Goats suffer a different destination. To them Jesus will say, "Depart from Me, you who are cursed, into the eternal fire prepared for the Devil and his angels!" (25:41). As for the untold millions who will have already died by the time of Christ's return, they will be raised from the dead to face a similar judgment. Those whose names are found recorded in the book of life will enter everlasting joy with the rest of the sheep, but all others will be "thrown into the lake of fire" for everlasting punishment (Rev 20:15). With so much on the line, it is important to understand the basis on which this separation will be made. More to the point: How can you ensure that you will be counted a sheep rather than a goat?

Born from Above

Among the Pharisees was a man of quality named Nicodemus. Less ironhearted than his fellows, Nicodemus felt drawn to give close and open-minded attention to Jesus' teachings. But the party line among the Pharisees said Jesus was a fraud, and so Nicodemus bided his time and kept quiet about his interest in the teacher from Galilee. When he was unable to master his curiosity any longer, he came to Jesus by night, using the cover of darkness to hide his actions. Finding the Lord, Nicodemus confessed belief that Jesus had come from God; but he was thinking of him only as a prophet, a man commissioned by God to spread a message among the people. Seeing

Nicodemus and Jesus by Bida. Nicodemus came to Jesus at night.

that Nicodemus had attained only a fraction of the truth, Jesus told him, "I assure you: Unless someone is born again, he cannot see the kingdom of God" (John 3:3). Recalling the distinction between sheep and goats at the final judgment, Jesus' words to Nicodemus show us that one becomes a sheep (enters God's kingdom) via *rebirth*. This raises an obvious question. Nicodemus is quick to ask it for us: "How can anyone be born when he is old? Can he enter his mother's womb a second time and be born?" (v. 4).

Jesus began his answer by saying, "Unless someone is born of water and the Spirit, he cannot enter the kingdom of God. Whatever is born of the flesh is flesh, and whatever is born of the Spirit is spirit" (John 3:5–6). This is a helpful start toward understanding rebirth. We see that it is spiritual rather than physical. It is a supernatural act in which God grants fallen humans a new spiritual nature and a status that conforms to his purity. It does not transform us in such a way as to end our pen-

Rebirth is a supernatural act in which God grants fallen humans a new spiritual nature and a status that conforms to his purity.

chant for sin, but it replaces a spirit dead to God with one that is alive to his will and presence, prepared to grow in godliness over time.

Alright. We know by now what rebirth is, but we have yet to learn how to *attain* it. Fortunately for everyone, Nicodemus pressed Jesus until he learned that rebirth is possible only by trusting in Messiah. Jesus put it this way: "For God loved the world in this way: He gave His One and Only Son, so that everyone who believes in Him will not perish but have eternal life" (John 3:16). Can it really be this simple? Absolutely.

Rebirth is possible only by trusting in Messiah.

There are no additional steps and no works to perform. Faith in the Son saves the soul, for this is the will of God who loves the world enough to make a fatal sacrifice of his holy Son.

For those who are not reborn through faith in Jesus, there remains only an expectation of judgment, for through death's door they bear their sins as a filthy garment that wards away the God and holy Judge of all people. Continuing his instructions on God's saving measures in the Son, Jesus said to Nicodemus, "Anyone who believes in Him is not condemned, but anyone who does not believe is already condemned, because he has not believed in the name of the One and Only Son of God" (John 3:18).

One wonders why anyone would refuse to believe in such a Savior as this, come to give us free pardon and life forever in the presence of God; but lest we believe only a madman would refuse belief, Jesus reported that the world prefers darkness over light (John 3:19). He often made this stark diagnosis of humanity's spiritual preferences. On one such occasion a bystander caught Jesus' drift and, being amazed at such a teaching, asked, "Lord, are there few being saved?" (Luke 13:22).

Christ by Rembrandt.

Apparently he expected Jesus' salvation would be broadly welcomed in the world, a fallacious expectation that is especially common today. To this Jesus responded by urging the man,

"Make every effort to enter through the narrow door, because I tell you, many will try to enter and won't be able once the homeowner gets up and shuts the door" (vv. 24–25).

Secured from Above

Salvation is a free gift, but it cannot be used as a license to flaunt God's pardon at the expense of his holy standards for living. Striving for obedience is a basic requirement for true Christian discipleship; so is staying on the narrow path till the end. Those who fall away after experiencing a season of affec-

Striving for obedience is a basic requirement for true Christian discipleship; so is staying on the narrow path till the end.

tion for Jesus should draw no confidence from their brief but discarded foray into Christian discipleship. They are to be counted among those whose "faith" flourished in shallow soil and mild sunshine only to wilt under pressure from trials and temptations (Luke 8:4–15). Not having a genuinely remade heart, the familiar darkness welled up from within and drew them away to destruction. Others keep up the show pretty well throughout their lives. They have a semblance of lasting faith, but in the end it proves to have been a feat of religion rather than a work of God. To these Jesus will say, "I never knew you! Depart from Me, you lawbreakers!" (Matt 7:23).

These facts should sober all who call themselves Christians. There is no conga line to glory; we walk instead an *anaconda* line along which the old Serpent strikes from the cover of thorns and roots which crowd the dis-

Those who fall away after experiencing a season of affection for Jesus should be counted among those whose "faith" flourished in shallow soil and mild sunshine only to wilt under pressure from trials and temptations.

ciple's footpath. Fortunately we do not walk the path alone. While Jesus on many occasions urged his followers to prove themselves true by continuing in his word (John 8:30) and remaining in his love (15:9–10), he also vowed that he would

Jesus vowed that he would never cast out those who had genuinely come to him.

never cast out those who had genuinely come to him (6:37) nor allow them to be snatched from his hand (10:28). Also, on the night of his arrest, Jesus prayed for all people throughout history who would believe in him. While speaking to the Father with great anticipation about his soon-coming restoration to glory in heaven, Jesus said, "Father, I desire those You have given Me to be with Me where I am. Then they will see My glory, which You have given Me because You loved Me before the world's foundation" (17:24).

We have a basic tension here. On one hand Jesus repeatedly warns that his followers must be diligent and persistent in their discipleship, else they will fall into destruction and prove that they were never genuine disciples. On the other hand Jesus promises that our place in his hand is secured forever. From this we conclude that true believers will persist in their faith, never falling permanently or completely away from a life that reflects Christ's teachings.

True believers will persist in their faith, never falling permanently or completely away from a life that reflects Christ's teachings.

Sure, there will be ups and downs for every disciple. Our love and obedience dim during seasons in which the light of Christ is blocked off by sin or by the hurts that press down on us, tempting us to doubt God's goodness. But true believers make it through such times. Is this because of their efforts or God's? The answer is *both*. Consider Paul's admonition to the Christians at Philippi: "Work out your own salvation with fear and trembling. For it is God who is working in you, enabling you both to will and to act for His good purpose" (Phil 2:12–13). If we could paraphrase this, we might say, "With awe for God's holiness and power, work hard to stay true to Christ. Do this because God himself works in your heart and mind to ensure that this happens."

This strikes a balance that calls the believer to take the discipleship task seriously while simultaneously comforting him or her with the assurance that almighty God is the ultimate Guardian of salvation.

City of Eternal Light

Death of the body is not death of the self. Hearts seize and brain waves fall flat, but this only ushers in a change of state. Exactly what kind of existence immediately follows a Christian's last breath is hard to say. We have no bodies at that time, of course, for the resurrection comes only at the end of this age when God comes to judge the quick and the dead and make all things new. If we are not embodied

Every follower of Christ experiences instantaneous welcome into God's presence at the time of death.

immediately after death, what sort of existence do we have? Are we merely spirits? Do we float around like ghosts? The Bible does not give us definitive information about this sort of thing, but we do know that Jesus promised the rebel who was executed alongside him on Golgotha that because of his

The Sistine Chapel (detail showing the martyrs in heaven) by Michelangelo.

newfound faith they would be together in paradise that very day (Luke 23:43). This means he had ongoing conscious awareness and personal identity immediately after he died by Jesus' side. This was not unique to him. Every follower of Christ experiences instantaneous welcome into God's presence at the time of death. One clear evidence of this is the apostle Paul's insistence that to be absent from the body is to be present with the Lord and that to die is to gain (2 Cor 5:8; Phil 1:21–23).

As for the final destiny of those who are redeemed, the

apostle John was given a vision in which he saw "the Holy City, new Jerusalem, coming down out of heaven from God, prepared like a bride adorned for her husband" (Rev 21:2). A herald standing at God's throne cried out in a great voice: "Look! God's dwelling is with men, and He will live with them. They will be His people, and God Himself will be with them and be their God. He will wipe away every tear from their eyes. Death will exist no longer; grief, crying, and pain will exist no longer, because the previous things have passed away" (vv. 3–4).

The New Jerusalem by Doré. The apostle John was given a vision in which he saw "the Holy City, new Jerusalem, coming down out of heaven from God, prepared like a bride adorned for her husband" (Rev 21:2).

One can only imagine how John's heart soared as the herald shouted out God's promise while the heavenly city, whose dimensions and brilliance were beyond all imagination, was lowered to the new earth. As he watched, God himself narrated the unfolding events.

Then the One seated on the throne said, "Look! I am making everything new." He also said, "Write, because these words are faithful and true." And He said to me, "It is done! I am the Alpha and the Omega, the Beginning and the End. I will give to the thirsty from the spring of living water as a gift. The victor will inherit these things, and I will be his God, and he will be My son. But the cowards, unbelievers, vile, murderers, sexually immoral, sorcerers, idolaters, and all liars—their share will be in the lake that burns with fire and sulfur, which is the second death" (Rev 21:5–8).

After this an angel took John "in the Spirit" (i.e., in a vision) to a high mountain. Together they watched new Jerusalem continue its descent from its unseen halls of manufacture in the reaches above space and time. "Her radiance was like a very precious stone, like a jasper stone, bright as crystal. The city had a massive wall, with 12 gates. Twelve angels were at the gates" (Rev 21:11–12). The angel then took a golden measuring rod in hand and set off to measure the city while John gazed at walls and celestial components made of

John on Patmos by Bosch. An angel took John "in the Spirit" (i.e., in a vision) to a high mountain. Together they watched new Jerusalem continue its descent from its unseen halls of manufacture in the reaches above space and time.

"pure gold like clear glass" (v. 18). Clearly human language failed him here. His expression is at once evocative and unimaginable. It represents his attempt to convey a new creation

John's expression is at once evocative and unimaginable. It represents his attempt to convey a new creation whose form and substance are without parallels on earth.

whose form and substance are without parallels on earth. When the angel had finished his task with the gilded rule, he announced that the city's dimensions totaled 1,400 miles in height, length, and width (v. 16). Twelve varieties of precious stones adorned foundations that ran far past eye's reach. Twelve massive gates gave entry to the city, and to John's eye it seemed that each of them was made of a single pearl. Just like his talk of transparent gold, we may be right to suppose that the gates are not *literally* made of pearl. Then again, perhaps they are! In any event they are massive and radiant with a measure of beauty never seen on earth.

The temple that stood in Jerusalem during Jesus' ministry was destroyed by the Romans in AD 67. Writing approximately 30 years later, John was eager to see the sanctuary in new Jerusalem, for the absence of such a sacred structure in earthly Jerusalem had been a source of shame and mourning for all Israelites. How glorious would the heavenly sanctuary be? John was eager to find out. But as he searched he learned that new Jerusalem has no sanctuary "because the Lord God the Almighty and the Lamb are its sanctuary" (Rev 21:22). This reminds us, as it surely reminded John, that the era of sacrifice for sins has passed. Thanks to Jesus' once-for-all atoning death on the cross, people of faith have direct access to God. There is no longer any need for daily rituals and sacrifices in any temple on earth or in heaven.

> *Thanks to Jesus' once-for-all atoning death on the cross, people of faith have direct access to God.*

Another era has passed as well: the era of darkness. New Jerusalem is bathed in unending light coming from the very center of glory. "The city does not need the sun or the moon to shine on it, because God's glory illuminates it, and its lamp is the Lamb. The nations will walk in its light, and the kings of the earth will bring their glory into it. Each day its gates will never close because it will never be night there" (Rev 21:23–25). Life in heaven is life in light—warm, inviting, *divine* light that permeates every atom of a world newly made by the God who will never let his glory fade or admit into new Jerusalem anyone or anything that harbors falsehood or bears enmity against his holiness (v. 27). In other words, life in light means citizenship in a city whose gates are barred against anyone who has not gladly bowed knee, head, and heart to Jesus Christ. Choose to be a citizen of the city of eternal light!

Part V
Jesus' Followers

Pentecost by Duccio.

Chapter 18
Tongues of Fire

"Listen to them," said the young priest hotly. He motioned to the crowds gathered along the roadside. By the hundreds they shouted praises to Jesus as he entered Jerusalem for Passover. "They hail him as if he were a king entering his imperial city. The whole world goes after him as we stand by and do nothing!"

"His triumph will be short-lived," his older companion assured him. "The Sanhedrin has not been idle while this Galilean worked his magic. We've a plan to put a stop to all of this. You will see. Jesus and his movement will be dead before Sabbath."

"Make a martyr of him, and he'll be more powerful than ever," the young priest warned. "From the grave his voice will break forth like thunder. Remember the prophets?"

"This won't be a martyr's death," replied the elder. "By Rome's help we will nail him to a cross. 'Anyone hung on a tree is under God's curse,'" he said, quoting Moses. "We'll see how much they love him then!" Laughing, he clasped his protégé on the shoulder, and together they followed in the wake of the doomed man.

Rebirth of the Phoenix

Though the above conversation is fictional, it almost certainly resembles real discussions that passed between ruling priests in the days before and after Jesus' crucifixion. The math was simple, they thought. Subtract Jesus and you nullify his movement. Little did they suspect that their plot would instead multiply Jesus' influence exponentially. Like the mythical phoenix whose fiery death led to glorious rebirth, the crucifixion of Messiah proved to be a passage leading to new and greater life for Jesus and his followers. The resurgence began on Resurrection Sunday, gained momentum with each of Jesus' subsequent appearances, and reached escape velocity 40 days

Like the mythical phoenix whose fiery death led to glorious rebirth, the crucifixion of Messiah proved to be a passage leading to new and greater life for Jesus and his followers.

postresurrection with Christ's ascension. After watching Jesus rise through the clouds, the disciples gathered with the rest of Jesus' followers in Jerusalem. They totaled about 120 people at this time, and they were "continually united in prayer" (Acts 1:14). The group consisted of the Eleven, other male and female disciples, Jesus' mother, plus four men who opposed Jesus' messianic claims until they saw him come back from the dead: Simon, James, Judas (aka Jude), and Joseph—the half brothers of Jesus himself.

If Jesus' brothers were conspicuous by their presence, there was another who was conspicuous by his absence: Judas Iscariot. He had been a part of the inner circle for three years, but he was dead now, having met his demise shortly after betraying Jesus. While the biblical testimony does not present the clearest of pictures regarding Judas' death, the memory of his traitorous act lived on in the naming of a field purchased with his blood money (Acts 1:19).[1] As for the disciples who remained, they discerned from Scripture that someone had to replace Judas.[2] The believers were due to receive the Holy Spirit, Jesus' final provision for their missionary embarkation, and so now was the time for the disciples to close their broken inner circle. As leader of the young church, Peter announced the qualifications that must be met by one who was worthy to replace Judas. Zeal for the risen Jesus was not enough. Heartfelt conviction that he was the miracle-working Messiah and divine Son of God made you a disciple, *not* an apostle. Apostles were defined as those who had been eyewitnesses to the life of Jesus and who had been sent out bearing authority derived from Christ himself.[3] Thus Peter said the chosen man must be one who had followed Jesus from the time John baptized him to the recent day when he was taken up to heaven (vv. 21–22). Such a man could speak not just of what

Apostles were defined as those who had been eyewitnesses to the life of Jesus and who had been sent out bearing authority derived from Christ himself.

In keeping with an ancient Hebrew faith custom, the disciples said a quick prayer for guidance and then cast lots.

he believed but of what he *knew to be true*. A quick check revealed that two men among them met these requirements: Justus and Matthias. The Eleven used a surprising method to decide between these candidates. We expect a long prayer meeting in which God's choice eventually emerged in their hearts, but in keeping with an ancient Hebrew faith custom, they said a quick prayer for guidance and then cast lots (v. 26; see Prov 16:33). Let the sovereign God ordain the outcome in a game of chance. This was a reasonable approach in the era before God sent the Spirit to indwell and guide believers. One method for casting lots was to place marked stones inside a jar and rattle them around vigorously. The first stone to fall out was the "chosen lot." If this was the method the apostles used, Matthias's designated stone was the first to fly from the jar. From this point forward he was counted among the Eleven, such that they were again *the Twelve*—the ordained witnesses to the life and teachings, death and resurrection, commission and ascension of Jesus Christ. There was much work to be done. Their hearts were bursting to get underway, but not yet. God was still working to draw all the pieces into place.

Wind and Flame

Harvest was a greatly anticipated time of year for the ancients. In part this was because it was never guaranteed to happen. Drought, plague, blight, war—these and a dozen other factors could cut off the food supply, starving whole regions. Understandably a plentiful harvest was cause for great celebration. In this spirit the Jews annually celebrated the close of the grain harvest with a festival called the Day of Pentecost. It fell 50 days after the Passover week kicked off, placing it sometime in late May or early June. The weather was more conducive to travel by this time of year, and so visitors swelled Jerusalem to portions greater than during Passover. Now more than any other time Jerusalem became a melting pot of nations and languages as Diaspora Jews (those who had been "dispersed" to lands outside Israel) made a pilgrimage to their ancestral homeland.

Pentecost by El Greco. As the city filled with pilgrims, Christ's followers sat solemnly together—watching, waiting, listening. At nine in the morning, it happened quickly and with force.

Jesus' followers, the full contingent of 120, packed into a house for Pentecost (Acts 2:1). Expectations were high. Jesus had ascended to the Father only days ago, newly promoted Matthias now rounded out the Twelve, and everyone devoted themselves to prayer as they awaited fulfillment of Jesus' mysterious promise that God's Spirit would baptize them (1:5). What would the baptism be like? Could they even imagine? As the city filled with pilgrims, Christ's followers sat solemnly together watching, waiting, listening. At nine in the morning, it happened quickly and with force. "Suddenly a sound like that of a violent rushing wind came from heaven, and it filled the whole house where they were staying. And tongues, like flames of fire that were divided, appeared to them and rested on each one of them" (2:2–3). Fear might have overcome them had the Spirit not filled them straightway and channeled their energies into a fantastic phenomenon that leaves modern readers spellbound. Though they were common Galileans who had little or no firsthand experience of the broad world outside Israel, the disciples "began to speak in different languages, as the Spirit gave them ability for speech" (v. 4). Their Jerusalem abode became the crossroads of the world, and God appointed them its multilingual wayfarers.

It was warm in Jerusalem this time of year. Houses were kept open to allow cooling breezes to waft through the interior. For this reason the commotion inside the house caught the attention of crowds coursing through the streets and courtyards outside. "Devout men from every nation under heaven" were drawn near by the inexplicable fact that Galileans were proclaiming the mighty works of God in languages native to such far-flung places as Egypt, Asia, and Mesopotamia (Acts 2:5–12).[4] Many were amazed. Others said wine had loosened Christian tongues, causing them to show off an unusual but not unprecedented command of Diaspora languages.[5] Meanwhile the disciples fell silent once the Spirit had accomplished his purposes, but quiet did not return because the

By God's cleverness the disciples had become the center of attention in festive Jerusalem. Now the stage was set. Now was the time to kick off the mission Christ had assigned them.

crowd outside continued their debate. By God's cleverness the disciples had become the center of attention in festive Jerusalem. Now the stage was set. Now was the time to kick off the mission Christ had assigned them.

Peter and the rest of Jesus' followers emerged from the house when they heard the crowd. The throng which greeted them consisted of pilgrims from afar as well as citizens of Jerusalem who wanted answers. Peter began by denying that any of them had taken alcohol at this early hour. Rather than spirits from the vine, their utterances had been made possible by God's Spirit in fulfillment of end-times prophecies announced through the prophet Joel (Joel 2:28–32). Earth's last great dispensation had begun, a time of untold duration in which God's redemption plan moves to completion. One foretold harbinger of this epoch was that God would pour his Spirit out on Jews and Gentiles alike, causing sons and daughters to prophesy, young men to see visions, old men to dream dreams, and lowly slaves to utter the hidden things of God (Acts 2:17–20). In this age, "whoever calls on the name of the Lord will be saved" (v. 21). The

Peter Preaching the Gospel by Fra Angelico.

fire that fell on the disciples earlier signified that God would give them utterance in the task of speaking the gospel in Jerusalem and abroad, calling all people to place their hope in Jesus. Thus empowered, Peter stunned his listeners by asserting that the terrible things done to Jesus by "lawless people" were actually foreordained by God (v. 23). God had made his own Son a curse and put him to death! Peter also stressed that he and many others had personally seen Jesus after he arose from death. Their commitments to Jesus were based on solid evidence, not wishful thinking. After hearing Peter say that Jesus' resurrection proved that God had made him Lord and Christ, the crowd was "pierced to the heart" and asked what they should do (vv. 36–37). Peter's response bears repeating in full: "Repent and be baptized, each of you, in the name of Jesus the Messiah for the forgiveness of your sins, and you will receive the gift of the Holy Spirit. For the promise is for you and for your children, and for all who are far off, as many as the Lord our God will call" (vv. 38–39). That morning, in a city set to celebrate the harvesting of grain, 3,000 people became part of a far greater harvest by expressing faith in Christ and requesting baptism. They were accepted into the Christian community without delay.

In the following days the believers "devoted themselves to the apostle's teaching, to fellowship, to the breaking of bread, and to prayers" (Acts 2:42). The presence of God in their midst was undeniable. Healing miracles and spectacular signs were performed as the Spirit empowered the gospel messengers, but holy fear gripped them also (v. 43). They banded together daily, counted their possessions as jointly held implements of their united cause, and worked their way from house to house sharing the news about Jesus with any who cared to listen. "And every day the Lord added to them those who were being saved" (v. 47).

Builder's Stone

One day soon after Pentecost, Peter and John headed up to the temple complex to pray during the hour of sacrifices. The courts were always crowded at this time. As they neared an entrance called Beautiful Gate, they met a crippled man whose custom was to sit and beg alms as people passed in to do their

St. Peter and St. John at the Beautiful Gate by Gustave Doré.

devotions. What better place to catch sympathy from good-hearted people? The man was well practiced. He had been disabled from birth and for more than 40 years had relied on the kindness of family and strangers. When he asked Peter and John for alms, Peter replied that they had no silver or gold to hand out, but what they did possess they would give freely. Peter then commanded him, "In the name of

Jesus Christ the Nazarene, get up and walk!" (Acts 3:6). Immediately the disorder in his lower legs was mended. "So he jumped up, stood, and started to walk, and he entered the temple complex with them—walking, leaping, and praising God" (v. 8). Once they were inside the temple, everyone recognized the man who daily posted himself at the gate. Astonished at his healing, they ran up and mobbed him as he danced all around Peter and John, both of whom the crowd began to admire for their healing powers. Unwilling to receive praise for a miracle done in Christ's name, Peter told the crowd that it was not by his power or goodness that the man had been healed (v. 13). He went on to call his audience to repentance and faith in Jesus, whom God will send again at the end of the age to restore the reign of righteousness over all the earth (vv. 19–21). When Peter started detailing God's promise of resurrec-

Peter called his audience to repentance and faith in Jesus, whom God will send again at the end of the age to restore the reign of righteousness over all the earth.

tion through Jesus, the priests and temple guardsmen became provoked. As Sadducees, these men disbelieved in resurrection or afterlife, and they resented the crowd's interest in Peter's message of hope. In a bid to stop the damages, they arrested Peter and John and held them overnight in jail, but it was too late to stop another surge of conversions. "Many of those who heard the message believed, and the number of the men came to about 5,000" (Acts 4:4).

The next day the priestly power players assembled and interrogated Peter and John about the healing. The healed man was invited also. He stood there, able-bodied and beaming, but the joy on his face was not mirrored by the dour religious leaders. "By what power or in what name have you done this?" they asked Peter and John, as if they had assaulted rather than healed the man (Acts 4:7). The priests could not deny the reality of the miracle or its effect among the people, but they sought to disprove that such a wondrous thing had been done through the agency of the Galilean carpenter whom they had executed atop Calvary. Would the Jesus mania never end?

Filled with the Spirit, Peter delivered a command performance in front of the spiritual rulers of Israel. He reiterated that the miracle was done in the name and power of Jesus Christ, whom God had raised from death. Forsaking all caution, Peter then closed his talk by describing Jesus as "the stone despised by you builders, who has become the cornerstone. There is salvation in no one else, for there is no other name under heaven given to people by which we must be saved" (Acts 4:11–12). This confirmed the Sanhedrin's worst fears. The crucifixion had failed to end the Jesus movement. Against all reason Jesus' disciples were going forward with his message, now adding scintillating claims of resurrection and healing to their list of absurdities. What should be done to quell their growth? The answer was simple: bar them from preaching. The Christian message was inherently appealing and promised hope to any who would only believe. No works or rituals were required, making the priesthood obsolete. Sensing the threat to their position, the Sanhedrin commanded Peter and John to stop preaching Jesus (v. 18). Indomitable Peter responded in just the way we would hope: "Whether it's right in the sight of God for us to listen to you rather than to God, you decide; for we are unable to stop speaking about what we have seen and heard" (vv. 19–20). Peter had walked on water with God, cowered in fear before unveiled divinity on a mountaintop, lost all courage in the face of Jesus' arrest, and then dined triumphantly with the risen Lord on a lakeshore in Galilee. He could not be intimidated by scheming men whose unbelief was driven by ignorance and spiritual destitution. Jesus' name would be on Peter's lips no matter the threats or ordinances of men. No doubt the Sanhedrin despised this response, but they were rendered powerless to harm the disciples because of the upwelling support Christianity had earned through the healing of the crippled man. The priests mumbled a string of threats and then expelled Peter and John from the assembly.

Newly freed, Peter and John reported their experiences to

the fellowship. Far from being discouraged, they took the opposition to be part of God's master plan. In prayer they confessed to God that Roman and Jewish authorities had come against Jesus "to do whatever Your hand and Your plan had predestined to take place" (Acts 4:28). Similarly, they judged that the oppositions they now faced were foreordained by God. Rather than exemption from hardship, they asked God to embolden them. In answer to this, "the place where they were assembled was shaken," and the Holy Spirit swept down upon them with renewed vigor, supplying fresh courage (v. 31). Stone by stone God built his church atop the cornerstone Israel's leaders had rejected.

Land for Sale

Within the span of 13 verses in Acts 4 and 5, Luke tells a dramatic tale of two parcels of land. Perhaps they were situated near one another outside Jerusalem, but, figuratively speaking, the fruit that grew up from them could hardly be more different. Here is the context. Shortly after Peter and John were threatened by the Sanhedrin, the young church reached a spiritual zenith it may never attain again until Christ comes to consummate our perfection. At this early juncture, all who believed "were of one heart and soul, and no one said that any of his possessions was his own, but instead they held everything in common" (Acts 4:32). None of the Christians had material needs because goods flowed back and forth between them in a circuitous stream of exchange. No leases. No rentals. No exchange of monies. Just make your need known, and it will be met.

None of the Christians had material needs because goods flowed back and forth between them in a circuitous stream of exchange. No leases. No rentals. No exchange of monies. Just make your need known, and it will be met.

People even sold houses and land in order to contribute to the charitable pot. Such was the communal state of emerging Christendom when two tracts of land came to the church's attention. The first was owned by a fellow from Cyprus named Joseph. Luke tells us that Joseph was nicknamed Barnabas by the apostles, a name meaning Son of Encouragement (v. 36). In keeping with this reputation Barnabas sold his land and donated all of the proceeds to the young church's coffer. No one forced him to do this. Repudiation of private ownership was never a requirement for membership in the Christian fellowship. In step with many of his fellow believers, however, Barnabas pitched his resources behind the effort to expand the church and serve needy Christians. His is a fine but neglected example for today.

Where there is encouragement and Christian sharing, the devil is sure to seek an inroad. He searched the Jerusalem fellowship for pretense, pride, and greed. Such faults he found in a married couple named Ananias and Sapphira. They ostensibly mimicked Barnabas's charitable act by selling some land

they owned, but when Ananias laid only *some* of the dividends at the apostles' feet, he made like he had held nothing back (Acts 5:2–3). Barnabas had been well received for his generosity. Ananias hoped to purchase the same high reputation without

The Death of Ananias by Rafael. "When he heard [Peter's] words, Ananias dropped dead, and a great fear came on all who heard" (Acts 5:5).

the matching sacrifice. The urge to seek approval among the pious is a force against which we all must contend. Ananias and Sapphira gave in and made a play for greater stature. Espying these motives, Peter told Ananias that he had not lied to men but to the Holy Spirit, the giver of inspired speech and discernment who had been so manifestly active in constructing the church since Pentecost (v. 4). By approaching the apostles with a falsehood, Ananias may as well have strode into God's own throne room with honey lips and a gut full of rot. "When he heard [Peter's] words, Ananias dropped dead, and a great fear came on all who heard" (v. 5). Some young men were present to witness this. They hastily wrapped Ananias' body and carried him out of doors in search of a burial plot.

Finding a suitable place, they committed to earth the body of one who sought self-aggrandizement in a church marked by self-sacrifice.

Around three hours later Sapphira presented herself before the apostles. No one had told her about her husband's death, and like anyone who believes they have hatched a winning deception, she was caught up in an ecstasy that blinded her to all signs of trouble. As she centered up in front of Peter, she expected to receive praise for her part in the giveaway. Possibly her delayed appearance was even designed to let the news percolate through the ranks, ensuring that she would catch maximal attention. Fixing Sapphira in his gaze, Peter asked if the field had been sold for the amount her husband had donated. She answered yes. "Then Peter said to her, 'Why did you agree to test the Spirit of the Lord? Look! The feet of those who have buried your husband are at the door, and they will carry you out!'" (Acts 5:9). With Peter's last words, she fell dead at his feet and was soon interred next to her husband.

It is difficult for modern believers to imagine Peter as prosecutor, the Holy Spirit as executioner, and young disciples as impromptu grave diggers. Here we come face-to-face with early realities that seem foreign or even contradictory to our modern experience of Christian community. What are we to make of this episode? First, *At this early mark in church history, God worked in extraordinary ways that have not been closely repeated in subsequent eras.* we must grasp the larger context of Ananias and Sapphira's deaths. At this early mark in church history, God worked in extraordinary ways that have not been closely repeated in subsequent eras. Only once in history did Jesus come to live, die, and rise again on our behalf, and only once has God initiated his church through the band of men who served as the chosen eyewitnesses to the life and teachings of Christ. As with any new historical movement, it was important to get it right from the start, or else there would be little chance of recovering truth down the line. Either Jesus' biography would be firmly established by the men who were commissioned to write and teach it, or else it would be jostled, mutated, and freely altered at every turn as people with no claim to knowledge or authority fashioned Jesus into whatever image they pleased. In this light it was vital that God establish the authority of the apostles and the trustworthiness of their teachings. When Ananias and Sapphira paraded a false claim of charity before Peter, they made a direct assault on apostolic authority and its uncompromising commitment to truth. Furthermore and even more significantly, it was necessary in this early era for God to demonstrate beyond question that the Holy Spirit was genuinely and powerfully involved in the life of the church. It was no idle promise when Jesus said the Spirit would indwell believers and guide them in truth (John 16:13).

It was vital that God establish the authority of the apostles and the trustworthiness of their teachings.

Second, the story of Ananias and Sapphira highlights our need to recover the fear of God that pervaded the early church. Five times in Acts we are told that fear came over the church or that they walked in fear of God (2:43; 5:5,11; 9:31; 19:17). How many churches resemble this today? God's presence was palpable among the first believers. May it be so for us today!

Third, we must not fall into the mistake of forming our doctrine of God based solely on the Scripture passages in which he forcefully judges sin. God's judgment against sin is a stark reality that we must not neglect, but we should stand in even greater awe anytime we see a demonstration of his undeserved love and grace toward sinners.

Dishonored for the Name

The episode with Ananias and Sapphira sobered the church but did not check its momentum in the least. As Luke reports it, "Many signs and wonders were being done among the people through the hands of the apostles" (Acts 5:12). With each miracle the apostles gained new renown, but always they deflected honor to the Christ in whose power the works were performed. Men and women came

With each miracle the apostles gained new renown, but always they deflected honor to the Christ in whose power the works were performed.

to faith in droves, and people were healed with such regularity that a river of stretchers and pallets flowed into Peter's presence from villages around Jerusalem (vv. 14–16). Unwilling to tolerate this, the ruling Sadducees arrested the apostles. It was little use. An angel sprang them in the middle of the night and told them to go to the temple "and tell the people all about this life," which they promptly did at daybreak (vv. 20–21). Soon the baffled temple authorities tracked down the absconded apostles and escorted them to a meeting of the Sanhedrin where the high priest asked why they had disobeyed the command not to preach about Jesus. Sounding a familiar

The Liberation of Peter by Caracciolo.

refrain, Peter answered, "We must obey God rather than men" (v. 29). This sharp retort nearly got Peter and his fellows killed, but a temperate Pharisee named Gamaliel intervened and suggested the apostles be put outside for a while. Once he was alone with the assembly, he advised them to be patient. If the Jesus movement is not of God, it will sputter and die. If on the other hand it *is* of God, opposition is useless. The council saw the wisdom in Gamaliel's assessment, and as a result they merely flogged the apostles and again forbade them from preaching. What effect did this have? The apostles "went out from the presence of the Sanhedrin, rejoicing that they were counted worthy to be dishonored on behalf of the name" (v. 41). As for preaching, they kept it up just as before. House to market, temple to court—the name of Jesus spread like healing fire.

Martyr's Blood

The church soon grew past its capacity to care for its needy members. Realizing this, the apostles called the host of believers together and explained that they were being distract-ed from preaching and prayer and thus found it necessary to appoint "seven men of good reputation, full of the Spirit and wisdom," who could manage the task of distributing food and care as necessity arose (Acts 6:1–4). The proposal was enacted immediately with the result that the apostles made greater im-pact than ever before. Even "a large group of priests became obedient to the faith" through the apostolic preaching (v. 7). Undoubtedly a great many of these priests had previously voted to execute Jesus and sup-press the emerging church, but by force of the Old Testament

Jesus was coming to be loved by many who had once hated him.

prophecies, the eyewitness testimony to the resurrection, and the miracles of mercy that changed lives daily, genuinely pi-ous priests could not hold back the tide of truth that washed against their hearts. Jesus was coming to be loved by many who had once hated him.

Of the seven men chosen to manage the church's charitable efforts, the best known was a young man named Stephen. He was "full of grace and power," and "great wonders and signs" were done as the Spirit worked through him (Acts 6:8). This made him a natural target. One day a group hailing from the Freedman's Synagogue cornered Stephen and tried to make him look foolish, but "they were unable to stand up against the wisdom and the Spirit by whom he spoke" (v. 10). Ashamed of their failure, these men accused Stephen of blasphemy, with the result that he was dragged before the Sanhedrin. He stood before them with an angelic face as capital charges were read against him (v. 15). When it was his turn to speak, Stephen masterfully traced the history of Israel's relations with God from the days of Abraham down through Solomon (7:2–50). In many ways it was an ignoble history filled with rebellious figures who taunted God and resisted his messengers. It was little different now. "Which of the prophets did your fathers not persecute? They even killed those who announced before-hand the coming of the Righteous One, whose betrayers and murderers you have now become" (v. 52). In response to this charge, the assembly became howling mad and gnashed their teeth at Stephen. He had not only touched a nerve; he gouged it down its length. Foreseeing the outcome of his trial, Stephen looked skyward and was granted a vision of what awaited him on the other side. "Look!" he exclaimed to his accusers, "I see the heavens opened and the Son of Man standing at the right hand of God!" (v. 56). The end came quickly after this. Screaming in force and blocking their ears from Stephen's blasphemies, the priests seized him and pushed him into open spaces beyond the city boundaries. There they could stone him without interference from the Roman authorities. A hail of stones broke Stephen's strength, pushing him to the ground. From a kneeled position, he called not for heaven's vengeance but for mercy. "Lord, do not charge them with this sin!" (v. 60). As Stephen lay dying, a zealous young Pharisee, a choice tool in the hands of those seeking to eradicate Christian faith, stood nearby and guarded the robes of his superiors. His name was Saul. Stephen's

The Stoning of Stephen by Rembrandt. From a kneeled position, Stephen called not for heaven's vengeance but for mercy. "Lord, do not charge them with this sin!" (Acts 7:60).

death pleased Saul, but he saw it as only the barest beginning of a pogrom that must run down every street and alley in David's city. Only by the letting of Christian blood would Israel's festering wound be healed. Such was Saul's diagnosis.

Growth through Suppression

Stephen's murder sparked off a wave of persecution that drove most of Jerusalem's Christians into the surrounding Judean countryside and beyond. It had never been safe to follow Christ; now it was downright deadly. Saul was lead thug in the roundup (Acts 8:3). Remarkably, the more he pushed for the church's annihilation the more broadly its roots extended. This was because "those who were scattered went on their way proclaiming the message of good news" (v. 4). By this means many people who otherwise would never have learned about

Jesus met him in the teachings of the Christians who had been hounded out of Jerusalem. Even the Samaritans got to hear the gospel when a Christian named Philip preached to them as he worked to keep out of Saul's warpath. They embraced his message eagerly (v. 8). Unlike everyone else in the Christian fellowship, the apostles held their ground in Jerusalem despite many threats, but when they heard that some Samaritans had converted to Christ, they risked a sortie by sending Peter and John to investigate. Finding their confessions convincing, the apostles prayed over the Samaritans and watched as even these people,

> *Many people who otherwise would never have learned about Jesus met him in the teachings of the Christians who had been hounded out of Jerusalem.*

so despised by good Jews everywhere, were gifted with the Holy Spirit (v. 17). More of the same happened on their return journey as Peter and John stopped off in dozens of stray villages, preaching a Christ whose adoration was quickly becoming a multicultural phenomenon (v. 25). Even an Ethiopian dignitary joined the movement when Philip obeyed the Spirit's prompting to loiter on a roadway near the Gaza desert. Philip intercepted the Ethiopian's chariot and found him reading from the book of Isaiah. News was traveling all around that Jesus had fulfilled the messianic prophecies, but the Ethiopian could not understand Isaiah. Philip gladly explained Isaiah's text and other Old Testament teachings about Jesus. The Ethiopian embraced all that Philip taught him and requested baptism when he spotted water. Philip obliged him and was then whisked away by the Spirit to a nearby city. There he kicked off a campaign to evangelize a string of coastal towns until he reached his terminus in Caesarea (vv. 38–40). Even there, in a city raised to Caesar's honor, people turned from false religion to the living Christ (10:16).

From Damascus to Rome

Meanwhile Saul continued his quest to extinguish the church's flame, but for all his exertions, he only managed to scatter embers throughout Israel and beyond, setting up a conflagration that eventually trapped even him. Being well positioned in the religious hierarchy, he asked and received from the high priest letters directed to the synagogues in Damascus (north of Israel, modern Syria), requesting that they should hand over to Saul any synagogue members who had joined league with the Christians. These would be arrested and taken to Jerusalem for trial (Acts 9:1–2). Saul's journey to Damascus changed history, but not in the way he anticipated. "As he traveled and was nearing Damascus, a light from heaven suddenly flashed around him. Falling to the ground, he heard a voice saying to him, 'Saul, Saul, why are you persecuting Me?'" (vv. 3–4). The voice was that of the risen Jesus. Contrary to all expectations, the Lord selected this antagonist to be his chief messenger to the non-Jewish world. Blinded and cowering to the ground, Saul listened as Jesus instructed him to go on to Damascus as planned. Saul's companions led him by the hand. Christ spoke to a disciple named Ananias and told him to meet up with Saul on Straight

The Conversion of Paul by Caravaggio. "As he traveled and was nearing Damascus, a light from heaven suddenly flashed around him. Falling to the ground, he heard a voice saying to him, 'Saul, Saul, why are you persecuting Me?'" (Acts 9:3–4).

Street. Though skittish due to Saul's venomous reputation, Ananias obeyed. Soon Saul was healed of his temporary blindness, baptized into the faith, and introduced to the Christian fellowship in that city. To Saul no less than his newfound (and wary!) brethren, the world had gone upside down. For Saul the shift was so significant that he decided to go by the name Paul, most likely in conscious imitation of Old Testament patriarchs who came away with new names after having profound experiences with God.[6]

In the years and decades that followed, the apostles kept

Jerusalem as their main base of operations, but they also scoured the nations, preaching Jesus as Messiah to Jews and non-Jews alike. Though a latecomer and a one-time archenemy, Paul was grafted into the apostolic circle since Christ himself had appeared to him and charged him with the Gentile mission. Controversy cropped up from time to time as Jewish Christians struggled to understand what kinds of expectations to place on Gentile Christians and how to interpret law in the context of Christ's grace, and always there was the need for instruction and encouragement, correction and admonition as the apostles sought to cultivate maturity and potency of witness among the churches. The New Testament books which follow after Acts are the inspired records of these efforts. As we will explore still further in the next chapter, from the earliest days of the church on through to the closing frames of the New Testament, the consistent claim of the Christians was that Jesus of Nazareth was God's Messiah, the divine-human Son of God who died for human sins and was raised to new life three days later. This is who they understood Jesus to be, and in their preaching they made it clear that it was all or nothing. Either you followed Christ as the

Opposition mounted in every city, but with tongues of fire the apostles and everyday disciples plied Christ's message among the peoples of every nation that lay within their reach.

risen Lord and Savior of your soul, or else you opposed him. Opposition mounted in every city, but with tongues of fire the apostles and everyday disciples plied Christ's message among the peoples of every nation that lay within their reach.

Shortly before he was executed in Rome, the apostle Paul wrote a letter to one of his protégés, a minister named Timothy. By this point Paul had given 30 years of his life to the cause of Jesus Christ. Many times he had been beaten, stoned, and whipped for his testimony. At a thousand points along life's trail, he could have ended his suffering by simply backing down from his claims about Jesus, but he never did so because he refused to go back on the truth. Jesus was alive from the dead. Against all his deepest expectations, Paul had seen this for himself. Reflecting back on this legacy and looking forward to his reward, Paul wrote to Timothy, "I have fought the good fight, I have finished the race, I have kept the faith. In the future, there is reserved for me the crown of righteousness, which the Lord, the righteous Judge, will give me on that day, and not only to me, but to all who have loved His appearing" (2 Tim 4:7–8). For Paul there could be no doubt that his faith was well-founded and that his every sacrifice for truth would reap eternal dividends. The question arises: Can we have that same confidence today? Unlike Paul none of us has seen the Lord on the road to Damascus. What we have are books, a collection of 27 altogether, commonly called the New Testament. In the next chapter we examine vital issues regarding the trustworthiness of these books.

Notes

1. In Matthew 27:3–10 we are told that guilt-stricken Judas returned his money to the priests and then hanged himself. The priests then used the money to buy a field that they dedicated as a burial ground for foreigners. The field became known as "Blood Field" because the priests had used "blood money" to purchase it. Matthew sees all of this as a type fulfillment of an event recorded in Jeremiah 32:6–9. Luke's account in Acts 1:18–20 seems to differ significantly. Taken in its most natural sense, Luke's report has Judas buying a field himself and then falling headfirst to his death while walking the property. The field became known as "Field of Blood" because Judas' innards spilled forth due to the impact of his fall. The differences between Acts and Matthew on this score are impressive and often trouble readers. However, it is incorrect to say that these variant reports compose an outright contradiction, for it is possible to suggest a scenario that harmonizes the discrepancies. No formal contradiction exists where a logically possible resolution can be deployed. The most common attempt at resolution goes something like this: Judas returned the money to the priests. The priests then purchased a field using Judas' money. Thus indirectly Judas purchased the field. As for his death, it is suggested that Judas hanged himself and subsequently his decomposed corpse fell from the noose and burst open. Possibly at this time the priests had not yet

purchased the field with Judas' money. If so, they may very naturally have chosen to purchase the field in which Judas hanged himself, thus simultaneously justifying both Matthew in his assertion that the field was called "Blood Field" because it was purchased with blood money and Luke (Acts 1:19) in his claim that the field's name derived from the fact that Judas' body burst open onto the ground. Admittedly, this scenario involves creative thinking. One may even doubt its feasibility, but one cannot deny that it counts as a logically possible harmonization, plus it is motivated by a recognition that when all facts are known Scripture in all its testimonies will cohere, broadly at least, since God is its author (2 Tim 3:16). Nevertheless, we should avoid forced, artificial harmonizations that risk leaving the reader incredulous. For more discussion on the nature of Scripture, see chapter 20, "A Gift of Words."

2. It is from Psalm 109:8 that the disciples most directly drew the conclusion that Judas had to be replaced, but they likely also inferred this need from the fact that Jesus had intentionally chosen 12 inner disciples from the beginning of his ministry as a visually compelling demonstration that the hope of Israel's 12 tribes were fulfilled in Jesus of Nazareth, the Messiah of God.

3. The 12 men (minus Judas) who throughout the Gospels are called "the disciples" are often referred to as "the apostles" in the rest of the New Testament, for they became the "sent ones" when Jesus personally commissioned them to be his authorized messengers in Jerusalem and abroad. The man chosen to replace Judas was considered an apostle because he had been an eyewitness to Jesus' life plus he received commission through the agency of the apostles whom Christ had chosen.

4. By "every nation under heaven" Luke merely means all the nations known to the Hebrew consciousness.

5. By "Diaspora languages" I mean the languages that were native to the lands outside Israel where many Jews had lived since Israel was sacked by foreign armies between the eighth and sixth centuries BC.

6. Perhaps the most gripping name change in the Old Testament is recorded in Genesis 32:24–32, where Jacob is renamed Israel after he wrestles with God. As for Saul's switching his name to Paul, it was common for Romans to bear three

names. Most likely "Paul" was one of the apostle's birth names but was not his preferred name until after his conversion.

Chapter 19
The Surviving Voice

Be careful what you say in the dark. Voices carry far in the chill of night because air becomes denser as it cools, meaning there are fewer gaps between air molecules as they compact together due to energy loss. Thus voices travel efficiently from molecule to molecule through a dim and sleeping world. Voices do not travel as far in daytime because they must compete with other sounds and because air molecules are spaced more widely apart due to warmer temperatures, creating microscopic voids that allow sound waves to dissipate into nothingness. If enough gaps and competing sounds are present, your voice soon dies out.

What of Jesus? Have gaps in time and information muted his voice? Have competing voices drowned him out? If so, we listen in vain for his words, for our only hope of hearing him hinges

Jesus' voice can be heard in the New Testament because a small band of men mastered his teachings and wrote them down without mixture of error.

on the survival of his voice. In this chapter I argue that Jesus' voice can be heard in the New Testament because a small band of men mastered his teachings and wrote them down without mixture of error. Listen closely and you will hear it going forth through the world's spiritual night.

Memoirs of Messiah

In AD 100 a child named Justin was born into the world at Flavia Neapolis, a city in Roman Palestine. His parents loved the pagan gods and laid great store by the ancient rites. They fostered these same devotions in young Justin. As he grew older, he pursued gods and philosophies in a quest for meaning. For years it was a fruitless search, but then sometime around age 30 he met an old man who had all the answers. Finding that a "fire was suddenly kindled" in his soul, Justin converted to Christianity and dedicated his life to defending it as "the true philosophy."[1] Why did Justin think Christianity was true?

Justin Martyr on Trial. Justin was willing to die as a public witness to the truth of the gospel.

How could he be sure that it was truly reflective of what Jesus believed and taught? After all, it was now more than 100 years after Jesus' crucifixion. Would any trace of Christ's true teachings remain? Justin believed so. He was convinced that the New Testament writings (which he called "the memoirs of the apostles") were reliable eyewitness accounts about Jesus' miracles, his teachings, his predictions of death and crucifixion, and his resurrection from the dead. Justin was so sure that the apostles had gotten it right that he was willing to die rather than renounce their teachings. Thus in 165 he chose to be executed rather than obey a Roman command to sacrifice to the gods. For this reason history has given Justin the surname Martyr, which stems from a Greek word meaning *witness.* Justin was willing to die as a public witness to the truth of the gospel. The question arises: Was Justin right to trust the New Testament writings?

Would *you* be right to trust them today?

Training the Twelve

Jesus did not broadcast his teachings randomly as he walked from town to town, hoping a few people might listen closely enough to remember what he said. Instead, at the outset of his ministry, Jesus did what many gifted teachers of the ancient world did: he chose a small group of men to be his dedicated students. These men recognized that Jesus had not recruited them simply to tag along on a sightseeing tour. To be a disciple was to be a serious student, a *worker*. And so for three years these men listened closely to Jesus' teachings, witnessed his extraordinary actions, and paid attention when Jesus explained the meaning of those actions. As for Jesus, he was intentional and strategic in his teaching efforts. He used proven teaching tools such as parables, repetition, and visual aids to make learning easier and embed the lessons deeply in each student's memory. Jesus also taught his disciples *how* to spread his message (Mark 6:7–11) and commanded them to give their lives to this task after his resurrection (Matt 28:18–20). In summary, the disciples were the official students of a dedicated, skilled instructor who provided them with practical teaching experience during his lifetime and bade them give their lives to this task once he left earth. The disciples suffered many early halts and hitches on the path to understanding, but they were sincerely dedicated to the tasks of comprehending Jesus' teachings and remembering them with accuracy.

The disciples suffered many early halts and hitches on the path to understanding, but they were sincerely dedicated to the tasks of comprehending Jesus' teachings and remembering them with accuracy.

A Disciple's Memory

Even if Jesus chose men to be his student followers and crafted his teachings to facilitate understanding and memory, how well would the disciples remember decades later when they and their associates set out to write the Gospels? Memories fade as brains age and time stretches far beyond sight of original experiences. Does this not cast doubt on the reliability of the Gospels? The first step to answering this challenge is to recognize that the disciples did not flee Jerusalem or divorce themselves from Jesus' story line once he departed (Acts 1:9). Instead, they returned to the city, gathered with other believers, and became the focal point of the ongoing controversy about Jesus. In the days, weeks, months, and years after Jesus' ascension, the disciples repeatedly defended their beliefs and explained Jesus' biography to anyone who would listen. Their memories of Jesus were rehearsed daily as they gave unbroken attention to spreading his teachings during the decades stretching between Christ's life and the writing of the Gospels. Therefore Jesus' teachings stayed fresh in their minds through the years as they preached in city after city, giving them no opportunity to forget or inadvertently muddle the truths they knew.

The Preaching of the Apostles by Gustave Doré.

Further, most of us today have lost touch with the potential powers of the human memory. Pens and notepads abound all around us. We write grocery lists even when we go to fetch only two or three items. When it comes to bigger memory tasks, we store reams of data in books and computers, not our minds. Lack of such tools forced the ancients to make better use of the brain's storage capacities. The Jews in particular were impressive in this regard. As a people to whom God had revealed his will in spoken and written words, Jewish students of religion were motivated to achieve herculean feats of memorization. This value was emphasized by Moses in particular. After giving God's revelations at Mount Sinai, he admonished the people, "These words that I am giving you today are to be in your heart. Repeat them to your children. Talk about them when you sit in your house and when you walk along the road, when you lie down and when you get up" (Deut 6:6–7). It is fitting that such care should be taken with words from God. By Jesus' era it was said that advanced students of Jewish religion were like a basketfull of books; they kept *everything* in their heads. Though Jesus' disciples lacked this level of formal training it is certain that from the moment Jesus called them to be his students, they knew that they were expected to comprehend and remember

From the moment Jesus called them to be his students, the disciples knew that they were expected to comprehend and remember his teachings.

his teachings. To do anything less would be to disrespect their teacher, especially since they believed he was Messiah. Thus we have every reason to suppose that the disciples locked Jesus' teachings into their memories and kept them untainted for the rest of their lives.

Finally, the disciples likely wrote down key portions of Jesus' teachings years before the Gospels were written. Possibly they even took detailed notes during Jesus' ministry, as was sometimes done by students of leading rabbis.[2] These deposits would have been available to support the memory and serve as handy source materials for writing the Gospels. Luke may allude to such things when he refers to his preparation for writing his Gospel (Luke 1:1–4).

Holy Reminder

Jesus' strategic teaching efforts and the prowess of well-honed memories put the disciples in a good position to understand and remember Jesus' life and teachings, but there was an additional factor that helped them preach and write with accuracy. I speak of the Holy Spirit, whom Jesus sent to help his disciples comprehend and remember his teachings (John 14:26). The New Testament shows that the disciples became aware of the Spirit's role in their writings. The Jews laid great stress on the distinction between inspired Scripture and ordinary writing. Rabbis even said the Scriptures "defiled the hands," a surprising phrase that meant Scripture should never be handled flippantly. Since becoming defiled required one to undergo a lengthy cleansing process, no one bothered to handle the biblical scrolls unless they were undertaking a holy purpose. Such was the regard Jews had for God's Word. To claim that a document was from God would be blasphemous if untrue, and yet this is the very claim the disciples made regarding the New Testament. For example, in 1 Timothy 5:18 Paul quotes the words of Jesus as found in Luke 10:7 and calls it Scripture. Not only was Paul convinced that Luke had accurately reported Jesus' life and teachings, he actually believed God had inspired Luke's Gospel. Similarly, Peter affirmed that Paul's writings are Scripture in 2 Peter 3:15–16. This designation would have borne a lot of authority given Peter's leadership role in the early church. Clearly the men whom Jesus appointed to spread his teachings believed they bore authority from God. We will examine the issue of inspiration more closely later in this chapter and the next.

Hard Facts

It is popular among skeptics to claim that the New Testament books were written as expressions of a growing Jesus legend, not as reports of true history. This claim flies in the face of available evidence. Even a cursory reading of the New Testament reveals that the authors repeatedly emphasize the role of eyewitnesses and hang their claims on the historical reality of the events they describe. For instance, when Luke discloses his methods and purposes at the beginning of his Gospel (Luke 1:1–4), he says his book is about "the events that have been fulfilled among us" as recounted by "the original eyewitnesses and servants" of Christ. He also says he researched these matters carefully before writing and that his reason for doing this was so his reader could "know the certainty" on which the Christian faith is based. Here is a man who has no place for legends, half-truths, or shots in the dark!

Luke says he researched these matters carefully before writing and that his reason for doing this was so his reader could "know the certainty" on which the Christian faith is based.

His focus is on the real Jesus and world-altering events that cannot be doubted. John similarly emphasizes the importance of *fact*. He is sure of what he has written and says he included only a small fraction of Jesus' doings (John 20:30 and 21:24–25). And like Luke he wants his readers to know Jesus as Lord and thus gain eternal life (John 20:31 and 1 John 5:13). Far from passing on shady legends, his goal was to convey assured truth.

Luke and John impress us with their emphasis on truth, but the most striking assertion that the New Testament witness is truthful comes from the apostle Paul. Paul bitterly opposed the young church as it roared through Israel like wildfire. As a zealot for pharisaic doctrines and the old ways of his fore-

The Apostle Paul by Rembrandt. Paul understood that the literal resurrection of Christ was the absolute basis of Christianity.

fathers, he wanted to eradicate Christianity. His campaign against the Christians drew praise from his elders and assured him that he would rise in power and position among Israel's priestly leaders. This all changed when Jesus supernaturally appeared to him on the road to Damascus. In a stunning reversal Paul poured the rest of his life into spreading truth about the same Jesus whom he had opposed. The foundation of his preaching was Jesus' resurrection. More than just a snappy preaching point, Paul understood that the literal resurrection of Christ was the absolute basis of Christianity. In 1 Corinthians 15:12–19 he said that if Christ's resurrection was not a real historical event, Christianity is a myth and Christians are liars. How could he lay his faith and personal integrity on the line like this? The answer is obvious. Like John, Luke, and every other New Testament author, Paul *knew* that Christianity was fixed on the sure foundation of truth.

Money and Movement

Religion has always been a best-seller. For this reason leaders of popular new religious movements rarely lack money. Avid disciples infuse the movement with cash, which all too often the leader uses for lavish personal upkeep and the operation of his publicity machine. Peel away the hype and you find a string of exaggerations, fabrications, and outright delusions that serve to inflate both man and movement beyond all reason.

What about the apostles of Jesus Christ? In Jesus' absence they led his movement from relative obscurity to empire-wide recognition. Did they become rich doing this? If so, it would be reasonable to suggest that they fabricated Jesus' biography, making both Jesus and their part in his mission more fantastic than reality warranted. However, evidence proves that the apostles won anything but riches for their devotion to Jesus. Monies that flowed into the Christian movement were quickly shunted toward needy widows and orphans rather than yawning apostolic coffers (Acts 2:44–45; 4:32–37). The apostles remained ever faithful to this ethic, for we see Paul performing his ministerial services free of charge in the decades after the church exploded into existence. To the Christian leaders in Ephesus he said, "I have not coveted anyone's silver or gold or clothing. You yourselves know that these hands have provided for my needs, and for those who were with me. In every way I've shown you that by laboring like this, it is necessary to help the weak and to keep in mind the words of the Lord Jesus, for He said, 'It is more blessed to give than to receive'" (Acts 20:33–35). To avoid placing financial hardship on the churches, Paul worked as a tent maker to provide for his needs and those of his fellow ministers (Acts 18:3). He encouraged all Christian laborers to emulate this model, as for instance when he said to Christians in Thessalonica, "For you yourselves know how you must imitate us: we were not irresponsible among you; we did not eat anyone's bread free of charge; instead, we labored and toiled, working night and day, so that

> *Monies that flowed into the Christian movement were quickly shunted toward needy widows and orphans rather than yawning apostolic coffers.*

we would not be a burden to any of you" (2 Thess 3:7–8). By word and deed Paul laid down a principle that all servants of the gospel must follow: ministers must serve in a manner that proves that their motives are spiritual rather than financial.[3] In conclusion, the money did indeed flow as the Christian movement grew, but the apostles always

The gathering of wealth and comfort was never a motive for spreading the good news about Jesus.

deployed it to meet the needs of fellow believers and gospel laborers. The gathering of wealth and comfort was never a motive for spreading the good news about Jesus.

Ambition

There are other forms of gain besides money. Did the apostles win fame and approval by preaching Jesus as Messiah and risen Lord? If so, perhaps they bilked a set of exaggerated stories for the sake of winning esteem from their peers. Does the evidence support this possibility? Absolutely not. Most Jews regarded the apostles as deviants from Israel's holy traditions. Gentiles cared little for Jewish traditions but shared the Jewish disdain for Jesus' followers and saw them as threats to civil society. In nearly every city they visited, the apostles were apt to be arrested and beaten for their testimony. Most of them were eventually executed because they would not shut up about Jesus. Would the apostles persist in such a self-destructive lifestyle if they knew their sermons were based on hype, wishful thinking, or outright fabrication? Of course not. Notice the things Paul suffered for his allegiance to Christ:

> Five times I received from the Jews 40 lashes minus one. Three times I was beaten with rods. Once I was stoned. Three times I was shipwrecked. I have spent a night and a day in the depths of the sea. On frequent journeys, I faced dangers from rivers, dangers from robbers, dangers from my own people, dangers from the Gentiles, dangers in the city, dangers in the open country, dangers on the sea, and dangers among false brothers; labor and hardship, many sleepless nights, hunger and thirst, often without food, cold, and lacking clothing (2 Cor 11:24–27).

Whole towns were outraged by the message the apostles preached. In Ephesus, a mob of craftsmen perceived that their livelihood was in danger because the Christian message was muting the demand for silver idols and shrines dedicated to the goddess Artemis. Led by a fiery purist named Demetrius, these men "rushed all together into the amphitheater" where the Christians were preaching. Paul was not present at the time, so the mob grabbed two of his traveling companions instead. When Paul learned of this, he tried to make his way into the amphitheater to take a stand alongside his companions, but friends prevented him from doing so because murder was in the hearts of the craftsmen. By slow degrees the city clerk talked the mob down from its furor (Acts 19:21–41). This sort of scene was

Ephesian craftsmen persecuted the Christians because their preaching undercut the idol-making business. Photo: HolyLandPhotos.org.

repeated in cities throughout Israel and beyond. Far from winning fame, the apostles were a scourge on the earth. Accepting no money and winning no fame for their labors, why would they persist in preaching if they had invented grand but untrue stories about Jesus? Or why would they drive on undeterred if, after years of reflection, they began to suspect that they had been too excitable during the week of Jesus' death and might have only imagined his resurrection? Obviously they wouldn't have continued if they even *remotely* suspected such a thing. Only a foundation of assured, life-giving knowledge could motivate a band of men to forsake all worldly comforts and remain true to a message which earned them so much pain and trouble.

Only a foundation of assured, life-giving knowledge could motivate a band of men to forsake all worldly comforts and remain true to a message that earned them so much pain and trouble.

Public Revelation

All major religions claim that private revelations or insights have come from God to select individuals in the past. In the Bible we think of God's appearing to Abram in Haran or to Moses in the burning bush. To the extent that Christianity, Islam, and Mormonism share Old Testament history as part of their foundation, they all rely on the possibility, indeed the *reality*, that private revelation has come from God in the past. Unlike Christianity, however, all of the revelations that make Islam and Mormonism distinct rest entirely on private revelations that were supposedly given to lone "prophets" who then branched off from the biblical tradition and started their own religion. Mohammed, for instance, is the sole author of Islam's holy book, the Qur'an. He said he wrote it on the basis of revelations given by Gabriel in the privacy of a desert cave beginning in his teenage years. Naturally Mohammed could not prove that such meetings actually occurred. People either

Fourteenth-century depiction of Mohammed receiving his revelation.

believed his claims or they didn't. Similarly, Joseph Smith Jr. founded Mormonism on the basis of mystical experiences which no one could verify. Preoccupation with mysticism ran in the Smith family, as it turns out. Joseph's father was a diviner and an avid treasure hunter. Smith Senior's fixation on treasure hunting was peculiar given the fact that he was born into late colonial America. How much treasure could be buried in a land which had never been inhabited by anything more than a thin band of hunter-gatherers? Perhaps he suspected that America actually had a storied but hidden history of civilization. In any case Smith Jr. adopted his father's interests and took them to new levels beginning at age 15 when God supposedly commissioned him to reestablish authentic Christianity, which had apparently gone missing some 18 centuries beforehand. This holy calling did not keep Joseph from using his father's pagan seer stones in the quest to find America's long-buried treasure. At age 22 he hit pay dirt. From a hillside near Palmyra, New York, Smith allegedly unearthed golden plates engraved with "reformed Egyptian hieroglyphics" that gave a historical record of Jesus' dealings with ancient American civilizations whose every trace had been obliterated

The so-called "Sacred Grove" (as it appeared in 1907) where Joseph Smith received the Book of Mormon in the 1820s. Photo: George Edward Anderson.

from earth. Convenient, isn't it, that young Joseph's find vindicated his father's quirky theory about treasure? Even more conveniently, only Smith and a few hand-picked "witnesses" ever saw these plates. Veiled by a curtain, Smith decoded the hieroglyphics as a secretary took it all down. The Book of Mormon is the result.[4]

To say the least, the origins of Mormonism and Islam are suspect. Dark caves and concealed spaces of the mind, furtive teenage boys receiving commissions from God Almighty, treasure-yielding hillsides and golden artifacts carefully hidden from inquiring minds—these are tales of hidden origins, subterfuge, and *deception*. The original converts to these new religions were in no position to question the founding revelations, nor could they stave off baseless legends that grew around the founding figure. After all, no one but the founder was "in the know" about what really did or did not happen at the advent of his religion.

The initiation of the Christian religion was entirely different. Jesus was a public figure making public claims supported by public actions. His miracles, his teachings, his transfiguration, the descent of God's Spirit at his baptism, his return from the dead—these and many other foundational events took place in the presence of witnesses. The apostles in particular were present to see and hear these things. Granted, they were privy to a lot of instruction that Jesus never shared with the wider public, but this instruction was an elucidation of his public actions and teachings. Hence Christianity, unlike Islam or Mormonism, was significantly founded on the basis of *public* revelation. No caves, trances, or elusive gilded plates were involved. Christianity's foundational claims were laid bare for all to see. Either Jesus really did feed 5,000 men with a handful of food, or else he did not. Plenty of witnesses were on hand to judge the matter. Either the voice of God really did boom from heaven on several occasions, verifying Jesus' status and authority, or else it did not. Again, witnesses were on hand to judge the matter. Jesus never slinked into town claiming he had received a private word from God and that on that basis everyone must follow him. Instead, he was with people, especially his chosen students, at

Miracle of the Loaves and Fishes by Lambert. Either Jesus really did feed 5,000 men with a handful of food, or else he did not. Plenty of witnesses were on hand to judge the matter.

every key juncture in his ministry. Therefore, had the Christian story line gotten out of control down the line, such that indefensible legends grew up in the name of Jesus, the apostles were in an ideal position to throw cold water on such exuberances and set the record straight. They were the authorities on the public revelations of Jesus Christ, and even they could not fudge Jesus' story since many hundreds of other people had kept pace with Jesus' doings well enough to act as secondary authorities on what did and did not take place. All of these people, therefore, would have been willing, able, and *eager* to quell any legends that exaggerated Jesus' story. This is especially true since Christians suffered persecution over their allegiance to Jesus. If misunderstandings and exaggerations of

Jesus' life and claims caused persecution, the apostles, backed by countless other witnesses, would have stepped forward to set the story straight and thus end the baseless persecutions. This never happened. It never happened because Jesus really taught what the apostles said he taught, really did what they said he did, and really did rise victorious on the third day.

Hail the Gods?

The apostles consistently turned away opportunities to glorify themselves. For instance, Peter was once sent by God to visit with a modestly prominent Gentile named Cornelius. This man feared God but knew little or nothing about Jesus. In a vision he was told to send for Peter. When Peter arrived, Cornelius "met him, fell at his feet, and worshiped him" (Acts 10:25). Here was one of many chances for Peter to accept praise and worship, but notice his response: "Stand up! I myself am also a man" (v. 26).

Paul once faced a similar test. He and Barnabas were preaching in a town called Lystra when Paul noticed that faith was dawning on the face of a crippled man in the audience. In a loud voice Paul commanded him to stand up. Never in his life had the man been able to do such a thing, but now he *The apostles consistently turned away opportunities to glorify themselves.* "jumped up and started to walk around" (Acts 14:10). Astounded, the crowd called out, "The gods have come down to us in the form of men!" Barnabas they took to be Zeus. Paul they decided was Hermes, "the god who leads in speaking."[5] The priest who officiated at the nearby temple of Zeus fetched oxen and garlands and, along with the crowd, prepared to offer sacrifices to Paul and Barnabas. The apostles "tore their robes when they heard this and rushed into the crowd, shouting: 'Men! Why are you doing these things?'" (vv. 11–15). They assured the crowds that they were mere men and that they had been sent by the one true God to announce good news. "Even though they said these things, they barely stopped the crowds from sacrificing to them" (v. 18).

What is most remarkable about this event is that Paul and Barnabas put themselves in danger by rejecting the people's worship. Unbelieving Jews who had dedicated themselves to snuffing Christianity soon tracked Paul and Barnabas to Lystra and rallied the people against them. Had Paul and Barnabas permitted the people to deify them, the prosecuting Jews would have been chased from town; but since the apostles emphasized their mere humanity the Lystrians were game for the pitch the Jews came to make. Heroes fall hard. If Paul and Barnabas were not miracle-working gods,

What is most remarkable about this event is that Paul and Barnabas put themselves in danger by rejecting the people's worship.

the people decided they must be hoax-performing charlatans. Incensed that they had been duped, the crowd stoned Paul until they believed he was dead. They then dragged him out of town and left him lying, but the disciples found him and gathered over him. Thereafter Paul arose and went to another city, ready to relive this experience if necessary in the campaign for truth.

Gospel Portraits

We get a good idea of what motivated the apostles when we examine the self-portraits they gave when writing or supplying information for Jesus' biographies. If they cared more for their reputations than for truth, they would have taken a free hand in depicting themselves as wise, spiritual, and quick to apprehend Jesus' meaning and purpose. They would have kept quiet about any blunders they made along the way. However, the picture presented in the Gospels could hardly be more different. The apostles are depicted as slow to understand, quick to misjudge, greedy for positions of honor, and unwilling to let children access Jesus. Furthermore they often spoke out of turn, misapprehended key events, struggled with unbelief, slept when devotion demanded wakefulness, fled like schoolboys at Jesus' arrest, and denied knowing him when surrounded by unbelievers. These and other unflattering depictions are spread throughout the Gospels. What can these be but signs that the apostles valued truth (even *embarrassing* truth) above all else when retelling the life of Jesus Christ?

Captured and Amplified

In his book *Church History,* Eusebius of Caesarea (c. AD 263–339) quotes from the writings of Papias, bishop of Hierapolis. Papias authored a five-volume work called *Exposition of the Words of the Lord,* which, sadly, has been lost to history except for select quotes which Eusebius and others set down. Papias was a Christian leader in the late first and early second centuries. He may have been born as early as the year 50. This means his life partially overlapped with the apostles and especially people who were directly or indirectly acquainted with them. In fact Papias knew the daughters of Philip the evangelist (Acts 21:8–9), possibly Philip himself, and may have been acquainted with the aged apostle John. Living in such a time, Papias had access to first- and secondhand information regarding the life and teachings of Jesus. His home base of Hierapolis was situated on a cultural thoroughfare, allowing him to quiz witnesses as they journeyed back and forth between the power cities of the region.

Ruins at Heirapolis. Papias's home base of Hierapolis was situated on a cultural thoroughfare, allowing him to quiz witnesses as they journeyed back and forth between the power cities of the region. Photo: HolyLand-Photos.org.

Scholars suggest that Papias may have written his books in the year 110 or earlier, and judging from the title and quotes that have survived we know the books recorded information he had gleaned about Jesus' teachings. Further, much like Luke's Gospel, Papias wrote his book for an individual person to whom he wanted to convey the assured truth about Jesus. In a fascinating quote that Eusebius preserves, Papias says in his prologue, "I shall not hesitate also to put into properly ordered form for you everything I learned carefully in the past from the elders and noted down well, for the truth of which I vouch. For unlike most people I did not enjoy those who have a great deal to say, but those who teach the truth."[6] Four important notes must be made regarding this passage. First, Papias is writing about his doings at an earlier phase of life, a time when the associates of the apostles were yet living. Very likely this was around AD 80.[7] Second, the people from whom he gathered information were disciples of "the elders," men whom the apostles and their associates appointed as leaders of churches that sprang up throughout the region (Acts 14:23; Titus 1:5). It seems that when Christians came through Hierapolis they naturally stopped in to visit the church there, where Papias presided, and they shared with him the information they had learned from their participation in the churches that the apostles had founded and entrusted to local elders. Third, Papias preferred these sorts of informants over big talkers who had "a great deal to say." This shows that Papias was a man of discernment, not one to fall prey to expansive storytellers who happened to strut through town.

Papias "noted down well" all that he had "learned carefully" from the elders, putting it into a "properly ordered form" for the recipient of his books.

Fourth, Papias "noted down well" all that he had "learned carefully" from the elders, putting it into a "properly ordered form" for the recipient of his books. Here is a picture of a man collecting Jesus' biographical information with care, accuracy, and integrity.

Papias goes on to describe the relative value he placed on various sources of information available to him. Recall that he is writing around AD 110 but is referring to his practices and values from 30 years previously, a time when the Gospels of Matthew, Luke, and John were either not yet written or were in the early stages of coming into circulation. Recall also that in this era Luke said, "Many have undertaken to compile a narrative about the events that have been fulfilled among us" (Luke 1:1). Papias says essentially the same thing in his prologue. After describing his habit of seeking testimony from those acquainted with the elders, Papias says, "I do not think that I derived so much benefit from books as from the living voice of those that are still surviving."[8] Most likely he is thinking of the same kind of books that Luke consulted—nonscriptural but helpful accounts of Jesus' life and teachings. Actually, these are the very sort of books Papias himself wrote in 110—nonscriptural but dependable accounts about Jesus. Thus it is clear that Papias is not denying the value of such writings in his quote above. To paraphrase him, he is saying "Why read books when you can conduct *interviews* instead?" This is a reasonable stance. And what a thrill he must have gotten from speaking with people who had such close links to the origins of Christianity!

Papias's preference in AD 80 for personal interviews does not mean that, when the Scriptures were all written and distributed in years to come, he felt the written texts were of lesser importance. Evidence from Eusebius demonstrates that Papias quoted from 1 Peter and 1 John in his books.

It seems more than reasonable to suppose that if we had Papias's entire five-volume production on hand we would find him quoting from all or virtually all of the New Testament books.

Other evidence indicates that he was also familiar with the book of Revelation and may have known the Gospels of John and Luke as well.[9] Since we have only a slim sampling of Papias's writings, and since in that slim sample we learn that he made use of several New Testament writings, it seems more than reasonable to suppose that if we had his entire five-volume production on hand we would find him quoting from all or virtually all of the New Testament books. This would demonstrate that Papias came to value the New Testament writings as the authoritative source for Jesus' surviving voice. This is just as we would expect it to be. When speaking of his preferences in AD 80, he naturally preferred to hear from witnesses who could recall their experiences and answer any questions he wished to put to them.

By the early first century the church had transitioned from relying primarily on the spoken surviving voice to the written surviving voice.

By the year 110 things were different. The apostles were long dead. Most likely the elders and their close associates were also dead. This means the interviews that Papias had so valued in former years were no longer possible. By the early first century the church had transitioned from relying primarily on the *spoken* surviving voice to the *written* surviving voice. Far from a handicap, this was actually a boon for the growth of Christianity. Once the voice of Jesus was captured in scrolls, it was amplified by many magnitudes. After printed news can travel faster, farther, and with greater permanence than that which is carried by fatigable, impermanent human messengers.

Once the voice of Jesus was captured in scrolls, it was amplified by many magnitudes. After all, printed news can travel faster, farther, and with greater permanence than that which is carried by fatigable, impermanent human messengers.

Writings True and False

It is popular for critics to claim that Christianity as we know it is not reflective of the true life and teachings of Jesus but is instead a contrivance invented by priests and politicians. The story typically goes something like this: There never was any such thing as officially sanctioned, eyewitness writings about Jesus or the movement that centered on him. Instead there arose in the century or so after Jesus a slew of incompatible accounts, some nearer to the truth and others farther from it. Different strains of Christianity produced these writings. Each offered variant depictions of Jesus, believed different doctrines, and adopted unique practices. The differences naturally bred competition between adherents. Each group thought their version of Christ ought to be the *only* version. One group eventually gained the upper hand by forming the right political alliances. This made them "right by might," and so they suppressed all other Christianities by burning "false" Scriptures, silencing errant preachers, and herding naïve Christians into the orthodox pen. Many truths were forever lost as a result of this takeover, but from time to time some are resurrected as ancient manuscripts are hauled up from earthen graves. So the story goes. Central to the plot is a collection of books discovered by a farmer in Egypt.

The Gnostic rediscovery. One day in 1945, Mohammed Alí Samman went digging for fertilizer around a large boulder near Nag Hammadi. Rather than fertilizer he found a jar that had been sealed shut for 1,600 years. At first he would not open it. Local lore said evil genies guarded treasure hordes, and Mohammed suspected the jar held gold. After deciding his love for gold outweighed his fear of genies, he arced his shovel down atop the jar, shattering it into a cloud of dust and stale air. In the aftermath he found neither gold nor genies but a stack of 13 leather-covered books. When he returned home, he showed them to his wary mother before storing them in his goat shed, but mom fetched the books later that night and used them to fuel her cook fire. Thus ancient texts wafted through the air in an acrid black smoke that settled quickly and ran along the ground, searching for its lost tomb. In the time it took to warm an old woman's stew, one priceless book and stretches of others were lost for all time.

Mohammed was mostly indifferent when he learned of this vandalism. Still, on the balance he saw no sense in burning the books, so he stowed them out of his wobbly mother's reach. Weeks later unexpected news arrived. Six months previously Mohammed's father had been murdered. The killer had

The cache of books found at Nag Hammadi in 1945.

eluded capture, but now some locals had tracked him down. Seizing his chance for vengeance, Mohammed rushed out with family members who brandished mallets and picks. They found the killer asleep by a roadside. Hearts pounding, they encircled the man and killed him. The police immediately suspected Mohammed. Knowing that his home would be searched, Mohammed passed the books off to a Coptic priest who then showed them to his brother-in-law who in turn sent one to Cairo for examination. Before word came back from the museum in Cairo, the remaining books were sold off in different directions, eventually passing through the hands of priests, bandits, and celebrities in places as far away as New York City and Ann Arbor, Michigan.[10]

This story began with a search for fertilizer. In one sense that is exactly what was found, for once they were retrieved and translated, the Nag Hammadi books set off an explosive growth of theories about Christian origins, early doctrines, and the true identity of Jesus Christ. Most of the unearthed books represent an ancient heretical movement known as Gnostic Christianity (explained below). The long-lost Gnostic Christians were finally regaining their voice, some said. Others went so far as to say that *authentic* Christianity had returned to the light of day, but do the Gnostic documents really present the true Jesus?

The truth about Gnostic Christianity. Those who hail Gnostic Christianity as authentic Christianity make two major claims. First, they say the New Testament was written late and misrepresents Jesus and early Christians. Second, they insist that the Gnostic Christian writings predate the New Testament and properly reflect Jesus and early Christian belief. These claims imply that the Gnostic Christians had it right about Jesus but that the so-called orthodox group gained the upper hand politically and extinguished Jesus' light. Further, they suppose that the Gnostic texts found at Nag Hammadi were shoved under the boulder in hopes of keeping the orthodox mob from destroying every last remnant of truth. Interesting claims. Does the evidence support them?

New Testament scholars commonly date all of the writings within the range of AD 45 to 95, which falls within the life span of Jesus' original followers.

First, though extreme skeptics date the New Testament books to a century or more after Jesus, their attempts wilt under examination. New Testament scholars commonly date *all* of the writings within the range of AD 45 to 95, which falls within the life span of Jesus' original followers.[11] Nonbiblical writings serve as key evidence for these dates. For example, Pliny the Younger served as governor of Bithynia for Trajan, emperor of Rome. In AD 112 Pliny wrote Trajan to report about

Trajan, emperor of Rome, AD 98–117.

the state of things in Bithynia. Among other things he mentioned Christians, whose expansive growth was undermining local traditions. Pliny executed those who would not renounce their "excessive superstition" about Jesus being God.[12] Here, from the pen of a dedicated non-Christian, is evidence that belief in a divine Jesus was widespread at an early date. Only an early dating of the New Testament writings can explain this, for it is *these writings alone* that present Jesus as God. In the Gnostic writings Jesus was a regular man who became host to a semidivine essence at his baptism. The Gnostics revered such men but did not worship them as God.

Second, it is insupportable to claim that the Gnostic Christian writings preceded the New Testament. The evidence is indisputable. By the late *first* century, perhaps shortly after AD 80, a Christian document known as the *Didache* or *Teaching of the Twelve* summarized basic Christian belief in clear conformity to the New Testament, apparently even quoting from Matthew's Gospel. By 160 Justin Martyr named all four New Testament Gospels as authoritative for the church. At what stage of development were the so-called Gnostic gospels at this point? Simply put, they did not exist. As early as

It is insupportable to claim that the Gnostic Christian writings preceded the New Testament.

140 a man named Marcion rejected orthodox Christianity and sought instead to combine it with elements of Greek Gnostic thought. Finding that the New Testament writings could not support this endeavor and finding also that there was as yet no such thing as a Gnostic Christian document, he edited

Luke's Gospel and Paul's epistles in such a way that fit his deviant desires. Thirty-two years later, in 172, a Gnostic heretic named Tatian took the four New Testament Gospels and edited them for the purpose of creating a harmonized text. That Tatian used the standard Gospels means that as late as 172 leading Gnostic Christians still had no genuine Gnostic Christian writings to which they could appeal. It was not until the later stages of the second century that Gnostic writings such as *Gospel of Thomas* and *Gospel of Judas* began to appear. Clearly the New Testament writings existed long before the revisionist Gnostic writings. Further, it is impossible that orthodox Scriptures represent a response to and suppression of Gnostic Christianity if in fact the orthodox Scriptures predate the Gnostic ascendancy of the second and third centuries.

Third, it is insupportable to claim that the Gnostic gospels reliably represent the teachings of Jesus. In fact they teach a series of beliefs that are contradictory to core Jewish beliefs about God and the world. For instance, they reflect the standard Greek Gnostic beliefs that spirit is good, matter is evil, and an evil god created this world. Try squaring that with the book of Genesis! The Gnostic gospels also teach that salvation is escape from matter and ignorance, that only the intellectually enlightened can be saved, and that females seeking salvation must become male since "females are not worthy of life."[13] These can scarcely be the beliefs of Jesus of Nazareth, an observant Jew and fulfiller of Old Testament prophecies.

The Gnostic gospels also teach that salvation is escape from matter and ignorance, that only the intellectually enlightened can be saved, and that females seeking salvation must become male since "females are not worthy of life."

In conclusion, Gnostic Christianity was exactly what it appears to have been: an odd syncretism between Greek philosophy and hollowed-out Christianity. The result was a movement that enjoyed a brief day in the sun before dipping forever below history's long horizon.

Canon and Transmission

Theologically speaking, the word *canon* refers to the list of books approved for inclusion in the Bible. Hence, to speak of the biblical canon is to speak of the God-inspired, authoritative books whose teachings define correct belief and practice. Our New Testament includes 27 such books. Are they the right books? Are the current manuscripts reliable copies of the originals? Following is an examination of these vital questions.

Before winning universal acceptance, each book had to be circulated, copied, examined, and discussed among the churches.

A gradual process. It took several centuries for the canon to emerge as a widely acknowledged fact. Recall that the earliest churches were founded by the apostles and their associates as they fanned out from Jerusalem. The churches depended on these men to teach them about Jesus and the Christian life. At first these teachings were strictly oral, but eventually (AD 45–95) the apostles wrote letters and Gospels, thus providing early Christians with authoritative "books" to guide them. Before winning universal acceptance, each book had to be circulated, copied, examined, and discussed among the churches. This was not a quick process. New churches cropped up in far-flung regions at a pace that outstripped the spread of Scripture. Thus many churches had few if any New Testament books. When new books reached these churches, they were accepted only after careful consideration and consultation with apostolic churches (churches personally founded by the apostles) since they were in a good position to judge the merits or demerits of candidate books. Apostolic authority was honored by all true churches at the advent

No central office pronounced the identities of the canonical books or forced their use in worship.

of Christianity, yet each and every Christian church was independent from external governing authority. No central office pronounced the identities of the canonical books or forced their use in worship. Understandably, it took several centuries for churches sprawled all over the map to build communicative ties and reach common consensus on the canon.

The various second- and third-century writings that introduced "alternative Christianities" were never considered for adoption into the canon because they were written long after the apostles and their beliefs contradicted the Old Testament and apostolic teachings.

As churches sifted through all the materials and ideas that came to their attention, doctrines that were contrary to apostolic teaching were rejected as innovation. A prime example came with the advent of so-called Gnostic Christianity. As inheritors of apostolic teachings, well-informed Christians knew that Gnostic teachings contradicted genuine Christian doctrines. Churches marked the distinction between authorized and heretical writings, and as Christians across the Roman Empire endured periodic persecutions that threatened death to anyone harboring Christian Scriptures, the canon began to emerge as a defined body of books. False writings you would allow the pagan authorities to seize; biblical writings you would die for. The various second- and third-century writings that introduced "alternative Christianities" were never considered for adoption into the canon because they were written long after the apostles, plus their teachings contradicted the Old Testament and apostolic teachings.

Witnesses to the canon. Many canonical books were widely recognized as Scripture from early on. For example, in AD 96 Clement of Rome quoted the Gospel of Matthew as Scripture. In 110 Ignatius cited Gospel material as Scripture. By 180 the apologist Irenaeus defended Christianity by appealing to many New Testament writings. In total scholars believe he used 22 of the 27 canonical books. A short time later an apologist named Tertullian charged Gnostic Christians with misusing "the instru-

Origen named all 27 books and noted that six of them (Hebrews, James, 2 Peter, 2 and 3 John, and Jude) were disputed. These six were debated for centuries, but their revered position was never shaken.

ment," by which he meant the canon. Only James, 2 Peter, and 2 and 3 John go unnamed by Tertullian. A few decades later Origen named all 27 books and noted that six of them (Hebrews, James, 2 Peter, 2 and 3 John, and Jude) were disputed. These six were debated for centuries, but their revered position was never shaken. In the fourth century the canon further emerged as an accepted fact. Eusebius of Caesarea listed 27 books that were accepted as Scripture. In 367 Athanasius listed all 27 books *In the fourth century the canon further emerged as an accepted fact.* as Scripture. He made no note about disputed books, which probably indicates that the debate had cooled. A little more than a decade later Jerome placed all 27 books into his Latin Bible translation. As for the disputed books, he believed that their history of acceptance proved them biblical. Augustine agreed that the 27 were canonical. Of the disputed books he said they should be approved because the apostolic churches had long accepted them. Finally, in 393 and 397 the Councils of Hippo and Carthage said the canon includes 27 books, no more and no less.

During the Reformation many Christian beliefs and practices were reexamined in light of Scripture. This emphasis highlighted the need to be certain about which books were genuinely from God. When Luther published a German Bible in 1522, he included all 27 books but sounded notes of disapproval over the disputed books. Despite his reservations the 27-book canon was not seriously questioned, and no sustained challenge has arisen in the churches since the Reformation.

The vast majority of all changes are easily detected and amount to nothing more than simple misspellings, synonym displacements, or mixing of homophones.

Preservation of the manuscripts. Skeptics claim that the New Testament books have evolved beyond all recognition since the day they were written. Amateur copyists, hapless monks, rogue theologians, sly politicians, folk from many quarters are said to have had a turn at corrupting the text by adding, deleting, and modifying at will. One popular critic emphasizes that the number of changes found in the existing manuscripts exceeds the number of words in the entire New Testament! Technically he is correct, but the implications are far less drastic than he claims. The vast majority of all changes are easily detected and amount to nothing more than simple misspellings, synonym displacements, or mixing of homophones (words that sound alike but are spelled differently, such as *their* and *there*). These sorts of mistakes have no impact whatsoever on the meaning

In cases where the original reading remains in dispute, textual scholars have rightly said that you could eliminate all such verses from the New Testament and yet not detract from a single doctrine.

of the books. In the few places where the changes potentially have theological importance, scholars are most often able to trace the text back to its original form with confidence. This is done by comparing the many surviving Greek manuscripts in

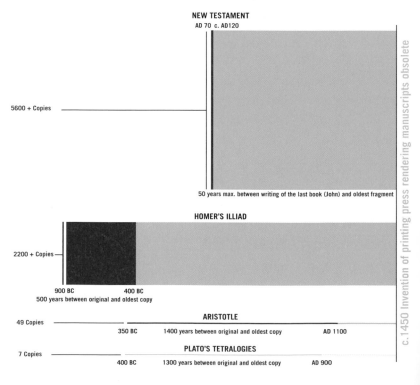

MANUSCRIPT AUTHORITY OF THE NEW TESTAMENT COMPARED TO OTHER CLASSICAL WORKS

NEW TESTAMENT
AD 70 c. AD120

5600 + Copies

50 years max. between writing of the last book (John) and oldest fragment

HOMER'S ILLIAD

2200 + Copies

900 BC   400 BC
500 years between original and oldest copy

ARISTOTLE

49 Copies

350 BC   1400 years between original and oldest copy   AD 1100

PLATO'S TETRALOGIES

7 Copies

400 BC   1300 years between original and oldest copy   AD 900

c.1450 Invention of printing press rendering manuscripts obsolete

Aside from inconsequential alterations, the manuscripts on which our New Testament translations are based are close replications of the original writings.

order to pinpoint the time at which the error arose as well as its possible cause. In this way scholars are able to determine the original reading in the majority of cases. In cases where the original reading remains in dispute, textual scholars have rightly said that you could eliminate all such verses from the New Testament and yet not detract from a single doctrine. In other words, none of the corrupted verses serves as the sole basis for a doctrine, so even if we dropped such verses from the Bible we could always point to undisputed verses elsewhere as support for the doctrine in question. Clearly, therefore, the variants are not very important. A fair assessment of the evidence reveals that the New Testament manuscripts have been preserved remarkably well through centuries of transmission, *far* better than those for any other ancient writing. Aside from inconsequential alterations, the manuscripts on which our New Testament translations are based are close replications of the original writings.[14]

Notes

1. A helpful summary of the life of Justin Martyr and many other Christian leaders throughout history can be found in *131 Christians Everyone Should Know*, edited by Mark Galli and Ted Olsen (Nashville: Holman Reference, 2000).

2. The scholar who has done the most to highlight the power of the disciples' memory and their possible use of notes to aid memory is Birger Gerhardsson. Advanced readers should consult his seminal book, *Memory and Manuscript: Oral Tradition and Written Transmission in Rabbinic Judaism and Early Christianity* (Copenhagen: C. W. K. Gleerup, 1961). For discussion of note taking, see page 202.

3. This is not to say that ministers ought not to be paid for their services. By God's design vocational ministers are to be financially supported by those whom they serve. Paul

expresses this in 1 Timothy 5:17–18. The reason Paul refused this privilege for himself was so that he could serve as an example of self-denial on behalf of the gospel.

4. For excellent information about Islam, Mormonism, and many other religious movements, see Walter Martin, *The Kingdom of the Cults: Revised, Updated, and Expanded Edition* (Bloomington, MN: Bethany House, 2003).

5. Richard N. Longenecker, *The Acts of the Apostles*, Expositor's Bible Commentary, volume 9 (Grand Rapids: Zondervan, 1981), 435.

6. Eusebius Pamphilus, *Church History*, Book III, chapter 39, as quoted in Richard Bauckham, *Jesus and the Eyewitnesses: The Gospels as Eyewitness Testimony* (Grand Rapids: Eerdmans, 2006), 15–16.

7. Bauckham, *Jesus and the Eyewitnesses*, 14.

8. Eusebius Pamphilus, *Church History*, Book III, Chapter 39. The quote as rendered above derives from the translation of Eusebius given by Christian Frederick Cruse, *The Ecclesiastical History of Eusebius Pamphilus* (Grand Rapids: Baker, 1989), 125.

9. See Bauckham, *Jesus and the Eyewitnesses*, 14.

10. Mohammed Alí Samman did not share the story of how he found the books until 30 years after the fact. Variations in numerous printed accounts make it difficult to know for certain exactly how events unfolded. The account given above is informed by several different sources, including http://www.nag-hammadi.com/history.html.

11. Among the better-known scholarly books that outline evidences for dating the New Testament writings early are: John A. T. Robinson, *Redating the New Testament* (Eugene, OR: Wipf and Stock, 2000), and Martin Hengel, *The Four Gospels and the One Gospel of Jesus Christ* (Harrisburg, PA: Trinity Press, 2000).

12. For a good discussion of Pliny and Trajan, see Gary R. Habermas, *The Historical Jesus: Ancient Evidence for the Life of Christ* (Joplin, MO: College Press, 1996), 197–201.

13. *Gospel of Thomas*, 114:1–3.

14. Three excellent resources for grasping the true quality

of existing New Testament manuscripts are Daniel B. Wallace, et al., *Reinventing Jesus: How Contemporary Skeptics Miss the Real Jesus and Mislead Popular Culture* (Grand Rapids: Kregel, 2006); Timothy Paul Jones, *Misquoting Truth: A Guide to the Fallacies of Bart Ehrman's* Misquoting Jesus (Downers Grove: IVP, 2007); and Doug Powell, *The Holman QuickSource Guide to Christian Apologetics* (Nashville: B&H, 2006).

The Inspiration of St. Matthew (detail) by Caravaggio.

Chapter 20
A Gift of Words

Ours is a world made by words. Not silent letters set to paper but divine commands sent forth into the void to call earth and sky, plant and creature to arise from nothing. All things exist because God in timeless counsels chose to erect a theater in which his glories would play to the rapt attention of men and angels. "Let there be . . .," he said, and his spoken words forged world and life.

Given once to make the world, God in latter days gave another gift of words to *remake* it. Unto a humanity marred by spiritual ruin, he spoke words of self-disclosure, hope, and redemption. As a result we have the Bible—a chronicle of past action, an interpretation of present realities, and a guidebook to future fate. But in what sense is the Bible God's Word? In this chapter we examine several basic characteristics of the Bible.

Inspiration and Authority

The word *inspired* is overused in our culture. We speak of artists being inspired to create beautiful works, or we say an athlete has turned in an inspired performance if he or she overcomes great odds. In these cases we mean a person looked within and found the will to excel or else was motivated by some excellence outside themselves. It is a heightening of natural abilities and efforts, nothing more.

The Bible means something entirely different when it reports that its authors were inspired. For instance, Paul says, "All Scripture is inspired by God and is profitable for teaching, for rebuking, for correcting, for training in righteousness, so that the man of God may be complete, equipped for every good work" (2 Tim 3:16–17). The word translated "inspired" is the Greek word *theopneustos*. Literally it means "God breathed" and more closely refers to breathing *out* than breathing in. In other words, Paul is saying that the words of Scripture were breathed out by God through the agency of the authors whom he guided. This means God himself is the ultimate source of Scripture. Above all other voices it is *his* that breaks through as we read. As Paul goes on to note, this makes Scripture the authoritative sourcebook for our beliefs and practices. By appealing to Scripture, we can teach truth, rebuke and correct error, and train ourselves for righteous living.

> *God himself is the ultimate source of Scripture. Above all other voices it is his that breaks through as we read.*

Peter also gives a helpful image of God's role in authoring the Bible. Speaking specifically of prophecies, he says, "First of all, you should know this: no prophecy of Scripture comes from one's own interpretation, because no prophecy ever came by the will of man; instead, moved by the Holy Spirit, men spoke from God" (2 Pet 1:20–21). Here we see that the meaning and ultimate genesis of prophecy were supplied by God, not human authors. The apostles believed every prophecy of the Old Testament was certain to be fulfilled. A helpful example is found in Acts 1:16 where Peter addresses the Christian community about the need to replace Judas. "Brothers, the Scripture had to be fulfilled that the Holy Spirit through the mouth of David spoke in advance about Judas, who became a guide to those who arrested Jesus." Here we see that Peter viewed Scripture as authoritative over the beliefs and practices of God's followers but also over history itself. If Scripture said Judas must be replaced, *he must be replaced.* This theme runs throughout early Christian preaching. Everything that happened to Jesus was seen as a fulfillment of what had been written in ages past. Also note that Peter identifies the writings of King David in Psalms 69 and 109 as originating in the person of the Holy Spirit. The same is true of the whole Bible. For this reason you cannot go wrong by believing and living what the Bible intends to teach, nor can you go right if you oppose it.

The Humanity of the Bible

Some people have supposed that the human authors acted as robots when they penned the biblical books. Commonly called the "dictation" view, this theory implies that God ar-

rested the minds and hearts of the biblical authors, putting them in a sort of trance which ensured that they had no real involvement in the selection of words, literary forms, and so forth. Most likely this theory arose due to select Old Testament passages in which prophets spoke in God's name. Exodus 5:1 is the first instance of this, where Moses went to Pharaoh and said, "This is what the LORD, the God of Israel, says: Let My people go, so that they may hold a festival for Me in the wilderness." Another familiar example is Jeremiah's call to ministry. "The word of the LORD came to me: I chose you before I formed you in the womb; I set you apart before you were

The erroneous dictation theory holds that the biblical authors were like robots as God commandeered their minds and will.

born. I appointed you a prophet to the nations" (Jer 1:4–5). In fact, the thus-says-the-Lord refrain runs throughout the Old Testament; without doubt it means that God communicated through his chosen agents by carefully selected words, but it need not imply the dictation view.

God inspired every word of Scripture, yet evidence suggests that the human authors were in full command of their faculties as they wrote. Notice again Luke's disclosure about his purpose and method for writing his Gospel: he saw that others had written about the life of Jesus, decided he would undertake the same task, discerned that he was in a good position to do this since he had "carefully investigated everything" in advance, and then engaged his chosen task in hopes of bolstering the faith of a man named Theophilus (Luke 1:1–4). Luke never says he received a direct supernatural commission (as through a vision or angelic visitation) to write his Gospel, nor does he indicate awareness that God directed what words or sources he should use in retelling the life and teachings of Christ. By all appearances Luke's book is *his* book, a product of efforts, desires, and knowledge gained in the course of a life devoted to Jesus. However, that is not the whole story about Luke's book or any other biblical book. Christ gave the apostles special authority to spread his message, and he sent the Holy Spirit to help them comprehend and recall his teachings. Luke shared in this apostolic authority because he labored closely with Paul and other apostles. As a result Paul felt justified in quoting Luke's writing as Scripture. In like manner Peter was confident that Paul's writings were inspired by God (2 Pet 3:16), and Peter was regarded as wielding the same authority in his writings.

God inspired every word of Scripture, yet evidence suggests that the human authors were in full command of their faculties as they wrote.

In summary, the apostles were genuinely in control of their minds while writing. It may even be that they did not know they were writing Scripture when they wrote the Gospels and letters that were later packaged into the Bible. Nevertheless they wrote with a consciousness of their God-given authority, a remembrance of Jesus' promise that the Spirit would guide them, and an awareness of the Spirit's presence to make good on that promise. Far from implying a dictation view of Scripture, the biblical evidence proves that the writing of New Testament Scripture was an organic process growing up from Jesus' selection of 12 dedicated students who were commissioned to speak and write as emissaries of the gospel.

Precision and Truthfulness

If the Bible comes from God and is an authoritative guide-book for belief and practice, it should be true in all that it intends to teach. As Hebrews 6:18 says, "It is impossible for God to lie." If God cannot lie, neither can his Book. It is important, however, to draw a distinction between precision and truthfulness. Webster's dictionary defines *precision* as "mechanical or scientific exactness." This means if I am asked to replicate *precisely* a conversation I had sometime in the past, I am required to recite word for word what was said. No summary version or proximate retelling is acceptable. My best hope in this situation is to produce an audio recording of the conversation. If the conversation was not recorded, I am out of luck.

The definition for *truthful* is somewhat more relaxed. One option Webster's gives is "corresponding with reality." Sticking with our previous illustration, if I am asked to give a truthful rendering of a conversation I had once upon a time, all that is required of me is that I give an account that represents everything fairly, such that I convey the event and its meaning with enough accuracy that you can trust what I have said. Some of my details may be imprecise but not *untrue*. This is the sort of testimony eyewitnesses give in courthouse trials every day. It is unreasonable to expect witnesses to provide precise replications of what was said or done in the past. Rather than precision, the standard is truthfulness. So long as a witness delivers a truthful testimony we regard their reconstruction of past events as reliable.

It is unreasonable to expect witnesses to provide precise replications of what was said or done in the past. Rather than precision, the standard is truthfulness.

The question arises: are the conversations and events recorded in the Bible *precise* renderings (having "mechanical or scientific exactness"), or are they sometimes less precise and yet wholly truthful? This is a sensitive topic that all serious Bible readers must face. The goal in the following paragraphs is to expose our presuppositions and expectations to biblical evidence. To achieve this we will explore the writings of Luke, using him as a test case for determining what approach he and other Bible writers may have taken. Luke is ideal for this inquiry because he stressed that he had investigated matters closely and wrote with the intention of setting things out in a comprehensible, convincing manner (Luke 1:1–4). Given such high goals, do we find him always precise in his writings, or does evidence suggest that truthfulness was his aim instead? Three brief studies will help answer this question.

Luke gives two separate accounts of Jesus' ascension to heaven. In his Gospel he reports that Jesus told the disciples to stay in Jerusalem until the Spirit came, so that they would be "empowered from on high" (Luke 24:49). Then, in the very next breath, Luke says, "Then [Jesus] led them out as far as Bethany, and lifting up His hands He blessed them. And while He was blessing them, He left them and was carried up into heaven" (Luke 24:50–51). When Luke retells the story in *Imprecision is not the same thing as untruthfulness.* the book of Acts, he has Jesus talking not just about the coming of the Spirit but also about the end-times and the commission to take the gospel to "Judea and Samaria, and to the ends of the earth" (Acts 1:4–8). No mention is made of Bethany. Instead, Luke simply says Jesus was with the disciples. Further, the report in Luke 24 has Jesus ascending while he is in the very act of raising his hands and pronouncing a blessing over his disciples, but Acts 1:9 simply says Jesus ascended right after restating the commission to take the gospel to the world. No mention is made of a blessing or raised hands. While it

Writers can give long and short versions of the same event without compromising truth. is important to note that there are no contradictions between Luke's two accounts, the differences are nevertheless easy to spot. Would we say these differences prove that one account is true and the other is not? Did Luke get it right one time and wrong the other? Of course not. Both accounts are true and can be harmonized. The differences indicate that one account may be more precise than the other in certain details, but imprecision is not the same thing as untruthfulness. We can also suggest that one account may be more comprehensive than the other. Writers can give long and short versions of the same event without compromising truth. Certainly the gist of both accounts is the same: Jesus met with the disciples, reiterated some key teachings, and then was taken to heaven as they watched. Luke has told the truth in both accounts, albeit with a mixture of precision and imprecision, comprehensiveness and brevity.

As another example which offers a different window on the same basic view, consider the story about Cornelius's conversion to Christianity. Acting as narrator in the initial version, Luke reports an exchange between Cornelius and an angel in which the angel said, "Your prayers and your acts of charity have come up as a memorial offering before God. Now send men to Joppa and call for Simon, who is also named Peter. He is lodging with Simon, a tanner, whose house is by the sea" (Acts 10:4–6). A few short passages later Luke records a conversation between Cornelius and Peter in which Cornelius recounts the angel's message. Notice that what Cornelius says does not correspond precisely with what Luke narrated previously. "Cornelius, your prayer has been heard, and your acts of charity have been remembered in God's sight. Therefore send someone to Joppa and invite Simon here, who is also named Peter. He is lodging in Simon the tanner's house by the sea" (vv. 31–32). The gist of both reports is the same, but they are by no means word-for-word identical. So the questions arise: Is either of these accounts pre-

St. Peter in the House of Cornelius by Gustave Doré.

cisely correct? Did Luke replicate the angel's words verbatim in verses 4–6 but then let Cornelius's loose rendering stand in verses 31–32? Possibly. In that case Luke as narrator has been precise, but Luke as reporter has allowed Cornelius's imprecise quote to stand uncorrected, which may indicate that other quotes in the Bible were also allowed to stand in a state that could be described as "imprecise but true." Another possibility exists also. Perhaps we have an indication that *neither* Luke nor Cornelius sought to give a verbatim rendering of the angel's words. Perhaps both of them only aimed to tell the truth. This too would indicate that the Bible may include quotes and descriptions that are true but imprecise.

As a final example, consider the three different times Paul's conversion experience is recounted in Acts. There are several notable differences between the three, but we will focus only on the differences which appear in a single sentence that is common to all three versions. When Luke as narrator records Paul's encounter with the risen Jesus, he reports that Jesus said, "I am Jesus, whom you are persecuting," in response to

The Conversion of Paul (detail from the Sistine Chapel) by Michelangelo. Paul met the risen Jesus on the road to Damascus.

Paul's question about the speaker's identity (Acts 9:5). Later in the book, when Luke records the first of two testimonies in which Paul recounts this event, he reports that Paul put Jesus' words somewhat differently: "I am Jesus the Nazarene, whom you are persecuting" (Acts 22:8). Here we see that "the Nazarene" has been added to the quote. The question arises: Did Jesus really say "the Nazarene" when he identified himself to Paul? If so, Luke chose not to include it in his original report, which means he was somewhat imprecise; if not, either Paul or Luke chose to add it to this first version of the testimony, most likely to add clarity since *Jesus* was a common name in that era. Again, this indicates that one of the accounts is truthful yet imprecise. Finally, when Paul gave his testimony a second time later in Acts, he dropped "the Nazarene" from the quotation (Acts 26:15). So what exactly did Jesus say on the road to Damascus? It may be most reasonable to say that we do not know *precisely* what words he uttered. What is clear is that he identified himself to Paul and thus changed his life forever.

The conclusion from these examples seems unavoidable:

Luke valued truth, as seen in the opening stanza of his Gospel, but that does not mean he felt bound to give precise renderings of everything he recorded in his books, nor did he feel obligated to "clean up" any loose quotes spoken by men such as Cornelius and Paul. What Luke *did* feel obligated to do was write in such a way that Theophilus could "know the certainty" of the things he had been taught about Jesus (Luke 1:4). That same certainty is available to you and me when we read the accounts given by the Holy Spirit through the agency of Luke.

The Voice of Jesus

On page 118 we asked the question, "Do we have the exact words of Jesus?" As you can now see, this question is directly related to the discussion about precision and truthfulness. When theologians tackle this issue, they ask, "Do we have the 'very words' (Latin: *ipsissima verba*) of Jesus, or do we instead have the 'very voice' (*ipsissima vox*) of Jesus?" If the very words, then we have precise renderings of what Jesus said. This would mean the Gospels replicate his words with something like "mechanical or scientific exactness." If on the other hand we have Jesus' very voice, we have truthful renderings of his meaning but not necessarily the exact words he uttered.

Though the New Testament is written in Greek, Jesus predominantly spoke Aramaic and Hebrew when teaching his fellow Jews throughout Palestine.

Before making comparisons of Jesus' words in several parallel accounts, we must investigate four lines of evidence that suggest at the outset that Jesus' words in the Gospels may be true but imprecise replications of what he really said. First, bear in mind that, though the New Testament is written in Greek, Jesus predominantly spoke Aramaic and Hebrew when teaching his fellow Jews throughout Palestine. Thus his words have already been translated from one language to another in the original manuscripts of the New Testament. This by no means introduces doubt about meaning, but since no two languages trade evenly, we are left to conclude that Jesus' words in the Gospels are already a step removed from exact replicas of his original utterances. Second, the Gospel accounts of Jesus' actions and teachings are condensed versions of what he said and did. Were full accounts given, "not even the world itself could contain the books that would be written" (John 21:25). A modern analogy is found in newspaper reporting, in which hour-long speeches are summarized in a few columns that convey the most important aspects of the speech. Third, the somewhat loose way in which New Testament authors cite Old Testament passages indicates that it was acceptable to forego precision and instead simply capture the meaning (or latent meaning) of a source. One example is how Luke records Jesus' citation from the book of Isaiah in Luke 4:18–19. Luke says Jesus located a specific place in Isaiah's writing and then read it off as the synagogue audience listened. A close look at the citation shows that Luke actually has Jesus pulling from portions of Isaiah 61:1, skipping backward to a slice of 58:6 and then bounding forward to pull from the first refrain of 61:2,

The somewhat loose way in which New Testament authors cite Old Testament passages indicates that it was acceptable to forego precision and instead simply capture the meaning (or latent meaning) of a source.

all while packing them together as if this were a seamless quotation of the prophet. Obviously this is no verbatim quotation of Isaiah. Further, the citation follows Isaiah's writing as it appears in the Septuagint, a reliable yet notably freehanded Greek translation of the original Hebrew Old Testament. Thus Jesus' quotation of Isaiah is several steps removed from absolute precision. In fact it is certain that Isaiah never uttered the sentences exactly as laid down in Luke 4:18–19. Now keep in mind that Jesus, Luke, and every author of the New Testament held the Old Testament to be nothing less than God's inspired Word. If such men as these felt comfortable exercising responsible freedom when quoting the Old Testament, odds are good that the evangelists felt the same freedom when reporting Jesus' words in the New Testament. Fourth, many scholars have discerned that ancient writers were held to a different expectation than modern writers. Writers today have the luxury of consulting audio and video recordings or reams of digital or printed material to lock down precise quotations or details. Thus modern readers expect high standards of precision. Ancient writers lacked these luxuries. Granted, we have argued that they had fantastic memories and may have used scraps of notes here and there to record key statements and events, but a survey of even the best writings from that era reveals that ancient writers were often imprecise in their reports.[1]

All four of the above factors predispose us to expect that Jesus' words as recorded in the Gospels are true but somewhat imprecise renderings of his original statements. The evidence seems to bear out this expectation, as two brief examples will show. First, when Jesus was with the disciples near Caesarea Philippi, he asked them what was being said of him by the crowds. Matthew, Mark, and Luke record this event. Importantly, all three evangelists record Jesus' question differently. Lining them up in the order in which they were likely written, we have:

> **Four factors predispose us to expect that Jesus' words as recorded in the Gospels are true but somewhat imprecise renderings of his original statements.**

> **Mark 8:27:** "Who do people say that I am?"
>
> **Matthew 16:13:** "Who do people say that the Son of Man is?"
>
> **Luke 9:18:** "Who do the crowds say that I am?"

You can see that no two versions are alike. Each evangelist is portraying the exact same statement, and so here we see that we have the "very voice" of Jesus rather than his "very words." Do we suffer loss because of this? Surely not. The meaning and intent of each version is the same. The differences are minor and possibly reflect emphases that each evangelist wishes to make, or else they are unintentional variations that are not vested with special meaning.

As another example, consider elements of Jesus' famous Sermon on the Mount. Both Matthew and Luke record portions of this episode. Matthew says the sermon occurred after

Jesus went up a mountain and sat down whereas Luke says he was on a mountain and came down a little ways to sit at a level place. It is easy to envision both descriptions being true without conflict. As for the sermon itself, notice the slight variation in the following parallel statements:

> **Matthew 5:3:** "Blessed are the poor in spirit, for the kingdom of heaven is theirs."
>
> **Luke 6:20:** "Blessed are you who are poor, because the kingdom of God is yours."

> **Matthew 5:11–12:** "Blessed are you when they insult and persecute you and falsely say every kind of evil against you because of Me. Be glad and rejoice, because your reward is great in heaven. For that is how they persecuted the prophets who were before you."
>
> **Luke 6:22–23:** "Blessed are you when people hate you, when they exclude you, insult you, and slander your name as evil, because of the Son of Man. Rejoice in that day and leap for joy! Take note—your reward is great in heaven, because this is the way their ancestors used to treat the prophets."

As is the case with Jesus' question at Caesarea Philippi, the variation between these reports indicates that we have Jesus' very voice rather than his very words. This means we have truthful renderings of important statements he made, not exacting precision of his every word. It is hard to see why this should bother us. The Bible aims to give us saving knowledge, not *exhaustive* knowledge. John sums up this strategy nicely when he explains that he wrote "so that you may believe Jesus is the Messiah, the Son of God, and by believing you may have life in His name" (John 20:31).

We have truthful renderings of important statements Jesus made, not exacting precision of his every word.

Bible in the Balance

If the Bible includes truthful but imprecise quotations and event descriptions, what does this mean about inspiration? Besides setting aside the dictation theory, it establishes beyond doubt that the human authors of Scripture exercised real presence and perspective while engaged in the writing task. Rather than overriding their person, God worked unobtrusively through humans to author books that promote faith, knowledge, and understanding. In the mystery of God's providence, he directs all events over the wide earth and yet does so without detection and without wrecking human agency. God's *God's work to inspire Scripture was not mere providence, but as a miraculous act it was nevertheless stealthy and was conducted in accordance with the fact that humans are free agents rather than puppets.* work to inspire Scripture was not mere providence, but as a miraculous act it was nevertheless stealthy and was conducted in accordance with the fact that humans are free agents rather than puppets. In the final analysis it is not possible for us to describe what it felt like for a biblical author to be inspired in this way. What we *can* describe is the result: books that are truthful revelations of God.

Balance is difficult to pull off when discussing the authorship of the Bible. Our tendency is to lay such emphasis on one reality that the other becomes obscured or essentially denied. Ironically, at the heart of most distortions is a mistaken assumption about what the Bible should look like if in fact God lies behind it as Inspirer and Guarantor of its full accuracy. For instance, unbelieving critics find it incredible that a book filled with evidence of human involvement can also be the inspired, unerring Word of God. They suppose that if the Bible is really God's Word it should have no trace of human contribution. What they seemingly expect is a golden scroll lowered from heaven by angels. Finding that the Bible has not come to us in this manner, they dismiss God's involvement altogether. Christians, on the other hand, are tempted to push a strictly supernatural view of the Bible, minimizing or denying the human role in an attempt to protect Scripture against skepticism. Unfortunately this stance shoots past truth and even guards the Bible against faith-friendly scholarship that can help forge faith-affirming answers.

It is best to regard Scripture as a product of God *and* humanity in which God ensured that we were given exactly the words he meant for us to have. True to human convention, the writings include descriptions that sometimes recount events and conversations with precision and sometimes with relative imprecision, sometimes in poetic style and sometimes in narrative, sometimes in summary form and sometimes more comprehensively. True to *divine* convention, the writings were given

> *It is best to regard Scripture as a product of God and humanity in which God ensured that we were given exactly the words he meant for us to have.*

without error, conveying knowledge of past, present, future, and eternal truths. The end result is not only a fully trustworthy Bible but also one that is defensible against skeptical criticisms insomuch as imprecisions or variations between parallel accounts do not reflect error but rather the habits of genuine human authorship. Far from being a defect or embarrassment, the Bible's humanity is proof of God's involvement in real human history. He has spoken to the human race not from the distant halls of heaven but through us, in us, and among us in the sacred writings. By his gift of words, we know him, love him, and receive the Son who came for us.

CLOSER LOOK

A Book without Errors?

Given God's involvement in its authorship, we expect the Bible to be entirely truthful. Theologians express this by saying the Bible is inerrant (free of errors). It is important to understand what is and is not meant by this.

First, divine inspiration secured the truthfulness of the

Bible's original composition but not the accuracy of the copyists who subsequently reproduced it or the translators who render Greek and Hebrew into modern languages. For this reason the doctrine of inerrancy applies only to the original manuscripts. Since these are lost to history, we must concede that the inerrant Bible is in some sense a bygone rather than a present reality. However, evidence shows that the manuscripts were transmitted with great care through the centuries, modern translators have a wealth of linguistic data that helps them make accurate translations, and our impressive store of ancient manuscripts allows us to ascertain the original readings to a degree that commends trust in the Bible as we have it today.

Second, inerrancy means the Bible is error free in all that it intends to proclaim. Sometimes we misinterpret the meaning or intention of Scripture, as when former interpreters believed the Bible intended to make scientific statements about the arrangement of the solar system. In such cases we inadvertently make the Bible teach error. God's Word is inerrant; our reading of it is not.

Third, inerrancy does not imply precision. Remember, the Bible is God's Word given through genuine human agency. The writings have every mark of the ancient culture and times from which they sprang. True to the literary style of that era, many biblical events and conversations are recorded in true but relatively imprecise form. Scripture may not provide precise replications in every case, but what is given is truthful. We have every reason to be satisfied with this arrangement. After all, these are the words that God has given as his authoritative witness in the world.

Fifth, inerrancy is a statement of faith that sums up a disciple's trust in God's Word. Certainly there are challenges to inerrancy that remain unresolved. Rather than erring on the side of skepticism when facing these challenges or accepting an obligation to prove inerrancy in every verse, we simply declare that we trust the message of Scripture and note that many past challenges were overturned once new information came to light.

Sixth, the doctrine of inerrancy is important and worthy of defense, but it must be kept in proper perspective. Christian hope rests on the truth of the liberating message Scripture conveys. Thus our chief proclamation is that humans can be saved by faith in the Son whom God sent to live, die, and rise again in our place.

Note

1. Darrell Bock has written a helpful essay that introduces this and other issues involved in the Gospels and the recording of Jesus' words. Please see Darrell Bock, "The Words of Jesus in the Gospels: Live, Jive, or Memorex?" in *Jesus Under Fire: Modern Scholarship Reinvents the Historical Jesus*, ed. Michael Wilkins and J. P. Moreland (Grand Rapids: Zondervan, 1995), 74–99.

Chapter 21
Deep Impact

Each of us is an author of history. By word and deed we help write the scroll that stretches from creation to the future final day. Our God-given purpose is to inscribe good rather than bad, doing our part to make the human story a tale worth celebrating. We mark the scroll personally but also indirectly through people whose lives we touch. What kind of history are you writing? What about Jesus? What kind of history has he written personally and through his followers? Below we examine three examples of how Jesus has shaped social history for the better.

A Woman's Place

Critics say Christianity suppressed women for 19 centuries and that it was only after it lost its grip on Western civilization that women emerged from long darkness. Is that true? Have Jesus and his followers inscribed a sexist agenda on history's scroll? To answer this, we must first set the sociohistorical context for Jesus' life and teachings.

The fabled Grecian city-states rose and fell long before Jesus was born in Roman Galilee, but their philosophies and out-looks lived on through the Romans who adopted and spread them during their conquest of the ancient world. Did this proliferation of the Greco-Roman worldview benefit women? Looking back to the heyday of Greece, we find that a wife was commonly confined inside her home unless she was escorted outdoors by her husband or a trustworthy male servant. Even most of her home became off-limits when male guests visited her husband. Imagine a wife whose movements are restricted even inside her own home! Not all Greek women were kept out of sight, however. Predictably, men were permitted to parade their mistresses publicly in demonstration of their prowess. The mistresses had their liberties, but ultimately they had it no better than their housebound rivals. Once their beauty faded, even the most accomplished mistresses were cast away, too spent and defamed to land a respectable marriage. Thus neither the home nor the arms of a married suitor offered shelter to the women of Greece, and there was little chance of their winning greater equality since education and the rights to public speech were reserved for males. It is fitting, therefore, that a female character in an ancient Greek play pronounces, "Surely, of all creatures that have life and wit, we women are of all unhappiest" (Euripides, *Medea*, 231–232).

The situation was little different in other ancient times and places. The Gnostic worldview, which flourished in parts of the Roman Empire during the second and third centuries AD, billed itself as the religion of intellect and transcendent insight, which is ironic given the fact that Gnostics touted men as spiritual and reasoned but held that women are by nature merely physical and sensual. This is sexism in its most thorough form. As we saw previously, the *Gospel of Thomas* took this as an indication that women had to become male if they wished to attain salvation! Not biologically, of course. What they needed was to change out their faulty feminine nature for the more capable male variety.

> *Gnostics touted men as spiritual and reasoned but held that women are by nature merely physical and sensual.*

Theologically the Jews knew better than to side with the Gnostics on this issue, but nonetheless everyday Jewish practice fell short of God's ideals. In Book II of his work *Against Apion*, Jewish historian Josephus says, "A woman is inferior to her husband in all things." Philo, a Romanized Jewish philosopher and a contemporary to Jesus, taught that "wives must be slaves to their husbands" (*Hypothetica* 7.3). In years to come, lesser Jewish authors continued propounding these misguided themes, saying such things as, "Let the words of Torah be burned up, but do not let them be delivered to women." By withholding education, Jewish men prohibited women from attaining the skills necessary to lift their gender from relative subjugation.

It was into such a world as this that Jesus stepped, introducing hope and freedom to women even on the day of his birth. That a peasant girl carried God's divine Son in her womb and then succored him, admonished him, and guided him through his formative years proves beyond doubt God's esteem for women and womanhood. Jesus fully understood this. As an adult, he often confronted prevailing views about women. Among his particularly daring moves, he depicted an impoverished widow as a model of true piety (Luke 21:1–4), used a woman searching for a lost coin as an analogy for God's quest to recover lost sinners (15:8–10), taught theology to an eager young woman who neglected her household duties in order

Jesus and the Woman of Samaria by Doré.

to listen closely (10:38–42), forbade men the license to look lustfully at women (Matt 5:28–29), condemned the prevailing custom that allowed men to wantonly divorce their wives and choose replacements (19:8–12), allowed women to accompany him as devoted followers (27:55), showed readiness to forgive and bless repentant women who had been caught in adultery (John 4:1–26; Luke 7:36–50), and, perhaps most shockingly of all, revealed himself to women first after his resurrection from the dead (Matt 28:8–10). All of these things made Jesus a disrupter of the status quo, a bold social reformer, one whose message was unwelcome among Jewish and Gentile traditionalists.

One of the most striking things about the early church is the fact that women were prominent members of the faith community and diligent, public laborers for the cause of the gospel.

Early Christians noted Jesus' example and laid emphasis on the value of women. One of the most striking things about the early church is the fact that women were prominent members of the faith community and diligent, public laborers for the cause of the gospel (e.g., Acts 18:24–26). This "liberalism" earned the church strong censure. Briefly, there were at least four ways in which Roman ideals for womanhood and domestic life were undermined by Christian belief and practice.

First, inspired by Jesus' lifelong celibacy and his commendation of that lifestyle, many Christian women chose to forego marriage in order to dedicate their lives to ministry. This was not well received among Roman traditionalists. It seemed to them that their daughters were getting uppity in the name of the invasive new religion from Israel, especially insomuch as celibacy was a direct assault on a father's customary rights of betrothal. From time immemorial Roman fathers had forged familial, commercial, and political alliances by dictating whom their daughters married. The Christian faith dared to offer a way out by affirming that a woman's conscience on such matters was bound to God alone. Additionally, celibacy threatened to exacerbate the growing birthrate crisis. Simply put, Roman women were not having babies. The nation's shift from agrarian to urban and traditional to contemporary made children less desirable to the average Roman woman; the unintended result was that homebred Romans were being overrun by immigrants. The Christian advocacy of celibacy only added to this problem. Christians, of course, did not aim to topple the empire. Their interests were in the moral freedom of women, not in the needs of a failing empire.

Second, the church granted membership to women whose

husbands were not Christians. It was customary for Roman husbands to dictate the religion of the home. Religious freedom was his alone; the household followed his gods and devotional habits. With the advent of Christianity, a growing number of Roman women shook off tradition, ditched their household's gods, and followed Christ alone. The fact that Christian women regularly strode out the door to attend worship services in neighboring homes only added to the husband's humility. Given the explosiveness of these strained marital relations, and given the fact that Roman men legally had the power to beat, imprison, and in rare cases execute their wives and children, Christian women were urged not to conduct their devotions in a cavalier attitude. Peter urged wives to be respectful and circumspect toward their non-Christian husbands in hopes that they would win them to the faith (1 Pet 3:1–2). Even so, Christian advocacy of a woman's freedom in these matters raised the hackles of Roman men.

> *It was customary for Roman husbands to dictate the religion of the home.*

Third, slave women were welcomed into the Christian fellowship. This too conflicted with a husband's right to dictate the religion of his entire household, but even more complex is the conflict that arose in cases where Christian female slaves were obligated to perform sexual favors for their masters or were forced into prostitution either as punishment or as a means of raising capital for the household. One can only imagine the hurt and desperation this caused the slaves, for their Christian morals indicated that sex was to be reserved for marriage alone. To the extent that the slaves protested to their masters, it would have seemed that Christianity had raised yet another threat against Roman social order.

> *She who is set free in Christ is set free to serve rather than while away in the bonds of repressive social custom.*

Fourth, ancient societies almost unanimously believed public life was a man's domain whereas women belonged indoors and uninvolved in the larger affairs of society. For instance, in his book *Special Laws*, Philo says, "Market-places and council-halls and law-courts and gatherings and meetings where a large number of people are assembled, and open-air life with full scope for discussion and action—all are suitable to men both in war and peace. The women are best suited to the indoor life which never strays from the house" (3.169).[1] While Christianity did not oppose suitable role divisions between men and women, it did oppose the sequestering of women or their prohibition from public affairs. So regularly did Christian women take to the streets, journeying to worship services, prisons, and homes of the needy, that the pagans suspected Christian women of gross immoralities. What are all these loose-living women doing in the streets and in one another's homes? The Christians knew the answer. She who is set free in Christ is set free to serve rather than while away in the bonds of repressive social custom.

In the following centuries the Christian impulse to alleviate oppressive cultural customs led incrementally to new freedoms for women. Ideally the pace of change would have been quicker. Looking back, we see that a great many Christian men (and women) were slow to recognize that certain of their cultural values did not reflect the values Christ had exemplified. Thus we sometimes find historical church leaders making harsh, derogatory statements about women and womanhood. All in all, however, Christian beliefs have been the major moral force in winning women equal status with men. The example of Jesus remains bold and liberating: women are in all ways equal to men, and society works best when both sexes are free to pursue the freedoms and roles that fit their abilities and God-given callings.[2]

Looking back, we see that a great many Christian men (and women) were slow to recognize that certain of their cultural values did not reflect the values Christ had exemplified.

Summing up, Jesus warmly received female disciples, extended uncommon mercies to outcast women, and countered social mores that suppressed women in the selfish interests of men. When asked where a woman's place is, Jesus' followers yesterday, today, and forever must say that it is with Jesus and wherever he may lead her.

Children and Childhood

As it goes for women, so it goes for children. Returning to the historical context that framed Jesus' life, we find that ancient cultures had a dim view of children. In urban centers, where adulteries and the pursuit of vanities essentially defined Roman womanhood, abortion was a common means of birth control. Typically it was accomplished by swallowing a poisonous mix of herbs that convulsed the womb and struck the child dead. Of the children who made it safely through to birth, half died before reaching their fifth year. Disease, poverty, and war played roles in driving this high mortality rate, but so did infanticide and infant abandonment, both of which were common practices. Ancient writing is littered with references to the drowning or dashing of deformed, weakly, or undesired infants. Among the Romans, the decision to keep, kill, or discard a newborn involved an inspection in which the father lifted the baby and examined it for defects and signs of infirmity. If he was displeased, the law permitted him to do whatever he wished.

Ancient writing is littered with references to the drowning or dashing of deformed, weakly, or undesired infants.

If permitted to live, undesirables were often abandoned at the community trash heap or a designated place where passersby could judge for themselves whether the child deserved to live. If by chance anyone rescued an abandoned child, they were free to graft it into their family, raise it as a household slave, sell it to traders, or even hire the child out as a prostitute. All options were open because such a child was redeemed as property, not as a person. Since most cultures valued boys over girls, infant daughters were discarded or enslaved at a higher rate than boys. As one Egyptian father wrote to his wife when he was away on business, "If you chance to bear a child, and it is a boy, let it be; if it is a girl, expose it" (Oxyrhynchus Papyrus 744).

A great many female prostitutes were forced to peddle themselves because they had been abandoned as infants, but even children who escaped abandonment and vocational prostitution were in danger of sexual exploitation. For instance, Greco-Roman culture held that the practice of sexual relations between men and boys was acceptable and even beneficial. Taking a note from military practices of the early Greek city-states, where soldiers were encouraged to pair up with one another, it was believed that homosexual relations between teacher and pupil deepened their relationship, facilitating greater learning and maturation. As for girls, their fathers commonly arranged for them to be married off even before they reached puberty.

Aside from the exploitations, childhood was a largely invisible stage of life. One widely cited illustration of this is the fact that the ancients tended not to count women and children when reporting the size of crowds. Following this custom, even the evangelists neglect to count women and children when reporting Jesus' miraculous feeding of the five thousand (Mark 6:44). This does not mean the disciples adopted full-scale the low pagan view of children, but it does hint at the generally impoverished view of childhood that touched even Jewish values.

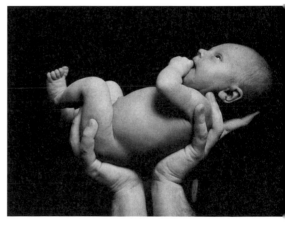

Finally, how did children occupy their time? Most were deployed into the fields or assigned household tasks to help meet their family's needs, and that is understandable given the conditions of the era; but even when education was feasible, it was neglected because dominant beliefs about intellect held that children were incapable of reason.

Summing up the status of children in the ancient world, W. A. Strange writes, "Children were marginal figures in the society of the ancient world. The central and key figure was the free adult male, able to bear arms and play his part in the religious, military and political life of the community. Women, children and slaves were peripheral figures. They found their place in society around and in dependence on the free adult males."[3]

What did Jesus do to help encourage greater rights and respectability for children? First, he demonstrated their value by allowing them to come to him. Being products of their time and culture, the disciples tried to ward off these diminutive invaders whenever they came seeking Jesus, but Jesus rebuked them for this. "Leave the children alone, and don't try to keep them from coming to Me, because the kingdom of heaven is made up of people like this" (Matt 19:14). Second, Jesus once set a child next to himself and told his ambitious disciples that unless they became humble like children they would not be permitted to enter God's kingdom

Jesus and the Little Children by Bloch.

(18:3). Furthermore, he said, "Whoever welcomes one child like this in My name welcomes Me" (v. 5). Here Jesus is in effect saying that though the world neglects children, he values them and identifies with their lot in life. But that is not all. He went on to say, "Whoever causes the downfall of one of these little ones who believe in Me—it would be better for him if a heavy millstone were hung around his neck and he were drowned in the depths of the sea!" (v. 6). Here we see Jesus as Defender of the innocent. A good measurement of our own discipleship can be had by gauging our efforts to help children.

Are we relieving needy children in the name of Jesus, or are we instead pouring harmful abundance into our lives and the lives of our own children?

Are we relieving needy children in the name of Jesus, or are we instead pouring harmful abundance into our lives and the lives of our own children? Third, Jesus once used a single lunch, the gift of a child, to feed five thousand men and an untold number of women and children (John 6:5–10). We are still talking about that child and his gift 2,000 years later.

Following Jesus' example, the early Christians advocated greater rights and protections for children. They vehemently opposed abortion and infanticide. Some of the earliest non-biblical Christian writings, such as the *Didache*, condemn infanticide; and, once Christianity became a legal religion in the Roman Empire, Jesus' followers lobbied politically for its prohibition. Abortion was equally abhorrent to Christians, as early literature testifies. Tertullian (AD 155–222), for instance, said Christians must oppose abortion because a fetus is nothing less than a human being (*Apology* 9). In 374, Emperor Valentinian was won over by Christian moral arguments and outlawed both infanticide and abortion. As for abandoned infants, Christians regularly took them in, raised them as their own, and granted them full human rights. Believers also pushed for the legal abolition of infant abandonment, and indeed Valentinian added this to his list of moral reforms.

> *Christians in every era have received the world's unwanted children in Jesus' name.*

The list of Christian reforms also includes a reduction in child marriage and an emphasis on every child's need for education. Christians in every era have received the world's unwanted children in Jesus' name.

Slavery

Slaves have labored under every day's sun since essentially the dawn of human history. No era has been free of slavery. It continues today in parts of Africa. It is not only Africans who have been victims, however. Blacks have owned blacks, whites have owned whites, and native peoples from every continent have subjugated one another. Skin color does not drive slavery; differentiation in power and guile does. Hunter-gatherers, warrior tribes, empire builders, all have been both subject and master in the slave equation.

Defeated soldiers were commonly forced into slavery, as when Julius Caesar awarded each of his soldiers a slave from among Vercingetorix's defeated infantry in 51 BC. Each soldier quickly converted his man into cash, a transaction which seems unfathomable to modern readers. The families of the enslaved soldiers were stranded and defenseless, and so they too were gathered and sent to market, where they would stand locked arm in arm in desperate hope that they would be purchased as a lot. Seldom did it work out that

Mothers and children, sisters and brothers were divided like coins in a sweaty palm.

way. Mothers and children, sisters and brothers were divided like coins in a sweaty palm.

So prevalent was slavery that more than half of the Roman population consisted of slaves in Jesus' era. From early Greece to Rome's dying day, from the rise of the pyramids to the destruction of Babylon's hanging gardens, the free lived in luxury at the expense of the enslaved.

More than half of the Roman population consisted of slaves in Jesus' era.

What was it like to be a slave? Undoubtedly it differed from case to case, but documented laws and practices give us a glimpse of the degrading lifestyle that many slaves experienced. To begin with, in the Greek and Roman eras slaves were legally classified as property rather than people. In Aristotle's words, "A slave is a living tool, just as a tool is an inanimate slave" (*Nichomachean Ethics* 8.11). The owner of a hammer can use (and abuse) his hammer in any way he likes without fear of legal reprimand. So too a master his slave.

In many cases slaves were offered the chance to purchase their freedom if the owner was willing to suffer loss of labor for gain of money. In hope of this, slaves spent years or even decades pooling their meager

Not only were slaves the property of their owners; they could be forced to act as their substitutes as well.

stream of income, but even up to the cusp of the momentous transaction the owner had the right to seize the savings for himself and retain his slave. History does not tell us how often this thievery took place, but since an owner could do it without consequence, it was probably done often.

Not only were slaves the property of their owners; they could be forced to act as their substitutes as well. For instance, in certain clubs and fraternities, a member who had infringed upon club rules or was late in paying dues was allowed to have his slave beaten in lieu of his paying up or suffering some other penalty. In a crude semblance to Christ's work on the cross, the innocent took the punishment for the guilty. Further, slaves were sometimes sent off by their owners to do dirty and violent deeds. If caught, the slave would incur all punishment. Finally, both male and female salves were subject to sexual exploitation. One way this manifested itself was when Roman wives who did not wish to bear any more children granted their husbands sexual access to their female slaves. Of course the slave had no choice in the matter even if she happened to be a Christian.

What impact did Jesus and his followers have on slavery? Though we might like to see a line in the Gospels where Jesus says something like, "Slavery is an abomination unto God and it must end," or perhaps an admonishment from Paul that Christians everywhere should unite and pull down the walls of slavery, no such lines exist. This was an era deeply steeped in the social acceptance of slavery. In fact the Roman Empire would collapse overnight if all its slaves were emancipated. Therefore, to confront the legality of slavery head-on would have been suicidal for the young Christian movement because the empire would not tolerate such an overt threat to its existence. Additionally, it is clear that Jesus, his apostles, and subsequent church leaders, regarded spiritual bondage as far more damnable than physical bondage. Thus, the tactic taken by Jesus and his followers was to teach first of all the need to escape spiritual bondage. As a secondary priority, they offered countercultural values and teachings that helped pave the way for the eventual abolition of slavery.

Jesus and his apostles offered countercultural values and teachings that helped pave the way for the eventual abolition of slavery.

Jesus set the tone in several ways. First, he dared to depict slaves as being capable of pleasing God (e.g., Matt 24:42–51). This is especially significant when contrasted with his consistently negative portrayal of Israel's religious leaders. Second, Jesus demonstrated that a slave's life is worth saving when he healed a slave whose master came to him in faith asking for help (Luke 7:1–10). Third, in some sense Jesus' dealings with women and children were transferable to slaves. Women and children held low station in ancient society, and yet Jesus repeatedly demonstrated their value by treating them with respect and love. By inference the same must be true for slaves. Fourth, Jesus' Golden Rule states, "Just as you want others to do for you, do the same for them" (Luke 6:31). Since no one desires enslavement, to impose it upon another is a clear violation of Jesus' ethic.

From these examples, we see that though Jesus never expressly forbade slavery, he did lay down teachings and examples that encouraged abolition. The early church understood this clearly enough. This is seen first of all in the letters of Paul. Speaking of Christian equality, he says, "There is no Jew or Greek, slave or free, male or female; for you are all one in Christ Jesus" (Gal 3:28). In another place he writes to a Christian slave owner and admonishes him to regard his Christian slave "no longer as a slave" but "as a dearly loved brother" (Phlm 16). This attitude was adopted so widely by early Christians that slaves flooded into the church and became key evangelistic agents as they shared the good news about Jesus with their fellow slaves and even the free members of their owner's household. Amazingly, some free Christians even went so far as to sell *themselves* into slavery as a means of freeing others. Notice what 1 Clement reports: "We know that many among ourselves have given themselves to bondage that they might ransom others. Many have delivered themselves to slavery, and provided food for others with the price they received for themselves" (1 Clement 55:2).

Amazingly, some free Christians even went so far as to sell themselves into slavery as a means of freeing others.

Aside from this, many Christians used their personal monies to buy freedom for slaves. Thousands were freed in this way. The famed fourth-century preacher John Chrysostom advised his congregation to purchase slaves, "and after you have taught them some skill by which they can maintain themselves, set them free" (*Homily 40* on 1 Corinthians 10). Roman observers were dumbstruck by the emancipation efforts of the Christians and regarded them as a threat to societal order.

Jesus' love for all people and his insistence on equality supplied the motivation for ending slavery wherever the Christian faith spread.

As Christians continued to multiply in the Roman Empire, bishops came to wield great influence on social and moral issues. Eventually this led to legal reforms that softened slavery. Throughout the centuries to come, Christians led the push to abolish slavery. William Wilberforce, an outspoken Christian, led the cause in England. He lived just long enough to see the first stage of slavery's abolition throughout the United Kingdom. Christian faith was also at the forefront of the American abolitionist cause. Jesus' love for all people and his insistence on equality supplied the motivation for ending slavery wherever the Christian faith spread.

Summary

Jesus never came out as a full-fledged social reformer because his primary aim was to save the eternal human soul. Had he explicitly led the charge against social abuses, he would have founded a social movement rather than a religion of spiritual liberation. Nevertheless, by his teachings and his examples, he fertilized a soil of salvation not just from sin's eternal penalty but the penalty of injustice in this lifetime.

There are a great many other ways in which Jesus has shaped history and culture positively. Christians in every land and age have reached out to the needy and the ostracized. Medical care, charitable giving, education, economic freedom, and even the rise of science are just a few examples of how Christ and his followers have inscribed good on history's scroll.[4] What part are you playing in this history?

Notes

1. Cited on page 32 of Margaret Y. MacDonald, *Early Christian Women and Pagan Opinion* (Cambridge: Cambridge University Press, 1996).

2. For a fresh look at what the Bible teaches about womanhood and capitalizing on modern freedoms, see Robert Lewis, *The New Eve: Choosing God's Best for Your Life* (Nashville: B&H Publishing, 2008).

3. W. A. Strange, *Children in the Early Church* (Eugene, OR: Wipf and Stock, 2004), 19–20.

4. Helpful resources for exploring the impact Christ and his followers have had throughout history include, Rodney Stark, *The Victory of Reason* (New York: Random House, 2005); Stark, *For the Glory of God* (Princeton: Princeton University Press, 2003); Dinesh D'Sousza, *What's So Great About Christianity* (Washington, DC: Regnery Publishing, 2007); Alvin J. Schmidt, *How Christianity Changed the World* (Grand Rapids: Zondervan, 2004); D. James Kennedy, *What If Jesus Had Never Been Born?* (Nashville: Thomas Nelson, 1994).

Chapter 22
Jesus in the Twenty-first Century

The world today is in the midst of seismic renovations. The process began some time ago. Consider the human journey over the past several hundred years. In the eighteenth and nineteenth centuries, cartographers completed their quest to document the globe. They filled in blanks on the world map only to discover wider blanks in cultural understanding. So many peoples and cultures, and what diversity from land to land! And so the world grew bigger even as maps brought it down to size.

World powers raced to conquer, colonize, and capitalize newfound lands. Western civilization encompassed the globe but failed to comprehend the world. Some myths and prejudices were overturned while others were unjustly canonized. In America, Indians were routed and blacks were chained. Representatives of the Christian consciousness protested slavery, but nothing changed until guns awakened. Hostilities ceased after many soldiers had fallen. In the aftermath, slavery was abolished, but the black man's freedom remained elusive.

In this same epoch scientists delved into Earth's bowels and found fossil bones and mangled stones that told tales of remote antiquity and primeval violence, of storied beasts reigning over a planet untouched by humankind. Then came new theories about life history and the relations between species. Christians wondered if the scientists had lost their minds; scientists wondered if they would lose their biblical faith. Some did; many did not. Atheists took the new data as proof that life had arisen without God whereas Christians insisted that God was the Maker of all, but among Christians disagreements arose about what timetables and modes of operation God used in creation and how Genesis should be interpreted. The debate continues today.

Ancient texts, etched in stone and clay, also came to light in Europe and Old World regions during the eighteenth and nineteenth centuries. Christians for nearly two millennia had believed that the Genesis accounts about creation and Noah's flood were entirely unique in the history of literature; but scholars and archeologists learned that several far-gone cultures had left earlier records, remembrances, and mythical stories about such things; and in some cases these texts bear surprising resemblance to Genesis. Exaggerated claims shot up among skeptics and committed non-Christians: the Bible had lifted content from the texts of surrounding cultures, they said, and reflects not God's revelations but the Hebrew quest for answers. Christian scholars countered this by demonstrating the uniqueness of the biblical testimony and its moral superiority to the other texts, but popular culture took no notice. It had already moved on.

Challenges and changes piled up faster in the twentieth century, making Jesus and his era seem more distant than ever. We banned God-talk from the laboratory and classroom. We split the atom and divided the family. Clever engineers learned to beam pictures invisibly through the air and catch them in TV boxes. Against all odds we reached the moon by rocket; against all reason we plumbed the moral abyss by free choice. Despots rose to power with alarming ease and regularity. We stopped them, but only after whole races were pushed to the brink of annihilation. When the menace passed, we pondered the good of humanity and humanity's God.

Positively, shapers of the twentieth century empowered women and desegregated blacks from whites. In piecemeal fashion we learned to be more respectful to groups that by long custom were unfairly marginalized. We also learned to be more insightful about history. Armed with unprecedented access to biographical and historical data, we looked back on people, events, and movements in a new light. We saw that some beliefs and practices of former times were ill founded (biblically and otherwise) and ought to be discarded. Unfortunately, we started to suspect that we had outgrown our ancestors so badly that they could no longer speak to us.

Now we have entered the third millennium of the Common Era, and we are a sight to behold. Our great-grandparents believed made-up fables about the starry hosts, but today's grade-schoolers know them to be nuclear furnaces whose radiological discharges are measured by machines that we send rocketing from Earth. We have robots crawling over Martian soil, tasting it and reporting back to us. Our telescopes glimpse sights from indescribably faraway sectors, and still the space blanket stretches on and on, far out of our grasp. Earth, we have discerned, is a small blue dot in a galaxy of more than 100 billion stars, and our galaxy is in turn just one of many billions. Generations before us believed Earth and humans were the center stage of creation. Now more than ever, scientific evidence shows that life depends on a fantastic balance of chemical and physical variables. It is only reasonable to conclude that life is rare and cannot arise apart from God, but is it necessary or even possible to believe that we earthlings are alone in this vast universe? Opinions differ. Only time will show who is right or whether the question really mattered in the first place.

Back on Earth, terrorists commandeer jet planes and brainwash zealous teens, deploying them on destructive errands aimed at defeating the Christian West, as if such a thing still existed. Scientists have mastered the human genome and are tackling microphysics. Your cancer is predictable now and can likely be removed; a century from now disease may not even exist. Questions remain, but now more than ever historians can describe the ancient development of nations and cultures. The stories of tribes, clans, and civilizations go back surprisingly far and are filled with verve and futility, promise and ruin. They impress us, appall us, and sadden us, and we wonder what link they have with us and the story we are living.

We are world travelers now and have felt firsthand travel's power to overturn provincialism and smug conservatism, and yet indiscriminate borders and moral liberalism are prescriptions for disaster. All people are by nature equal before God, but worldviews, religions, and moral values are not. Much of the world is under bondage to harmful ideologies, and yet no one is allowed to say so. No one believes in all religions; many believe in none whatsoever, and we are discouraged from believing one to the exclusion of all others.

Ours is an era of climactic questions, the most important of which is, "What should we do about Jesus?"

Traveler's Choice

Traveler came to a fork in the road. A sign was erected there. He stood before it, shouldering his great pack of belongings, and read the message repeatedly. "Jesus is the way, the truth, and the life," it said. "No one goes to the Father except through faith in him." Traveler vaguely recognized it as a paraphrase of a biblical verse he had heard sometime in the past.

An arrow on the sign pointed to the narrower of two paths. Traveler looked at it and shuddered. There would not be room to take his things and his indulgences if he went that way. Then he looked left and saw that the other path was broad and appealing. Well worn, too. On that path he could take everything with him and gather still more during the journey. Surely that was the better way. But what of Jesus? Traveler had heard good things about Jesus, but he was uncertain of the truth. And he stood there trying to decide.

Presently he noticed a man walking toward him. He was coming from down the broad path with a wide grin on his face. "Jesus of Nazareth cannot help us any longer," cried the man from a distance. Traveler saw that he was well dressed and carried a gigantic pack of possessions on his back. It didn't seem to weigh him down at all. "Doubt is my name," announced the man once he had drawn up before Traveler. "Listen, man," said Doubt. "This here is the twenty-first century. The world is hardly the same place it was when Jesus came." He slapped the sign with an open palm and said, "Think about it, Traveler! Back in Jesus' day most folks believed Earth was flat and lay under an arcing black dome in which greater and lesser lights were fixed. They thought their narrow patch of the globe was the entire world! They knew nothing about people on the other side of the globe. I don't fault them for these shortcomings. How could they have known better? The point is, theirs is a lost world. It is mothballed in ancient texts and dusty myths."

"There was a lot they didn't know back then," Traveler agreed, "and it's true that things are different now. I have wondered if we can think of Jesus the same way his followers thought of him back then. Maybe we have outgrown what they wrote in the Bible?"

"Compared to them we are a new humanity," continued Doubt, pleased with the direction of Traveler's thoughts. "Science dawned and gave us the only second birth we need. We are free from superstition now, and yet this sign says we must allow Jesus and his followers to set the religious agenda for all time? Come on! Shall we trade our rockets for their donkeys, too? It's a bad move, I say, and there's no sense in it. What sway can events or people in first-century Palestine hold over enlightened citizens of our day? Doesn't reason say we should reject the old beliefs?"

Traveler was just about to admit that he didn't know for sure how to answer Doubt's questions when a voice called out, "Truth is persistent!" Traveler and Doubt turned to look down the narrow way. A woman was picking her way toward them. She was in no hurry. A look of serenity enlivened her face, which surprised Traveler since she carried no pack of possessions and indulgences. She was dressed plainly and unadorned by jewelry.

"What do you mean, 'Truth is persistent'?" Traveler asked after she arrived and introduced herself as Faith.

"Truth outlasts all fads and theories," asserted Faith, "and it cannot be unseated by new discoveries. Truth is like a granite wall set against a child's fisticuffs. There's no use beating against it."

Faith then fixed her gaze on Doubt and said, "You say the

world has changed and grown in knowledge since Jesus' day. You are correct, but that does not count against Jesus' truth or the testimony of Scripture. Our race may yet be in for greater surprises as our instruments pierce earth and sky, mind and matter. But so what? All truth belongs to God, and whatever was true of Jesus' life and teachings 2,000 years ago remains so today."

Doubt sighed heavily and said, "You're working from an outdated conception of truth, Madam Faith. Perhaps it's better to speak of what is right or helpful. Jesus was right for the people of his time. *Some* of them, anyway. But right for everyone for all time? Come on! How can one religion, springing from a particular time, culture, and geographical location, lay claim to universal relevance?"

"An excellent question," admitted Faith. "I grappled with it once myself. But I want to know what you think, Traveler. Under what conditions could events in Jesus' life have bearing on all of history and humanity?"

Traveler closed his eyes and rubbed his temples, shutting out the world. He had a knack for solving these sorts of puzzles, and this was one he wanted very badly to solve. He turned the question over and over in his mind, looking at it from all angles. He thought of Jesus and the broad movements of human history, of the long roll of humanity from pole to pole and age to age. After a while an answer started to emerge. He rehearsed it in his head and then said it aloud. "If Jesus' life was embedded in real human history and yet somehow transcended history as well, it could have application for all times and places."

Faith nodded approvingly. "That's correct, Traveler. Jesus is relevant now and forever because he was sent from heaven to become a man and represent humanity in a life of perfect righteousness. He is just as much for the twenty-first century as he was for the first and those that passed before. We are learned in this age of science," Faith said in deference to Doubt's perspective, "but we need Jesus just as badly as did the Dark Ages. He is the man for all mankind. His life and works shower mercies over all the ages. You've only to cup your heart and receive the healing waters."

"That all sounds great," countered Doubt with a hint of

sarcasm, "but isn't it all just superstition? I mean, there's little of anything believable in Jesus' biography when judged by the light of reason. Don't we need to sober up and face the world as it really is rather than place our hopes in a fairy-tale ending?"

Faith regarded him kindly and with something like pity. "Are miracles so hard to believe?"

"Science has disproved them," Doubt stated matter-of-factly. "Never once has a miracle been confirmed by a qualified scientist. On the contrary, many supposed miracles have been examined and found wanting once the tools of science were applied."

Faith raised herself more erect and said, "I should say first of all that science certainly has not overruled Jesus' miracles. Those were nonrepeatable events dating some 2,000 years ago, and you can be sure that no scientists were running around collecting evidence. But enough of that. For you, Doubt, the larger issue is this: you mistakenly believe that your disbelief in Jesus' miracles stems from scientific evidences against them. In reality, your disbelief in his miracles follows from your disbelief in God. You prejudge that Jesus never performed miracles because you've already concluded that no God exists to perform them or that if God exists he does not bother tinkering in our affairs. I wonder, can you prove that you are right? Can you scientifically disprove God's existence or his involvement in the world, Doubt?"

"I hardly need to," Doubt answered dismissively. "The burden of proof is *yours*. You say God exists and monkeys with his machinery. Show me, Faith!"

"As to God's existence," replied Faith, "that hardly needs arguing anymore. Scientists and philosophers alike have turned from their infatuation with naturalistic atheism. The universe itself lured them into theism instead. Consider the data from cosmology, the science that studies the how and why of the physical universe. The data proves hands down that the universe has existed for only a finite time and that it sprang into existence from nothing. If the universe began to exist, clearly it had a Beginner. If it began from nothing, clearly the Beginner created all things. This means the universe belongs to him in every sense *belong* can have. Thus he can do with the machinery whatever he pleases. Miracles are impossible, Doubt? Hardly! To God they are merely a choice to interrupt the usual course of events.

"As to showing you that God has in fact done such things, there is a record of them that you can take up and read. The miracles of Jesus are documented by eyewitnesses in the New Testament."

"But can we be sure that they've gotten it right in the Good Book?" asked Traveler. "That seems to be key to it all. Does the New Testament get it right about Jesus?"

"I couldn't have put a finer point on it myself," added Doubt. "I say we cannot be sure, and if we cannot be sure, *why bother?*"

"It comes down to this," answered Faith. "The Bible says God created a path out of darkness. Jesus is that path. His first followers believed that and gave up everything to tell the world. You tell me that the world has changed since Jesus came. I tell you that insomuch as it has changed for the better is has changed *because* he came. The human race has outgrown many false beliefs, and Christians have shed a fair share of misunderstandings and unbiblical biases, but

the truth of Jesus stands unchallenged. He is alive now and forever, Traveler, enrobed in glory and immortality. He offers himself as Savior and Brother. Will you choose to believe?"

Traveler bowed his head in thought. His pack seemed heavier than before, and he shifted uncomfortably under its weight. A message of hope and love had come to him, and it burned his heart to think of what it had cost the Son of God. He reflected on the fact that many millions had believed this gospel through the centuries and forsaken the dark for a life in light, receiving freedom from the penalty of sin.

"Will you believe?" Faith repeated.

"Yes!" Traveler answered with sudden joy. "Yes I will!"

"Wait!" objected Doubt. "Can it really be so simple? And think of what you must forsake to follow him."

But Traveler wasn't listening to Doubt anymore. He unshouldered his pack and set his feet on the narrow path that leads to life everlasting.

And you watch as Traveler picks his way down one of two paths.

Which one will you take?

LOOKING
FOR ADDITIONAL RESOURCES?

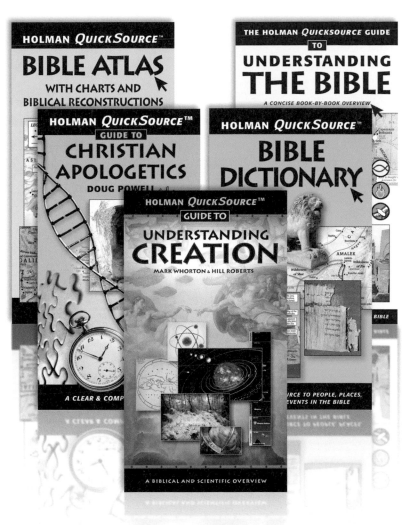

Holman QuickSource™ Guides are designed to help you develop a deeper understanding of the Bible — from the people, places and times, to defending your faith in a modern age.

PUBLISHING GROUP

Visit your local retailer or BHPublishingGroup.com for more information.